FOR ESTHER LOCK

Contents

Publication of this volume was aided by a generous grant from the Scouloudi Foundation, in association with the Institute of Historical Research. It was further assisted by a grant from The Isobel Thornley Bequest Fund of the University of London.

Acknowledgements

In writing this book I have incurred the debt of gratitude to many individuals and organisations. The following is an attempt to say thank you to those friends, colleagues, archive and library staff whose advice and encouragement have made this work possible. Firstly, the Economic and Social Research Council who funded my PhD research between 1992 and 1995, and the Institute of Historical Research, from whom I received a Scouloudi Fellowship in 1996 to complete that research. Secondly, I have received help and advice from many librarians and archivists but I would particularly like to mention the following: the Archives Office of Tasmania, the Corporation of London Record Office, Darwin College, Cambridge, the London Metropolitan Archive, the Public Record Office, and the Royal Philanthropic Society. Thirdly, I would like to acknowledge the help and advice of the following individuals: Brenda Assael, Kelly Boyd, Pene Corfield, Pam Cox, Martin Daunton, Andrew Davies, David Eastwood, Clive Emsley, Vic Gatrell, Tim Hitchcock, Peter King, Christine Linehan, Tim Meldrum, David Philips, Roland Quinault, Deborah Ryan and James Ryan and Andrew Wood. I would particularly like to thank Pene Corfield and Tim Hitchcock, without whose unflagging support and criticism I would not be writing these words today. Finally my greatest debt is to my parents Ellen and Allan Shore who have supported me both financially and emotionally, to my brothers Timothy and Ian, and to Laura Manison and Heather De Silva whose friendship has been invaluable.

Heather Shore
April 1999

Abbreviations

AOT	Archives Office of Tasmania
CLRO	Corporation of London Record Office
DNB	*Dictionary of national biography*
HO	Home Office
LMA	London Metropolitan Archive
MEPO	Metropolitan Police Office
OBSP	*Old Bailey sessions papers*
PP	Parliamentary Papers
PRO	Public Record Office
SC	*Select Committee*

List of Tables

Introduction:
'Inventing' the Juvenile Delinquent

'There is a youthful population in the Metropolis devoted to crime, trained to it from infancy, adhering to it from Education and Circumstances, whose connections prevent the possibility of reformation, and whom no Punishment can deter; a race *'sui generis'*, different from the rest of Society, not only in thoughts, habits, and manners, but even in appearance, possessing, moreover, a language exclusively of their own.'[1] – William Augustus Miles

'The primary causes of juvenile delinquency, like that of crime in general, are deeply implanted in the fallen nature of man, and the vicious constitution of the present state of society.'[2] – William Beaver Neale

Written respectively in 1839 and 1840, these extracts reflect a contemporary concern with juvenile crime in the early nineteenth century, and its perceived symbiotic relationship to societal mores and social behaviour. In the first extract, William Augustus Miles communicates the increasing fear of crime, distilled into the relentless march of the criminal class. For him, juvenile criminals were the product of a 'race', one which had evolved out of the special circumstances of the metropolis – a separate, and dangerous, entity, with its own creed, language and symbols. In both these extracts there lies the implicit message that something has been created that is out of the control and care of society's jurisdictions. The criminal class then, was the prodigal son of respectable society – the juvenile delinquent its potentially malleable heir. Consequently juvenile crime provoked both despair and expectation. Such children and youths could be saved and reincorporated into respectable society, or they could fall, and be absorbed, into the life of the hardened criminal.

Indeed in this period popular rhetoric sought an explanation for juvenile crime with recidivism at its core; persistent juvenile offending became an emblem for social breakdown and domestic instability. Whilst anxiety over the behaviour of youth was not new, in the nineteenth century a number of factors combined which brought the issue of juvenile offending sharply into focus. In the early decades of the century the groundwork for both political and public debate was established, highlighting an area of concern which would be central to the discussion of crime and delinquency henceforth.

1 W. A. Miles, *Poverty, mendicity, and crime*, ed. H. Brandon, London 1839, 45.
2 W. B. Neale, *Juvenile delinquency in Manchester: its causes and history, its consequences, and some suggestions concerning its cure*, Manchester 1840, 7.

1

Historians have generally located the public 'invention' of juvenile crime in the late eighteenth and early nineteenth century.[3] During this period there was a flood of pamphlet literature and parliamentary reports, which dealt with the apparent increase in crime, many specifically focusing on the perceived rise in juvenile crime. Simultaneously, these years witnessed the development of what essentially remains the modern penal system. At the start of the nineteenth century children who committed crime were, in theory at least, treated no differently from adults. From capture to commitment to trial and punishment, on paper, all were administered to in the same way. Only very young children were exempt, since under the ordinances of the established legal formulation known as *Doli Incapax* children less than seven years of age were not to be found criminally responsible for their actions.[4] However, by the 1840s and 1850s, a new system to cope with juveniles had started to evolve.

Consequently an understanding of the continuities and discontinuities that occurred in the early nineteenth century is vital. This study will show how, in that period, juvenile offenders became such a potent element of the debate about crime and punishment. Correspondingly we will see that not only did perceptions of youth crime shape the public and private debate, but that that debate, and particularly its legislative consequences, profoundly shaped the experience of the criminal justice system for children. Yet the experience of crime changed in other ways too. Developments in policing, the proliferation of voluntary philanthropic organisations, and shifts in workplace practices all contributed to changing experiences and, perhaps, expectations for children. Nevertheless, familiarity can be found as well, in this discussion of the lives of early nineteenth-century juvenile criminals. Debilitating environments, wretched poverty, minimal literacy and education, still remained. The descriptions that the children provide of their interactions with older criminals, receivers of stolen goods, the highways and byways of the underbelly of the metropolis, the networks of crime and criminals which sustained and fed their offending, existed as they did in the London of Jonathan Wild, or earlier in Elizabethan and Stuart London. Indeed the developments in this period need to be set in the context of a broader history of crime and of responses to criminality. The role of the juvenile offender, as both the progeny and progenitor of criminals, was central. Juvenile criminals were, after all, for many commentators, the genesis of the professional criminal, the origin of 'the monster roots of vice'.[5] As the years of

---

[3] S. Magarey, 'The invention of juvenile delinquency in early nineteenth-century England', *Labour History* [Canberra] xxxiv (1978), 11–27; M. May, 'Innocence and experience: the evolution of the concept of juvenile delinquency in the mid-nineteenth century', *Victorian Studies* xvii (1973), 7–29; L. Radzinowicz and R. Hood, *A history of English criminal law and its administration from 1750*, V: *The emergence of penal policy*, Oxford 1990, 113.

[4] A more substantial discussion of *Doli Incapax* can be found at pp. 8–9 below.

[5] H. Worsley, *Juvenile depravity*, London 1849, 119–20.

the early nineteenth century unfolded, much of this debate focused on the problem of the persistent juvenile offender. It is clear from both recent and historical texts that the juvenile recidivist was a 'bogeyman', a social barometer.[6] The issue of this figure was particularly problematic in the context of reformation and criminal responsibility. Thus the degree to which a child was 'hardened' dictated his or her responsiveness to, or eligibility for, reformation. Criminal responsibility rested less on age or gender than on this conflict between innocence and experience. Thus, far from seeing juvenile offenders as 'stunted little men' (or women), what concerned and discomfited contemporary commentators, was that these were children, but with adult experiences, adult mannerisms.[7] The people at the core of understanding and exploring such conflicts were to be the major contributors of information about juvenile offenders in the earlier nineteenth century. These people, who might usefully be referred to as social investigators, acted for a variety of reasons. Some carried out research on behalf of parliamentary inquiry, others for the press, some on their own mission of reformation and reclamation. Commentators such as Mary Carpenter, W. B. Neale, Charles Dickens, Henry Mayhew, W. A. Miles, Thomas Jevons, Thomas Wontner, Henry Worsley and Thomas Beggs shaped the views of politicians and public alike. Much of their work was impressionistic and highly subjective. These were formative years for the expression of evidence through statistics, yet these writers had limited access to statistical data and there were no real penal professionals from whom to gather information.[8] Indeed, outside legal, police and prison circles, these people were the expert opinion. There is little doubt that their work was treated to close scrutiny by parliamentary select committees, and often influenced legislative response. For example, William Crawford and Samuel Hoare, members of the 1815 Committee for Investigating the Causes of the Alarming Increase of Juvenile Delinquency in the Metropolis, both became vociferous campaigners; Crawford as one of the first Inspectors of Prisons, Hoare through his involvement with the Refuge for the Destitute and the Prison Discipline Society. William Augustus Miles contributed to the 1835 Select Committee on Gaols.[9] Mary Carpenter figured

---

6 D. J. West, *The young offender*, London 1967, 29; A. Hagell and T. Newburn, *Persistent young offenders*, London 1994.

7 M. D. Hill, 'Practical suggestions to the founders of the reformatory schools', in J. C. Symons (ed.), *On the reformation of young offenders*, London 1855, 2.

8 Whilst individuals did hold salaried offices in prison and houses of correction, or on the prison hulks (for example, the superintendent of hulks, John Capper), the extent to which people such as this represented 'penal professionals' is debatable. Having said this, however, many of the people who held office within such institutions did submit evidence to the various select committees and commissions.

9 *Report from Select Committee of the House of Lords Appointed to Inquire into the Present State of Gaols and Houses of Correction in England and Wales*, PP, 1835, xi–xii. Miles's evidence is in the 2nd Report (xi. 394–400), 3rd Report (xii, appendix, pp. 275–9), 4th, 5th Reports (xii. 439, 508–15, and appendix, pp. 5–24).

strongly in the Select Committee on Criminal Juveniles in 1852, and published a number of well-received books and pamphlets on the subject.[10]

However, these nineteenth-century commentators did not generally offer a critique of social organisation. They may have criticised penal arrangements but there was little indictment of political agendas. Instead their writing has the feel of exploration. They were outraged by immorality, ignorance, cunning, poverty, in the same way as missionaries exploring lost civilisations. For example, writing about juvenile crime in 1849, Thomas Beggs commented:

> A large proportion of the population were found to be grovelling in the veriest debasement, yielding obedience only to the animal instincts; brooding in spiritual darkness in a day of gospel light, and as much shut off from participation in the blessings of Christian privilege as if they had been the inhabitants of another hemisphere.[11]

Although rather verbose and hyperbolical, these narratives were not necessarily untrue. Some overstatement is to be expected given the social background of such voyagers. Seen through the lens of their own domestic comforts, the environments they visited provided a stark contrast; there was little acknowledgement of social relativeness. Moreover, it was often the case that elite observers sought out extreme situations: when Henry Mayhew and John Binny visited the 'London Underworld', they looked for the worst examples. Similarly, when William Augustus Miles interviewed juvenile boys in 1835, he visited the *Euryalus* prison hulk and spoke to boys destined for transportation.

What this indicates is a strong relationship between the contemporary political perception of juvenile crime and the wider public stereotypes and representations generated by such people. Whilst it is impossible to gauge how widely these writers were read, judging by the amount of duplication between contemporary pamphlets and the evidence aired in the various select committees of the period, the decision-makers were certainly aware of this literature. Because of the work (and often the assumptions) of these urban explorers, persistent juvenile offending became emblematic of contemporary debate about, and legislative enactment for, the treatment, punishment and care of juvenile offenders. Yet the discussion about juvenile reoffending in the early nineteenth century has to be balanced against the fact that many of those children who populated the prisons and houses of correction of the metropolis, had been placed there by means of summary processes. A substantial proportion of juveniles in custody had not been found guilty of a felony, had not been tried by jury, and in some cases had had

---

10 *Report from the Select Committee on Criminal and Destitute Juveniles*, PP, 1852, vii. For Carpenter's evidence see pp. 89–140.
11 T. Beggs, *An inquiry into the extent and causes of juvenile depravity*, London 1849, 2. See also G. Pearson, *Hooligans: a history of respectable fears*, London 1983, 130–1.

minimal contact with the court system. Large numbers of juveniles were committed for vagrancy and other misdemeanours; other 'disorderly' children had been brought in front of the magistrate by parents or guardians.[12] Before the Juvenile Offenders Act of 1847 there was little systematic recording of summary convictions. This discounts any large-scale quantitative analysis of summary jurisdiction.[13] The actual extent of persistent offending is guesswork. Summary treatment of crime, along with the unobtainable proportion of unprosecuted and undetected crime, undermines any attempt at precise measurement. The only certainty, in the early nineteenth century, was the belief that juvenile crime was rising and indeed was threatening to undermine that fragile edifice called society.

Many juvenile reoffenders would have started their 'careers' by being processed summarily. This was increasingly the case as the century progressed and legislation permitted the extensive application of summary procedures. Whilst the debate over the extension of these powers was protracted and often pettifogging it was essential to the development of attitudes to, and treatment of, the young offender. A series of acts regulating the behaviour of problematical youth established what would become the basic form for the treatment of juvenile offenders from the mid nineteenth century onwards. The Juvenile Offenders Act of 1847 allowed children under the age of fourteen to be tried in the petty sessions, summarily, a further act of 1850 raised the age limit to sixteen. Between 1854 and 1857 a series of Reformatory and Industrial School Acts replaced prison with alternative institutions as the locus of punishment for juvenile offenders.[14] As Margaret May has commented:

> For the first time in a legislative enactment Parliament recognised juvenile delinquency as a distinct social phenomenon and accepted responsibility not only for young offenders, but also for children who, although not in conflict with the law, required 'care and protection'.[15]

However, there was more to the debate than merely the recognition of child criminality. It also focused attention on ways of treating offenders, how to

---

[12] 'Disorderly' apprentices could be imprisoned under the Vagrancy Act. However, children presented to the magistrate by their parents were more likely to find their way to the Refuge for the Destitute, Philanthropic Society or Marine Society. (Parents also applied to these institutions directly.)

[13] For further discussion on the quantifying of summary crime see R. B. Shoemaker, *Prosecution and punishment: petty crime and the law in London and rural Middlesex, c. 1660–1725*, Cambridge 1991, 16–17, 320–1.

[14] 1847: Juvenile Offenders Act (10 & 11 Vict. c.82); 1854: Reformatory Schools Act (& 18 Vict. c.74); Middlesex Industrial Schools Act (Local) (17 & 18 Vict. c.169); Reformation of Youthful Offenders Act (17 & 18 Vict. c.86); 1855: Youthful Offenders Amendment Act (18 & 19 Vict. c.87); 1856: Reformatory and Industrial Schools Amendment Act (19 & 20 Vict. c.109); 1857: Industrial Schools Act (20 & 21 Vict. c.3); Reformatory Schools Act (20 & 21 Vict. c.55).

[15] May, 'Innocence and experience', 7–29, esp. p. 7.

stop them reoffending, and strategies of reformation. A fundamental feature of these public discussions was the categorisation of offenders. Types of criminal could be categorised by their crime: robber, thief, burglar, or by the extent of their delinquency. Hence, juvenile criminals were early on divided into distinct moral categories.

For example, from its earliest years in the late eighteenth century, the Philanthropic Society, one of the earliest and most enduring institutions to deal with delinquent children, divided its children by classification.[16] Those children who were orphans or children of convicted offenders, but not necessarily offenders themselves, were placed in the Manufactory. Those children who were 'delinquent' were placed in the Reform. In the 1790s, in institutions aptly named, the Reform literally provided moral and social education, whilst the Manufactory was concerned with more practical skills and employment. By 1804 the Reform had already become punitive, delinquent boys only moving up to the Manufactory after demonstrating good behaviour:

> All boys admitted on account of own delinquency, are sent in the first instance to the reform . . . 'sufficiently reformed' they are transferred to the manufactory, and placed on the same footing with the rest of the boys.[17]

Moreover, amongst the Reform boys, a further division existed. Thus the boys were differentiated into 'good' boys, who had got into trouble through external factors, such as peer pressure, or simple temptation; and 'bad' boys, who were seen as confirmed, and 'hardened' juveniles. In May 1816 the *Report of the committee for investigating the causes of the alarming increase of juvenile delinquency in the metropolis* articulated the first real conceptualisation of juvenile delinquency. Despite confusion about the disposition of the juvenile delinquent, a system was identified involving such 'bad', if unfortunate, lads:

> It was found that Juvenile Delinquency existed in the metropolis to a very alarming extent; that a system was in action, by which these unfortunate Lads were organised into gangs; that they resorted regularly to houses, where they planned their enterprises, and afterwards divided the produce of their plunder.[18]

Such systems of classification closely followed the ethos of late eighteenth- and early nineteenth-century voluntarism.[19] Hence the traditional trinity of

16 Founded in 1788 in London, the Society, renamed the Royal Philanthropic Society in 1952, still exists today providing for young offenders and children in care.

17 *An account of the nature and present state of the Philanthropic Society*, London 1804, cited in W. B. Sanders, *Juvenile offenders for a thousand years: selected readings from Anglo-Saxon times to 1900*, Chapel Hill, NC 1970.

18 *Report of the committee for investigating the causes of the alarming increase of juvenile delinquency in the metropolis*, London 1816, 5.

19 See, for example, D. T. Andrew, *Philanthropy and police: London charity in the eighteenth century*, Princeton, NJ 1989; D. Owen, *English philanthropy, 1660-1900*, Cambridge, Mass. 1965.

'those who will work', 'those who can't work', and 'those who won't work', was translated into those children who were on the fringes of delinquency, but who with assistance and some discipline, could pull away from the abyss; those who had fallen into delinquency because of hard times; and those who had abandoned themselves to crime. By the mid century, Mary Carpenter was enunciating a two-tiered model of 'perishing' and 'dangerous' juveniles, again echoing the rhetoric of provision for the 'deserving' and 'undeserving' poor:

> That part of the community which we are to consider, consists of those who have not yet fallen into actual crime, but who are almost certain from their ignorance, destitution, and the circumstances in which they are growing up, to do so, if a helping hand be not extended to raise them; – these form the perishing classes: – and of those who have already received the prison brand, or, if the mark has not yet been visibly set upon them, are notoriously living by plunder, – who unblushingly acknowledge that they can gain more for the support of themselves and their parents by stealing than by working, – whose hand is against every man, for they know not that any man is their brother; – these form the dangerous classes.[20]

Carpenter was communicating the feelings of many of her predecessors and contemporaries that, at the core of juvenile offending, there existed boys who were responsible for a great many offences. Further there was the suggestion that such boys were 'dangerous', and a danger to the redeemable 'perishing' juveniles.

Hence, from the early years of the nineteenth century, parliamentary reports, prison returns and social enquiries were concerned most about those children who offended many times. The very conceptualisation of 'juvenile crime' also provoked a more intense enquiry. The subject was newsworthy. Repeat offending was seen as an issue in all offending, both adult and juvenile. However, emphasis was laid particularly on juveniles since it was felt that these persistent offenders would grow into adult offenders:

> These young beings continue to herd in their dens of iniquity, to swarm in our streets, to levy a costly maintenance on the honest and industrious, to rise up to be the parents of a degraded progeny of pauper children, or to people our gaols until they are audaciously wicked enough for transportation – in either case to be a drain on our resources, a festering plague-spot to society.[21]

Such highly-charged rhetoric was accompanied by changes in penal and criminal law that may have encouraged a process whereby those children who were previously labelled as naughty, unruly and mischievous, were now seen as defiant, insubordinate, refractory and as potential juvenile criminals. Moreover, this process was facilitated by the possibility of categorising them

[20] M. Carpenter, *Reformatory schools for the children of the perishing and dangerous classes and for juvenile offenders*, London 1851, repr. London 1968, 2.
[21] Ibid. 352.

as juvenile offenders. Whilst there had always been an awareness of youthful delinquency, it was only in the early nineteenth century that a clearly identifiable label, the 'juvenile offender', emerged and became embedded in the social and political lexicon.

Underpinning the debates about levels, type and incidence of juvenile crime was the issue of age, which focused upon the question of the extent to which a child who offended was responsible for his or her actions. Throughout much of the early nineteenth century, it was felt that the existing custody arrangements could only encourage reoffending. Hence, it was imperative to determine the boundary between young and adult offenders and for that boundary to shape the punitive response to juvenile criminals. The aim was to keep child criminals out of adult penal institutions (although not out of institutions *per se*). The difficulty lay in deciding upon the age of maturity and responsibility. Moreover, this was not simply an issue of fixing a specific age limit. Rather, it meant a re-evaluation of criminal responsibility.

This issue had already featured on the agenda of the Philanthropic Society. In 1796 the Society had appointed a subcommittee to enquire into and report on the first seven years of the Society's existence. On the whole it seemed that the older children had proved less amenable to reformation. Of the 176 boys, fifty-one had absconded, thirty-one of the absconders being aged thirteen or more. The committee therefore suggested that these older boys should not be admitted to the Society in future since they were 'so far advanced in years as affording little chance of their being reclaimed'.[22] Over the years the matter of age was variously discussed within the Philanthropic Society. Correspondingly, parliamentary debate also examined the issue of a juvenile's age, and of its integral relationship to criminal responsibility.

This was a debate with seasoned precursors. Since the Anglo-Saxon laws, parliamentary and legal dialogue had frequently broached the subject. The argument was based upon the principle of *Doli Incapax*, which meant that the guilt of the child rested on the child's recognition of guilt, rather than on the actual criminality of the deed itself.[23] In the early seventeenth century it was assumed that:

> An infant of eight yeares of age, or above, may commit homicide, and shall be hanged for it, viz. If it may appeare (by hyding of the person slaine, by excusing it, or by any other act) that he had knowledge of good and evill, and of the perill and danger of that offence. . . . But an infant of such tender yeares, as that he hath no discretion or intelligence, if he kill a man, this is no felonie in him.[24]

---

[22] *Report of the committee appointed to examine the state of the Philanthropic Society*, London 1796, abstract 04, cited in J. Carlebach, *Caring for children in trouble*, London 1970, 10–11.
[23] The literal translation of *Doli Incapax* is 'incapable of being sorry', i.e. incapable of understanding.
[24] M. Dalton, *The countrey justice, conteyning the practise of the Justices of the Peace out of*

With property crime, and other offences, this criterion of knowledge of self-guilt had to be established.[25] Moreover, the factor of age also had to be considered. During the early modern period, various age limits were established and changed, but it was not until the nineteenth century that age and criminal responsibility were linked by statute.

However, the working-out of this relationship was fraught with confusion and dissatisfaction, much of it resting upon the seemingly arbitrary nature of the setting of age parameters. As the MP for Pontefract, Mr Milnes, noted in 1850:

> In England the Law had never laid down a distinct rule as to the age under which a child could be convicted, except, as he had been informed, that no legal conviction could be had of an offender under seven or eight years. But how little that rule, if it existed, had been adhered to in practise, might be inferred from the fact that Lieutenant Tracy, the governor of Westminster Bridewell, had had under his charge one boy not much over five years old, and ten more under eight years.[26]

Complicating the issue of age was the familiar division between 'dangerous' and 'perishing' juveniles. Clearly it was felt that tender age did not automatically correlate to innocence or inexperience. Thus a close connection was made between the age of the offender and the number of convictions: should the child of twelve, for example, who had been in custody many times, be treated differently from the lad of sixteen who had appeared in court on his first conviction? Reclamation depended less on the age of the juvenile than the degree to which he/she was 'hardened'. Age and experience were not identical.

Commentators also held a number of perceptions about criminality and its relationship to both masculinity and femininity. Another set of stereotypes came into play in such an arena. One of the perennial features of all juvenile offending is its overwhelmingly masculine character. The landscape of youthful offending, and particularly of persistent youthful offending, is framed almost exclusively as male territory. Indeed, throughout the recorded history of juvenile crime, prosecutions of boys have heavily outnumbered those of

their sessions ... 6th edn, London 1635, 244–5; A. W. G. Kean, 'The history of the criminal liability of children', *Law Quarterly Review* liii (1937), 364–70.
25 The case of William York, a ten-year-old boy convicted for the murder of a five-year-old girl at the Bury assizes in 1848, provided a striking example of the principle of *Doli Incapax*. William's attempts to bury the child, and the cleansing of blood from his body, meant that there was an acknowledgment of self-guilt. The issue was not simply that the child had killed, but that he recognised, by burying the body and cleansing himself, that this act was wrong: Anon., *The laws respecting women as they regard their natural rights or their connections and conduct . . . also, the obligations of parent and child, and the condition of minors . . . (etc) in four books*, London 1877, 429–30.
26 Speech on Juvenile Offenders Bill in *Debates of the House of Commons* (hereinafter cited as *Hansard*), 3rd ser. cx. 767–83.

girls.[27] Historically, early nineteenth-century opinion also saw juvenile crime as a male problem. Few urban explorers considered female offenders in their portrayals of criminal subcultures. When females had a strong presence in these narratives, it was in the standard role of the prostitute or criminal moll. Moreover, their role was corrupting, as girls became 'women' – the implicit suggestion here being that the sexual nature of their transgressions placed them beyond hope of redemption. Many accounts of juvenile boys linked their increasing delinquency to the influence of such women and girls. Thus William Augustus Miles, after interviewing eleven girls in the Westminster Bridewell about their life-styles, commented that 'young thieves – boys who lived entirely by plunder – lived, slept with, and kept them . . . that all stolen goods were consequently "fenced" or disposed of before the boys came home . . . that the girls frequently maintained the boys by the wages of their prostitution'.[28] Edward Gibbon Wakefield expressed a similar view. He noted in 1831:

> that a large proportion of the boys above twelve years of age, and even some younger, committed to Newgate, have been connected with women; a fact of which there is constant proof, since these boys are every day visited by their mistresses, under the name of 'sisters'; and the greater part of their conversation in the prison, which is sometimes, and might be always, overheard, turns upon their amours.[29]

Essentially, girl thieves were seen as peripheral to boys, and not really considered in their own right. This determination to categorise boys as thieves and girls as prostitutes provokes a number of questions. At the very least the gender dimension in prosecution policy and the organisation of custody needs to be considered. For example, the Philanthropic Society extended their facilities to female juveniles up until 1845. However, such girls were generally the offspring of offenders rather than offenders themselves. Moreover, no girls with 'unchaste manners' were accepted into the Society, as they were apparently difficult to place. By 1817 the Society had decided to stop taking in girls with criminal records. This came after a period during which restraint of the girls had proved arduous, with several absconding and attempting to communicate with the boys.[30] The Refuge for the Destitute and the Bridewell also took in female juveniles, in some cases recommended

---

[27] A detailed quantitative examination of the gender bias in juvenile offending and the punishment of juveniles can be found in the statistical appendix at the end of this book. An informative analysis of women and crime in the nineteenth century can be found in L. Zedner, *Women, crime, and custody in Victorian England*, Oxford 1991.

[28] Miles, *Poverty*, 45.

[29] Wakefield based his writings on his own prison experiences. In 1828 he had been sentenced to three years in Newgate for the abduction of an heiress: 'Facts relating to the punishment of death in the metropolis', cited *The collected works of Edward Gibbon Wakefield*, ed. M. F. Lloyd Pritchard, London 1968, 187–267 at pp. 200–1.

[30] Carlebach, *Caring for children*, 11–12, 14.

by the magistrates, in others brought by their guardians. A substantial number of these girls were seen as being out of control, and having 'loose habits'. Typical entrants to the Bridewell house of correction in 1835 were the fourteen-year-old, brought in by her father: 'a Girl of violent, wild, and disobedient Character, quite beyond the Control of her parents'. Another fourteen-year-old was brought in by her friends: 'This young girl is addicted to pilfering, has followed loose habits, and associated with very bad characters.'[31] However, it is clear that female juvenile 'unruliness' was emphasised in these institutions. The entrenched notion that female violence and assertiveness was unnatural permeates such commentary on juvenile girls, underscored as it was by implied sexual patterns of behaviour.

There was some discussion of juvenile prostitution in the early metropolitan police select committees, with concern being voiced over the link between lodging-houses and the trade in juvenile prostitutes.[32] More emphasis was placed on the female offender in the 1820s through the activities of Elizabeth Fry. Her work was closely related to that of other prime movers in the field of criminal reform, in particular those involved in the Refuge for the Destitute, an institution which was primarily involved in the 'rescue' of juvenile offenders.[33]

The best evidence for the historian of female juvenile offenders has to be sought in an institutional framework. Increasingly, with the establishment of the industrial and reformatory schools, female juvenile behaviour came under scrutiny. Like their male counterparts, girls were also classified. Not surprisingly, sexuality was the major determinant in the treatment of juvenile girls. Both Michelle Cale and Linda Mahood have commented on the early branding of boys as thieves and girls as prostitutes. The precocious sexuality of these girls was as threatening as the boys' propensity to theft. It was felt that not only did these girls need to be protected but also that society needed to be protected from their offspring and the results of their actions. Fundamentally, such girls were the progenitors of the future generation of criminals.[34] In other words, in all cases, the prognosis appeared gloomy. Here was a complex problem for reformers to explore and the judicial system to process.

The following study will to some extent reflect the contemporary concern

---

[31] SC Gaols, PP, 1835, 3rd Report, xii. 419–25, evidence of Mr N. Nicholls.

[32] Report from the Select Committee on the State of the Police of the Metropolis, PP, 1817, vii. 153–4, evidence of John Smith.

[33] The Refuge for the Destitute was founded in 1804, the female refuge opened in the Hackney Road in 1811, and the male refuge a few years later in Hoxton. In 1849, when their government grant was reduced, the male refuge closed. The female refuge continued and in 1923 moved to Dalston where it merged with the Elizabeth Fry Refuge.

[34] M. Cale, 'Girls and the perception of sexual danger in the Victorian reformatory system', History lxviii (1993), 201–17; L. Mahood and B. Littlewood, 'The "vicious" girls and the "street-corner" boy: sexuality and the gendered delinquent in the Scottish child-saving movement, 1850–1940', Journal of the History of Sexuality iv (1994), 549–78; L. Mahood, Policing gender, class and family, London 1995.

with male juvenile property offenders. The history of reformatory institutions, described above, necessarily belongs to the latter part of the nineteenth century, and to the twentieth century. However, the institutional treatment of boy and girl offenders will be dealt with in this study as part of the wider story of juvenile crime that is provided. The chapters following offer a broadly sequential journey through the process of becoming a juvenile offender in the early nineteenth century. This journey does not constitute the 'real' or the 'imagined' experience of being a juvenile offender. Rather, the intention is to provide a more nuanced history than those to be found in previous accounts of juvenile delinquency in the period. In particular, an attempt has been made to impart a sense of experience, and to ask fundamental questions about who these children were? Where did they come from? How did they work and play? How did they view their capture, trial and the punishments that awaited them? To even begin to think in these terms, to catch hold of some essence of past lives, is clearly dependent on the sources. Even for the historian well-provided with sources, the real, but essentially unobtainable, objective is to be able to sit back, to try not to bend them into the desirable shape, but to let them tell their own story. The sources, of course, are a problem. Sources that record criminals, examine them, question them, are shaped by the agenda of the creator – the social investigator, the prison chaplain, the philanthropist and the magistrate. These authorities present a particular construction of criminality, dependent on time and place, on political or economic rationales. Yet within these constructions the voice of the poor can be teased out and captured.[35]

First are the registers of criminal indictments, of prisoners, of transportation, from which we can assemble and analyse quantitative data to produce a clearer view at least of indicted juvenile crime. Data extracted from the Middlesex criminal registers that ran from 1791 provides information about change over time, about typologies of offending, age and gender distributions, trial outcome and punishment.[36] Information of this kind helps to anchor the qualitative nature of the following chapters into a more empirical structure. Second are the textual sources which result from the various public debates; the parliamentary select committees on crime, policing and punishment and the contemporary pamphlet literature produced by the societies and individuals who were contributing to the debate on juvenile crime. On the one hand, in chapters 1 and 5, such reports and pamphlets on juvenile delinquency are used to delineate the lines of debate and argument, the character of elite perceptions of juvenile crime. On the other hand, the unwitting testimony left in these reports is used in conjunction with the third class of source to travel through the process of becoming delinquent. The *Old Bailey sessions*

35 T. Hitchcock, P. King and P. Sharpe (eds), *Chronicling poverty: the voices and strategies of the English poor, 1640–1840*, London 1997; S. Humphries, *Hooligans or rebels? an oral history of working class childhood and youth, 1889–1930*, Oxford 1981.
36 PRO, HO 26/1–56, Middlesex criminal registers, series 1, 1791–1849.

papers, the trial reports of proceedings at the Old Bailey, and, from 1835, the Central Criminal Court; newspaper reporting; police reports; criminal petitions and indictments, provide information on the nature and process of offending and capture described in chapters 2 to 4. Furthermore, these sources, along with the records of the reform movement, are combined in the description of the strategies of punishment and reformatory experiments in chapters 6 and 7. Yet another form of unwitting testimony survives which provides the element of experience running through chapters 2 to 7. These are the accounts of the various interviews with juvenile and youth offenders which took place during the 1830s, interviews with children held on the *Euryalus* hulk and in various custodial institutions,[37] which elicited the subjects' comments on their own offending behaviour, on their familial circumstances, on their relationships with other criminals, on police and prison, on their experience of custody and on their ability to reform. These accounts and interviews are probably unique for the period. Whilst lives of criminals had always been fed to a voracious public, in the guise of last dying testaments and Ordinaries Accounts, these accounts pre-empt the writings of the Revd John Clay and Henry Mayhew who brought a new dimension into investigations of the lives of the criminal and the poor.[38] Thus they attempt to question, not merely describe, criminal behaviour. Whilst such material needs to be viewed critically it provides at least a snapshot of the lives of juvenile offenders in the early nineteenth century.

Thus, the *leitmotif* of what follows is an examination of the person of the juvenile criminal. The intention is to humanise the figure of the juvenile criminal of the early nineteenth century, to put flesh on 'his' bones. Historically, people who offend have often been reduced to categories or discussed as if they were separate subspecies. Partly this is a natural consequence when research involves a group of people for whom little evidence exists outside the records of the criminal justice system. When attempts are made to describe their lives, the portrayal always focuses upon the extreme elements, rarely the commonplace. Whilst personal information about such people will inevitably be tied into their offending (for example, if home life is discussed stress is generally placed on the negative), investigation of work, home, play, school, as well as the experience of the criminal justice system, can be used to contribute to a more holistic approach to the juvenile offender. This 'normalising' of the juvenile is not predicated on any particular model of humanity or human nature. It is common sense to suppose both innocence and

[37] PRO, HO 73/16, notebooks 1, 2, 3; rough notebooks, vols iii, iv, v; HO 73/2, pt 2, loose papers.
[38] H. Mayhew, *London labour and the London poor*, IV: *Those that will not work, comprising prostitutes, thieves, swindlers and beggars by several contributors*, first edn, London 1861–2, repr. London 1967. For a discussion of the prison reports of John Clay see J. Bennett, *Oral history and delinquency: the rhetoric of criminology*, Chicago–London 1981, 65–88; there is a useful discussion of the interviewing techniques of Henry Mayhew in this book at pp. 11–40, 41–64, 265–74.

experience amongst such children. However, the criminalisation and subsequent treatment of children, at any period, is suspect. Whilst some children were clearly out of control, in the early nineteenth century a system was established that often criminalised the most mundane behaviour, and that put its energies into the control of the most vulnerable members of society.

This study is overwhelmingly concerned with early nineteenth-century urban Middlesex. There are several reasons for this choice of time and place. To some extent the timing reflects the chronology of the debate about juvenile crime. Whilst it would be untenable to argue that the juvenile offender was 'invented' in the nineteenth century, it is clear that it is only in the nineteenth century that elite anxieties and constructions of delinquent youth are matched by legislative enactment. Whilst it might be unwise to go so far as to posit a 'moral panic', there does seem to have been a concentration of concerns around juvenile crime in this period. Of course, many periods have crisis points when criminality and disorderly behaviour come sharply into focus.[39] We need only look at the fear of the vagrant and disorderly poor in the sixteenth century, or the concern with idle and disorderly apprentices in the seventeenth and eighteenth, to see a relationship between public concern and the emergence of prescriptive writings or rogue literature delineating the boundaries and dangers of criminality.[40] There is no neat historical paradigm to explain these outbursts of concern over delinquent youth.

Yet the anxiety around juvenile crime in the early nineteenth century has come to be seen as something of a watershed because of its coincidence with the striking social, economic and political changes that were occurring. Indeed, the pamphlet literature evolved most rapidly in the post-Napoleonic war period. Arguably this was a period when concerns about education, reform, policing and poverty were being voiced. In the 1820s and 1830s alone the country experienced the passing of the Factory Acts, the establishment of the Metropolitan Police, Catholic Emancipation, the Great Reform Act and the New Poor Law. The debate about juvenile crime was only one strand in a series of debates around the problems of the poor, and particularly the criminal poor, which evolved and materialised into a series of legislative enactments concerning the criminal trial, policing, prisons and industrial schools. Moreover, anxieties about the criminal poor were strongly focused on the problematic nature of the urban poor. Thus the reports and pamphlets and essays were markedly directed at metropolitan crime, indicating a strong concern with the products and problems of urbanisation rather than industrialisation. The role of London, of the metropolis, was pivotal. Thus, the construction of crime in this period was profoundly influenced by the construction of the metropolis. The metropolis offered diversity, opportunity, shelter, anonymity and knowledge. The 'safe harbour' London provided for

[39] Pearson, *Hooligan*.
[40] P. Griffiths, *Youth and authority: formative experience in England, 1560–1640*, Oxford 1996.

thieves had been commented upon by Henry Fielding in the mid eighteenth century:

> Whoever indeed considers the Cities of London and Westminster, with the late vast Addition of their Suburbs, the great Irregularity of their Buildings, the immense Number of Lanes, Alleys, Courts and Bye-places; must think, that, had they been intended for the very Purpose of Concealment, they could scarce have been better contrived. Upon such a View, the whole appears as a vast Wood or Forest, in which a Thief may harbour with as great Security, as wild Beasts do in the Deserts of Africa or Arabia.[41]

The image of the City as encompassing and devouring, Cobbett's 'infernal Wen', was remarkably persistent. Without the surveillance and order that was seen to have characterised rural areas, or even provincial towns, London was considered a magnet to the criminal and the corrupt. It drew them and sucked them into the vortex of crime. Only in London, with its comparative size and density, was the theory of the criminal class, the underclass, really tenable. Thus mythologies about nurseries of crime, of the criminal 'underworld', found fertile ground in the imagined city of vice. Clearly this perception of London crime needs to be untangled. Commentators did remark on juvenile crime in rural areas, in the factories of the industrial north, in the larger towns like Birmingham, Liverpool, Glasgow.[42] Yet the omnipresence of London, its importance in popular perception, clearly justifies its central focus in this examination of urban juvenile crime.[43]

The study that follows addresses the complexities surrounding the incidence of juvenile crime in an urban, metropolitan setting in the early nineteenth century. Three certain statements can be made concerning this period. Firstly, that there was a rise in recorded juvenile crime; secondly, that a substantial public debate, and consequently literature, was developed; thirdly, that various penal and legal strategies to deal with juvenile offenders were worked out in this period. The relationship between these three factors prompts two immediate questions. To what extent was the rise in recorded juvenile crime a product of the public concern, or vice-versa? And how closely did the development of legislation parallel the views of contemporary commentators? Moreover, the public debates of the time were implicitly informed by stereotypical understandings of child criminality, heavily

---

[41] H. Fielding, *An enquiry into the causes of the late increase of robbers, &c with some proposals for remedying this growing evil*, London 1751, cited in R. Porter, *London: a social history*, London 1994, 152.

[42] C. Emsley, *Crime and society in England, 1750–1900*, 2nd edn, London 1996; Radzinowicz and Hood, *Emergence of penal policy*, 69–73.

[43] Thomas Plint's work on crime in England had argued that by the mid nineteenth century juvenile crime had decreased. However the highest concentration of juvenile offenders in the late 1840s (categorised by Plint as those aged under twenty) was to be found in Middlesex: *Crime in England, its relation, character and extent as developed from 1801–48*, London 1851, 158–72, esp. p. 160.

informed by changing notions of class and of the conceptualisation of a criminal class. Juvenile offenders were often the victims of short-sightedness and over-zealous philanthropy. Hence they were crowded into institutions for the sake of reformation, they were fed restricted diets and placed in silence and separation for the sake of control, they were shipped to colonial territories apparently for the sake of themselves. To humanise them, in all its grandiloquence, is to view them, criminal or victim, as people, children, and not merely as objects of moral or penal policy-making. Often these were ordinary children in extraordinary situations. Both statistics and public debates have reduced historical juvenile offenders to a social problem; hence the individuality of children like John Leary, William Allnut, Hannah Briant, Hugh Farrell, Henry Thompson, William Cook and Caroline Gadberry is lost in the mire of numbers and rhetoric. The contours of such individualities will be explored in this book; for the real testimony of these children, and others like them, is their progress through and appearance in the records of the institutions that 'saved' them, 'reformed' them, controlled them, and punished them.

1

Debates: Causes and Explanations

'The concept of the juvenile offender, with all that implies for penal policy, is a Victorian creation.'[1]

Leon Radzinowicz, in his masterly study of the development of the criminal law from the eighteenth century, is not alone in drawing attention to the correlation between the emergence of a juvenile justice system and the increasingly visible categorisation of the 'juvenile offender' in the nineteenth century.[2] Yet Radzinowicz, like others, fails in that simple correlation to satisfy the more complex demands of an investigation into historical juvenile crime. The statement needs further qualification. Statistically, it is certainly possible to argue that the number of juvenile offenders to be indicted for felony increased significantly in the early nineteenth century. For both male and female offenders indicted in this period youth was the overwhelming characteristic.[3] Moreover, impressionistically, the evidence seems to suggest that a wholesale rise in both indicted and summary juvenile crime was occurring. However, argument based determinedly on a line of thought which follows such a linear path of development needs to be modified in a number of ways.

Firstly, without comparative age information for the early modern period, the nineteenth-century increase in juvenile crime cannot be rigorously tested. Secondly, whilst the language of criminality in the nineteenth century is recognisably similar to our own, this does not mean that similar debates did not exist and circulate in previous centuries. Certainly Paul Griffiths has pointed out the imprudence of underestimating the issue of youthful delinquency in the early modern period, rightly pointing out the problematic

---

1 Radzinowicz and Hood, *Emergence of penal policy*, 133.
2 See, for example, Magarey, 'Invention'; May, 'Innocence and experience'; I. Pinchbeck and M. Hewitt, *Children in English society*, II: *From the eighteenth century to the Children's Act 1948*, London 1973, 431–95.
3 In 1797 those aged 25 and under formed 37% of all offenders indicted in Middlesex. By 1847 the young formed 61% of all those indicted. This increase is even more marked when the age is narrowed down to those aged 16 and under. Thus the number of indictments in this age group rose sharply between 1807 and 1817, and by 1847 this age group formed 15% of all indictments compared to 3% in 1797: see appendix 2, p. 165. For comparative information on the rates in the country see P. King and J. Noel, 'The origins of "the problem of juvenile delinquency": the growth of juvenile prosecutions in London in the late eighteenth and early nineteenth centuries', *Criminal Justice History: An International Annual* xiv (1993), 17–41.

nature of a literature which 'present[s] the experiences of Georgian or Victorian youth as entirely distinctive'. Arguably, the shift that has been identified in the nineteenth century hinges on a closer relationship between rebellious youth and property offences. Concern about youth in the earlier period, as Griffiths remarks, 'encompassed behaviour regarded as antisocial because it complicated the progress to adulthood, including irreverence, immorality, domestic disorders or even the "seditious" implications of conviviality and play'.[4] Whilst such concerns continue in the later period, public anxiety increasingly tended to objectify the relationship between youth and property crime, a factor reflected in the historical treatment of juvenile crime. However, whilst the most visible components of this debate centred on the forms of trial and punishment of children, the underlying issue of wayward and disobedient youth remained.

Perhaps the biggest shift between concepts of unruly youth in the early modern period and delinquent youth in the later period resulted from the changing form of the household. By the early nineteenth century apprenticeship was no longer a major life-cycle experience. Even before the repeal of the Statute of Artificers in 1814 apprenticeship had declined in many industries.[5] Generally, the children who provoked concern during the early nineteenth century were not noted for being apprentices. Many were unemployed or underemployed, or employed in short-term, menial and unskilled occupations. A further effect of the decline of apprenticeship was in household composition; in many cases children stayed in their parental home longer, and even when earning could not necessarily afford to live away from home. In the eighteenth century and earlier 'living in' as an apprentice or domestic servant constituted a common stage in the life-cycle between leaving home and establishing your own household. Increasingly, in the late eighteenth and nineteenth century adolescents and young adults either stayed in the parental home or alternatively lived with relatives or in lodgings.[6] The potentially conflictual relationship between live-in apprentice/servant and master commonly remarked on by early modern writers was thus less an issue in the later period.

Nevertheless, such changes in life-cycle experience and apprenticeship patterns do not constitute a full explanation for the changing focus of debates around youthful delinquency in the early nineteenth century. It is clear that concern was now expressed less about the delinquencies of youth *per se* and more about certain categories of youth, particularly the working-class youth

---

4 Griffiths, *Youth and authority*, 126–31, 129.
5 M. J. Daunton, *Progress and poverty: an economic and social history of Britain, 1700–1850*, Oxford 1995, 275–6; P. Horn, *Children's work and welfare, 1780s–1880s*, London 1994, 20–1.
6 M. Anderson, 'The emergence of the modern life-cycle in Britain', *Social History* x (1985), 69–87; R. Wall, 'The age at leaving home', *Journal of Family History* iii (1978), 181–202.

and the youth of what was conceived as the criminal class. Moreover, the line between these two categories was blurred; more often than not they were seen as one and the same thing. Clearly the semantics of this debate need to be disentangled to provide a clearer picture of the inter-relationship between discourse and changing practices in the period. Furthermore, there are noticeable chronological shifts in emphasis in the writing. For example, the early select committees and commentaries on juvenile crime tended to contextualise the problem, such as it was, within a broader social spectrum. Hence, the relationship between juvenile crime and poverty was considered, as were the morals of the poor, the decline of employment, and the relative merits and de-merits of education for example. The causes of juvenile offending were as often sought on the street as within the arena of the criminal justice system. Already, though, in this period (c. 1810–c. 1825) there was an increasing willingness to site the problem of juvenile offending within the justice system, particularly in the context of the courts (and specifically around the issue of summary jurisdiction) and within the prisons. This reflects the re-emergence of the penal debate, which had been more or less in abeyance since John Howard's ground-breaking work of the 1770s. A dialogue on prison discipline was emerging that was centrally concerned with the issue of classification and segregation within prisons. The concept of reform, embodied in the reformatory, was also explicit in this debate, contrasting with the more punitive regime of the prison. The extent to which juvenile offenders would benefit from a more punitive or more reformatory regime was a particular focus of concern. The debates on the appropriate penal practices for juvenile offenders, which will be considered more closely in later chapters, marked a high point in the criminalisation of children and youthful behaviour. Previously there had been at least some acceptance of the pressure of external factors, such as poverty and unemployment. Increasingly though, crime was seen as something inherent; during the 1820s and 1830s juvenile crime was linked to a much narrower explanation, which was characterised by reference to criminal subcultures and the existence of a criminal class.

It is clear from the social commentary circulating in the second decade of the nineteenth century that there was a widespread belief in the rise of crime. Contemporaries, in London especially, were increasingly voicing their concerns about the perceived increase in population, the crush of humanity in the metropolis, the rising tide of iniquity and poverty. The scales were balanced with immorality on the one side, and demographics on the other. Immorality was supposedly the direct result of population growth. William Fielding, the magistrate son of Henry, ascribed the rise in crime to 'the increase in the profaneness of the times, and from the increase of a very profligate population, which has met with no impediment, nothing to correct it'.[7]

---

[7] *Report from the Select Committee on the State of the Police of the Metropolis*, PP, 1816, v. 126–7.

Accordingly, an increased population led to an increased youthful under-class resulting in a rise in juvenile offending.[8]

The 'rise' of juvenile crime

Whilst the earliest pamphlets from the Philanthropic Society drew links between the Poor Law and the youthful destitution which they saw as its consequence, the first attempt to outline the problem and its causes thoroughly was the 1816 *Report of the committee for investigating the causes of the alarming increase of juvenile delinquency in the metropolis*. This committee, formed in 1815, visited nearly 800 delinquent children whose names they had obtained from Newgate lists of condemned boys, and from subsequent visits to Newgate and other prisons. The report voiced the impressions that the visitors had received, and gave the following as the principal causes:

The improper conduct of parents;
The want of education;
The want of suitable employment;
The violation of the Sabbath, and habits of gambling in the public-streets;
The severity of the criminal code;
The defective state of the police;
The existing system of prison discipline.[9]

In a nutshell, these 'causes', particularly the first four, became a mantra for the vast majority of commentators, whatever their background or interests. Parental neglect, lack of education, lack of religious observance, too little employment, and too much street life. Other themes arose. The perils of what was broadly seen as the criminal class and the subculture they inhabited, entailed corruption by 'hardened' criminals, both adult and children, and the jeopardy of disorderly houses and flash-houses. More generally commentators referred to the corrupting effects of popular culture – attendance at fairs and markets, executions and the general effect of Sunday papers. Others commented on increased opportunity, the exposure of property being seen as a particular inducement to criminality.

However, more shrewd observers remarked on the relationship between the rise in crime and the changes in policing and penal practices. The activities of the police, the process of remanding prisoners, the increased willing-

---

8 The statistics available for the population of Middlesex were insufficiently precise. However, even given the limitations of the figures which were published in the Parliamentary Papers, it is clear that the Middlesex population had a very large proportion of young people. For example, calculations based on information from 1821 showed that those under 15 represented 32.9% of the Middlesex population. However, for a substantial number of the population (20.3%), no ages were returned, making any clear correlation's complex and imprecise: *1821 Census*, PP, 1822, xv. 197.
9 *Report . . . juvenile delinquency in the metropolis*, 10–11.

ness of victims to pursue prosecutions, were all mentioned as factors contributing to the supposed increase of crime.[10] Some commentators went so far as to recognise a dichotomy between the actual amount of crime and the public perceptions of a crime-wave. For example, in 1828 J. H. Capper, superintendent of the hulks, stated that 'the increase of crime has not been much beyond the increased population of the country; I do not state that it has not increased, but not to that extent that seems to be the prevailing opinion'.[11] Others felt that the increase had been exaggerated, that the incidence of juvenile crime had, in fact, changed little. James Miller, of the 1815 Committee, felt this to be the case: 'I am inclined to think not so much as is generally supposed; I apprehend they are more known from being more investigated.'[12] Similarly Middlesex magistrate J. T. B. Beaumont was rather non-committal when asked about the increase in juvenile depredators: 'I am not aware of the fact, that there is an increase in youthful culprits; though that may be the case.'[13] As mentioned earlier, some felt that the change was less to do with declining morals, and was more symptomatic of a rise in population: 'I think that the town has now a body of people that must be more indigent than they were before such an increase of population, the poor children now being in such vast numbers, their parents have not the means, nor the Magistrates the means, of providing them with work'; 'Can you state to the Committee any reason why . . . the number of juvenile depredators should have increased? – I am not aware of any reason why it should, except from the population in general having increased.'[14] However, if some were prepared to voice contrary opinions, or at least maintain ambivalence, the vast majority agreed with the opinions of the 1815 Committee that 'Juvenile Delinquency existed in the metropolis to a very alarming extent' and concentrated their enquiry on models of explanation.

Secondary causes of juvenile delinquency

Whilst it was widely acknowledged that increasing juvenile crime had profound consequences for the pattern and volume of crime more generally, there was also some attempt to explain what had changed to produce this situation. While there seemed to be an agreement that the morals of the lower orders in general had not changed, or indeed had improved, there was a pronounced crisis over youth. Several reasons were given for this. There was

---

[10] SC Police, PP, 1817, vii. 423, evidence of Richard Birnie esq.; ibid. 495, evidence of Francis Hobler esq.; Report from the Select Committee on the Police of the Metropolis, PP, 1828, vi. 48, evidence of H. M. Dyer esq.
[11] Ibid. 110.
[12] SC Police, PP, 1816, v. 169.
[13] Ibid. 88.
[14] Ibid. 127, evidence of William Fielding esq.; ibid. 77, evidence of Robert Baker esq. (police magistrate, Great Marlborough Street).

a sense that the younger, poorer members of society had been neglected. John Smith, special constable and beadle in St Giles parish, spoke to the 1817 Police Committee about the swarms of children to be found sweeping the causeways of Russell Square, using 'dreadful' expressions and consuming alcohol.[15] The members of the 1815 committee were particularly critical of parents:

> the number of boys is very small whose original tendencies to do wrong have not sprung from the improper conduct of their parents; trifling faults, punished with disproportionate severity; undue indulgence, in permitting their children to be absent from school; allowing them to attend fairs and other places of indiscriminate resort: these are often the result rather of weakness than of design. But if the errors of parents have done much, their vices have contributed still more to encourage the criminal propensities of their children; and as the depravity of the ignorant seldom consists in the indulgence of a single vicious habit, the temptations to which their families are exposed become multiplied.[16]

In 1831, when John Any Bird Bell, the son of Kentish donkey drivers, was tried and subsequently executed for the murder of Richard Taylor, great emphasis was placed on the 'depravity' of Bell's parents. Bell was recommended to mercy on account of his youth, 'and the profligate and unnatural manner in which he had been brought up'.[17]

It is clear that there were a number of reasons which contributed to an increase in juvenile indictments and prosecutions. However, many of the reasons offered were hardly new. Parental neglect, the abuse of alcohol, unemployment, poverty, thief-taking, gambling, fairs and markets, irreligiousness, and the decline of indoor apprenticeship had all been cited at one time or another by social commentators in the previous century.[18] In the 1770s Jonas Hanway had commented on the numbers of apprentices abroad at night. Spectators in the eighteenth century had often denounced the spread of luxury and its constituents: gambling, fairs, pleasure-grounds and the tavern.[19] In the late seventeenth and early eighteenth centuries, the Society for the Reformation of Manners waged war against immorality and

15 SC Police, PP, 1817, vii. 155.
16 Report . . . juvenile delinquency in the metropolis, 11–12.
17 Times, 30 July 1831, 4, col. b; 2 Aug. 1831, 4, col. a.
18 S. Welch, 'A letter upon the subject of robberies, wrote in the year 1753', appendix to A proposal to render effectual a plan, to remove the nuisance of common prostitutes from the streets of this metropolis &c., London 1758, 54; W. Smith, Mild punishments sound policy: or observations on the laws relative to debtors and felons . . ., London 1778.
19 For discussion of social life (and lawlessness) in the early modern period see M. D. George, London life in the eighteenth century, London 1925, repr. London 1996; J. A. Sharpe, Crime in early modern England, 1550–1750, London 1864. The reference to Hanway is from George, London life, 269, from J. Hanway, The citizen's monitor, London 1780 (repr. of his The defects of the police, the cause of immorality and the continual robberies committed, particularly in and about the metropolis, London 1775).

ungodliness.[20] Hanway, the Fieldings and Patrick Colquhoun had all commented on the policing of the poor.[21] On the whole, though, they failed to isolate the juvenile criminal as a specific entity. It is possible that wartime was significant in explaining the rise in indictments of juveniles. Firstly, during the war surplus juveniles would have been absorbed by the armed forces and navy. Then, after the wars, it was remarked that demand for such boys had considerably dried up. Thus by 1828, when Alderman Wood was queried about the likelihood of boys obtaining a naval training through the Marine Society, he answered:

> but they are now very guarded about the morals of the boys they take, because they have got such a choice, and they will not take our thieving boys; in the time of war we got off a great many, but now they will not take the bad boys.[22]

However, the 'crisis', which had some of the hallmarks of moral panic, might well have subsided had it not been for the spiralling pressures of metropolitan life, and the augmentation of institutions to cater for the poor and the criminal. Debates about prison detention and reform had emerged in the 1770s and 1780s. The long period of wartime gave the government institutions and employees greater experience with penal detention. Techniques employed in the hulks and prisoner-of-war camps provided the basic framework in which custody became the main secondary punishment. Jeremy Bentham drew his plans up for the Panopticon in 1791, elements of which were incorporated into the first national penitentiary, Millbank, in 1816.[23] Consequently, it was the increasing tendency to use custodial punishment for juveniles, after the cessation of war in 1815, that resulted in a further intensification of the debate over the next few decades.

Primary causes of juvenile delinquency

There was a general agreement about parental neglect, and lack of education and religious training, which was firmly rooted in contemporary opinion. However, the search for understanding took commentators much closer to

---

[20] The Society for the Reformation of Manners was originally formed in the 1690s, experiencing a revival from the 1780s.

[21] P. Colquhoun, *A treatise on the police of the metropolis: explaining the various crimes and misdemeanours which at present are felt as a pressure upon the community: and suggesting remedies for their prevention*, London 1796; Hanway, *The defects of police*; Fielding, *Late increase of robbers*, and *An account of the origin and effects of a police set on foot by his grace the Duke of Newcastle in the year 1753, upon a plan presented to his grace by the late Henry Fielding, esq. To which is added a plan for preserving those deserted girls in this town, who become prostitutes from necessity*, London 1758.

[22] SC Police, PP, 1828, vi. 85.

[23] The Holford Committee, which was set up in 1810 to consider the possibility of a national penitentiary, was chaired by George Holford (MP), and included, amongst others, Samuel Romilly and William Wilberforce.

the mechanisms of the criminal justice system itself, and to its parallel world on the streets, the criminal 'underworld'. Thus in 1816 Robert Raynsford, the Hatton Garden magistrate, attributed the increase to:

> the pressure of the times, and the indigence of parents in the lower classes, occasion a number of their children to get out from home; having no means of obtaining a livelihood, they go out into the streets, and we all know the young mind is open to be corrupted; they get amongst the common thieves, and they make those young children the instruments of their depredations.[24]

The 'street' thus represented a place of corruption and contagion to young people, the language used to describe the virulent subcultures of the street mirroring the concerns about custodial practices. On the 'street' corruption could be accomplished by older, more 'hardened' thieves, who had pragmatic reasons for using vulnerable children: 'they are made the instruments of other persons who might be fearful of committing those offenses themselves, because they would most likely suffer the punishment of the law'.[25]

To some extent this was probably a valid point, since it was generally recognised that children would not suffer capital punishment. Many juveniles at this time would be acquitted, transported or discharged prior to sentencing. Raynsford pointed out that negotiation between the police, magistrate and prosecutor often arose:

> When a child has been committed for further examination, we do not tell the prosecutor himself, but we find the means of giving him a hint, that if he does not wish to prosecute, he may afford us an opportunity of discharging him, being fully aware it would be the ruin of that child, and that he would be lost forever.[26]

Undoubtedly young thieves were a vulnerable group. However, the older thief, the 'hardened' criminal, the corrupting adult, was transmogrified into a generic figure, representing not only the corrupter of youth but also intimately connected to those corrupting institutions, the flash-house and the disorderly-house.

Flash-houses were essentially public-houses in 'rough' areas. They were generally portrayed as criminal or 'underworld' pubs where deals could be struck, gambling took place, and protection was afforded to its regulars. Amongst the police and magistrates the argument pivoted around the extent to which they could be of use to the police (i.e. in keeping the villains in one place), and the degree to which this was offset by the negative effect the presence of such houses had on the morals of the lower orders, particularly those of the children. Flash-houses were often accused of being nurseries of crime.

[24] *SC Police*, PP, 1816, v. 56.
[25] Ibid. 56.
[26] Ibid. 57.

A typical 'narrative' of the gravity of the relationship between juveniles and flash-houses was provided by William Crawford, to the 1817 Police Committee:

> The number of houses of resort called flash-houses, is a very serious evil: at those places I understand that almost every practise prevails that is calculated to inflame the criminal propensities of youth. I have received accounts of those houses from different boys, who concurred in the main features of the statement: at those places they generally assemble, and divide themselves into distinct parties or gangs, selecting a young man as their captain; they then 'work', as they term it, in certain districts, one party in the daytime and another at night; they are seen in the streets in small parties of two or three, and at stated times the whole company meet, and divide their plunder; one boy stated that his party divided 400l. in one night. The system of dividing into companies is regularly adopted at flash-houses.[27]

There is some suggestion that men like Crawford, in this early stage of his philanthropic work, may have been impressionable. They seem to have taken much of what the boys told them at face value, treating their source material rather uncritically. Really, it is impossible to say to what extent such systematic organisation existed. Certainly, those police officers and magistrates who gave evidence to the 1816 Police Committee seemed to have had mixed feelings about the role of flash-houses.[28] For example, Mr Phillip Holdsworth, a former upper marshal of the City of London, denied knowledge of any flash-houses:

> Not one; whenever there is, it is stopped immediately, and upon a very different opinion from what prevails in the county: In the county, they conceive them to be very useful to the officers, that they meet there whoever they want: In the city, as soon as a house of the sort is attempted to be established, the man has notice; and if he persists, he loses his licence.[29]

Obviously there was a political agenda here, highlighting the traditional dichotomy between the City and Middlesex county. It is hardly credible, given that the City jurisdiction covered the Field Lane area (the beloved thieves' den of social and literary commentators in both the eighteenth and nineteenth centuries), that suppression was so effective. In the same paragraph of his evidence Holdsworth denounced juvenile gangs, 'trained up by adepts'.

In a sense, these examples of faction and diversity give real indications of the problems involved in reading such sources. Much of the evidence

---

[27] SC Police, PP, 1817, vii. 429.
[28] A notorious keeper of disorderly houses, Mrs Cummins was married to a watch-man of the St Giles parish, who had been, 'very active in securing thieves': ibid. 154.
[29] Ibid. 262.

gathered is impressionistic, forming mythologies, perhaps, of the criminal subcultures. However, evidence of training-grounds for juveniles occur throughout the period. There is a certain shift in emphasis. Hence the flash-house is suppressed and its alleged role taken over by the common lodging-house. In 1835 William Augustus Miles noted that:

> there are lodging-houses kept by old thieves where juvenile offenders herd together, and their constant intercourse tends to complete corruption. It is in these hotbeds of vice that they revel in the fruits of their plunder; and though extremely young, they live with girls, indulging in every kind of debauchery.[30]

Though the location had changed, the language remained the same. More-over, it is clear that the line between the police and the policed was a fine one. Community inter-relations and thief-taking practices emphasised the fact that the officers often both lived and worked in the same spaces as their prey. And, of course, many police, parochial officers and watch-men would have been drawn from these same communities, and from the same class.

The conduct of the police was an issue. At a time when the police were still inventing themselves into something like an organised force, disagree-ments were rife.[31] The major substance of these debates was around the issue of 'blood money'. Essentially thief-taking, this was attributed to the insuffi-cient pay allowed for officers. The accusation was that officers 'allowed' thieves to commit a number of crimes, thus making them a more remunera-tive prospect. J. T. B. Beaumont, a Middlesex magistrate, felt this to be a par-ticular danger for juveniles:

> all they see and hear is calculated to make them believe they may rob without fear of punishment, for in their thoughtless course they do not reflect that the forbearance of the officers will continue no longer than until they commit a 40l. crime, when they will be sacrificed.[32]

Concrete evidence of such practices had been glaringly provided by the noto-rious 1816 trial of Bow Street officer George Vaughan. Vaughan specialised in setting up robberies and burglaries and was eventually found guilty of con-spiracy with two other police officers; he was also found guilty in a separate trial of aiding and abetting a thief, John Donnelly.[33] It is probable that

---

30 Miles, *Poverty*, 45.
31 For literature on the policing of London prior to the 1829 Metropolitan Police Act see R. Paley, ' "An imperfect, inadequate and wretched system"? Policing London before Peel', *Criminal Justice History: An International Annual* x (1989), 95–130; C. Emsley, *Policing and its context, 1750–1870*, 2nd edn, London 1996; S. H. Palmer, *Police and protest in England and Ireland, 1780–1850*, Cambridge 1988.
32 *SC Police*, PP, 1816, v. 65. A 40l. crime was an offence attracting a £40 reward. This issue is dealt with most strongly in the Police Select Committees for 1816, 1817 and 1818. In this context 'police' is a generic term for all types of pre-1829 law enforcement, i.e. Bow street officers, patrol-men, police-officers, the Watch etc.
33 See *Times*, 23, 25 Sept. 1816; OBSP, seventh session, 1816, no. 824, pp. 374–9, for the

Vaughan was also willing to manipulate justice in the case of children. For example in February 1814 Vaughan pursued three boys, Moses Solomon and Joseph Burrell, both aged nine, and eight-year-old John Morris as they cracked a window in Watling Street, stole some oranges and nuts, cracked the window of Mr Atkinson's shop in Lombard Street, and attempted to 'star the glaze' at Mr Grosvenor's shop in Holborn:

> I belong to Bow-street. On Monday the 7th of February, I saw the three prisoners in Holborn, at the shop window of Mr Grosvenor, and while they were there, the prisoner Burrell put his hand into his right hand pocket and pulled out a knife from that pocket: at Mr Grosvenor's window he opened the knife and put it to the putty of the window, and as soon as he put it to the putty of the window I saw the glass fly across.[34]

As they were in the process of removing a pair of shoes, they were apprehended by Vaughan: allowing the boys to remove goods from the house made the charge capital, thus providing him with a more remunerative reward.

Whilst the ambiguity felt about the role of policing was implicit in the early select committees, there was also some recognition that improvements in policing had occurred. Thomas Evince, a Surrey magistrate, agreed with the 1816 Select Committee that the increase in juvenile crime was in part due to an increased vigilance on the part of police officers, and also of 'parochial constables who are attending at the water-side and the wharfs'. The Bow Street magistrate, Richard Birnie, also attributed some of the increase to the activity of the police; 'there are more pick-pockets and younger branches of thieves detected than there used to be: at Bow-street we have a larger establishment than at other offices, and our men patrol the streets and fall in with them more than the men at other offices'.[35] Birnie felt that there had been an increase in petty crime, rather than in crime *per se*. These types of minor offences were more likely to be committed by juveniles.

The prosecutor was also implicated in the explanation of the juvenile 'crime-wave'. It was felt that the decline in the severity of laws and the increased willingness of victims to prosecute, combined with various acts for the payment of prosecutors' fees, had resulted in an increase in the number of juvenile prosecutions pursued. Talking to the Select Committee on Criminal Laws in 1819, an insurance broker, Mr Samuel Garrett, discussed the unwillingness to prosecute, stressing, 'that if I were robbed fifty times I could not conscientiously prosecute the offenders, knowing that it would subject them

---

trial of George Vaughan and John Donnelly. See also L. Radzinowicz, *A history of English criminal law and its administration from 1750*, II: *The clash between private initiative and public interest in the enforcement of the law*, London 1956, at pp. 333–46 for an account of the 1816 trials.
[34] OBSP, third session, 1814, no. 208, p. 126.
[35] *SC Police*, PP, 1816, v. 64; *SC Police*, PP, 1817, vii. 423.

to capital punishment'.[36] In part, this was indicative of a growing revulsion at the idea of capital punishment for anything but murder. In the same year Thomas Fowell Buxton spoke in the House of Commons on the barbarity of capital punishment. In his memoirs he wrote, 'I conjecture that no man on the committee goes so far as I go – namely, to the abolition of the Punishment of death; except for murder.'[37] The cumulative effect of such attitudes was the movement, led by Sir Samuel Romilly, to repeal a number of capital crimes. In 1808 the death sentence was removed from picking-pockets, and in 1820 from stealing in shops.[38] However it was not until the accession of Victoria that capital punishment was limited to murderers.[39]

For other commentators unwillingness to prosecute prior to this period had less to do with humanitarianism and more to do with the cost of prosecution. The cost incurred in absence from work was also a great drawback. In 1778 an act had been passed authorising the courts to pay expenses in felony cases if the accused was convicted,[40] and John Eardley Wilmot certainly believed that this had encouraged prosecutions: 'it may have had an indirect tendency to multiply crime', especially since it had meant greater numbers 'contaminated' by prison.[41] In 1826 further legislation was included in Peel's Criminal Justice Act, which he felt addressed the situation, where 'the public interest loudly demands reparation from the offender'.[42] Two years after the passage of Peel's legislation the Marlborough Street magistrate, H. M. Dyer, was asked whether he thought it had caused the rise in crime. Dyer answered that:

> it is but fair to observe, that there is a greater inducement now to persons to prosecute since there has been greater liberality in allowing expenses; and that this circumstance has produced a greater number of prosecutions in proportion to the real number of actual offenses.[43]

---

36 *Report from the Select Committee on Criminal Laws &c*, PP, 1819, viii. 105.

37 Sir T. F. Buxton (Ist Bart.), *The substance of a speech of Thomas Fowell Buxton, esq. MP in the House of Commons, March 2nd, 1819: on the motion of sir James Mackintosh . . . "that, a select committee be appointed, to consider of so much of the criminal laws as relates to capital punishment or felonies . . .",* London 1819; C. F. Buxton (ed.), *Memoirs of Thomas Fowell Buxton, baronet: with selections from his correspondence edited by his son, Charles Buxton, esq. BA.,* London 1848, 87.

38 Larceny (pickpockets), 48 Geo. III c.129 (1808); Repeal of Capital Punishment for Stealing in Shops, 1 Geo. IV c.115 (1820).

39 V. A. C. Gatrell, *The hanging tree: execution and the English people, 1770–1868,* Oxford 1994, 566–85, 591–5.

40 Expenses for Prosecutions, 18 Geo. III, c.19 (1778).

41 J. Eardley Wilmot esq., *A second letter to the magistrates of Warwickshire on the increase of crime in general, but more particularly of juvenile delinquency, with a few observations on the causes and remedies of this increasing evil,* London 1820, 10.

42 Criminal Law, 7 Geo. IV c.64 (1826), *Hansard,* 4th ser. xiv. 1230 (1826), cited in Emsley, *Crime and society,* 146.

43 *SC Police,* PP, 1828, vi. 48.

Whilst the search for understanding continued, there was an increasing shift in emphasis towards exploring possible treatments and punishments which could be directed at juvenile offenders. By the later 1830s and 1840s the debates had developed a strongly punitive rationale. On the journey to this harsher attitude commentators and penal professionals sought to find some solution which would minimise the damage which full incorporation into a criminal justice system designed for adults could inflict on children. For many people summary jurisdiction provided the answer. Thus, during the 1820s, a two-tiered debate emerged concerning the processing and treatment of juvenile crime: separate trial and separate custody of children. Both of these were significant, as they signalled a process which would result in the large-scale criminalisation of children and consequently exacerbate the problem of juvenile offending.

Summary trial and jurisdiction

For those concerned with the welfare of juvenile offenders, one of the most controversial issues was that of summary jurisdiction.[44] Summary jurisdiction gave the magistrate or the bench the right to adjudicate immediately upon a matter. There was no jury present and trial could take place in front of one or two magistrates. All potential offenders first appeared before a magistrate. Depending on the severity of the crime, and/or quality of evidence, and willingness of the prosecutor, the accused would be committed for trial at a superior court. For this period the accused was committed to custody, on remand. Meanwhile, an indictment was prepared and the case passed on to the grand jury. The advocates of summary jurisdiction felt that it should be available to try crimes below a certain value or level of seriousness; crimes below a certain value committed by juveniles (though as Peel had pointed out the act of fixing the age of the juvenile was an arbitrary task); and crimes attracting a relatively 'mild' punishment – a fine, a flogging, or a short term of imprisonment.[45]

The main problem with the conventional procedure was that it raised concerns for the moral well-being of the prisoner during the period of remand. Many of the accused could spend weeks or even months in custody. It was not unusual, in the unreformed prisons, for remand prisoners to be mixed with those serving out their sentences. Even in those establishments which served as transitional prisons, such as Newgate, there were few

---

[44] For fuller discussions on summary jurisdictions see Radzinowicz and Hood, *Emergence of penal policy*, 618–24; Shoemaker, *Prosecution and punishment*; J. Styles, 'From an offence between men to an offence against property? Industrial pilfering and the law in the eighteenth century', in M. Berg, P. Hudson, and M. Sonenscher (eds), *Manufacture in town and country before the factory*, Cambridge 1983, 173–208.
[45] 'Juvenile Offenders Accused of Larceny', *Hansard* xx. 997–8 (1829).

attempts to separate boys from men, or known offenders from first-timers. Since children were viewed as fundamentally impressionable, the association of prisoners caused great disquiet. The effect of such intercourse was discussed in worrisome, invasive, corporeal terms – of 'contamination', 'contagion', and 'corruption' (a medical language reflected in the pamphlet literature which advocated 'cures' and 'remedies' to deal with juvenile crime).[46] Summary jurisdiction, it was said, would decrease the potential for 'contamination' to a considerable extent by cutting out the remand period, and processing offenders quickly and cleanly, thereby avoiding the glare and ceremony of the superior courts. It was felt that children, where possible, should be kept out of these courts. For inexperienced offenders it was crucial that they did not get too established within the mechanisms of the criminal justice system.

Forms of summary jurisdiction were already being used to process an extensive range of actions and behaviour. As Robert Shoemaker has pointed out, the pre-industrial definition of crime was much broader:

> while a narrow range of theft offences dominate the records of prosecuted felonies, misdemeanours include, in addition to property offences (theft, fraud, trespass), significant numbers of vice offences (keeping a disorderly or unlicensed alehouse, prostitution, gambling), regulatory offenses (neglect of office, failure to repair the highway, selling goods underweight), poor law offences (idleness, vagrancy, bastardy), and offences against the peace (riot, assault, defamation).[47]

Indeed, for the upholders of public morality, there was a fine line between misdemeanour and felony. Whilst the major distinction between the two was in mode of trial, the fact that many of these moral offences (such as gambling, vagrancy and disorderly behaviour) were 'victimless' meant little to the rhetoric of criminality. Theft (petty pilfering), trespass, prostitution, gambling, idleness, vagrancy, riot and assault were all offences which could be committed by young people. Such activities were often seen as the province of delinquent youth, disorderly apprentices and girls of 'loose habits'. Moreover, during the early nineteenth century there was an extension of summary powers (although it took another twenty years for them to be properly extended to juvenile offenders).[48] The Vagrancy, Malicious Trespass and Police Acts of the 1820s widened the net, giving the magistrates extensive powers over delinquent, if not excessively criminal, behaviour.[49] For example, the 1829 Police Act, allowed a policeman to apprehend:

46 See, for example, Neale, *Juvenile delinquency in Manchester*; Wilmot, *A second letter to the magistrates of Warwickshire*. However, this language was not peculiar to the early nineteenth century: Fielding, *Late increase of robbers*.

47 Shoemaker, *Prosecution and punishment*, 6.

48 H. Shore, 'The social history of juvenile crime in Middlesex, 1790–1850', unpubl. PhD diss. London 1996, 84–95; Radzinowicz and Hood, *Emergence of penal policy*, 620–1.

49 An Act for the Summary Punishment, in certain Cases, of Persons willfully or

All loose, idle and disorderly Persons whom he shall find disturbing the Public Peace, or whom he shall have the just Cause to suspect of any evil Designs, and all Persons whom he shall find between Sunset and the Hour of Eight in the Forenoon lying in any Highway, Yard, or other place, or loitering therein, and not giving a satisfactory Account of themselves.[50]

These acts gave the police extensive powers and the capacity for intervention into the lives of delinquent children. Indeed, Susan Magarey has argued that these acts specifically targeted the sorts of behaviour associated with young people, thus causing a rise in juvenile prosecutions.[51] Yet the extent to which these acts merely formalised the existing policies of many magistrates has to be considered.[52] Prior to the acts there are some indications that magistrates were using their own discretion when faced with juvenile offenders. To some extent the acts that appeared in the late twenties and thirties merely codified procedures that were already being used, making such powers more systematic and universal.

It is clear that in the 1810s, the period which experienced the principal rise in prosecutions of juveniles for indictable crime, substantial numbers of young people were being committed to Bridewells and houses of correction on charges of vagrancy and for other misdemeanours.[53] Indeed, there are

---

maliciously damaging, or committing Trespasses on public or private Property, 1 Geo. IV, c.56 (1820); An Act for consolidating and amending the Laws in England relative to Larceny and other Offenses connected therewith, 7 & 8 Geo. IV, c.29 (1827); Vagrancy Act, 5 Geo. IV, c.83 (1824); An Act for Improving the Police in and near the Metropolis, 10 Geo. IV, c.44 (1829).

[50] 10 Geo. IV c.44, cl. VII.

[51] Magarey, 'Invention', 18–21.

[52] It could be argued that there was a general shift in legal history in the period between 1790 and 1850, during which legal control of working-class behaviour became much more vigorous. For example, the Combination Acts of 1799–1800 made common-law bans on work-place practices more effective. In other words, they formalised and strengthened policies which were already being used in practice.

[53] Figures published in the *Report of the Select Committee on the State of the Police of the Metropolis* of 1818, from the Tothill Fields Bridewell in Westminster, and from the house of correction, Coldbath Fields in Clerkenwell, indicate a considerable amount of juvenile vagrancy in the years between 1815 and 1818: Tothill Fields Bridewell indictments for ages 7–19: felonies – 250, vagrancy/idle and disorderly – 232, other misdemeanours – 109. The figures from Coldbath Fields house of correction break down into specific offences. Rogues, vagabonds, disorderly persons, disorderly apprentices, reputed thieves and jugglers accounted for 56% of all committals of offenders under the age of 20. Of committals for all ages, 53% come from these categories. Felony accounted for 27% of the under-20 committals, and for only 18% of all age committals. Whilst it would be reasonable to expect some level of unreliability, these tables do seem to indicate a fairly significant level of vagrancy amongst the committals to these two institutions. However, these were places supposedly of correction and reformation, so perhaps it is natural that higher levels of vagrants and petty offenders would feature. Yet a similar table for the City of London prison and house of correction at Giltspur Street, show that a significant number of committals (all ages) to the prison were vagrants – 38% The house of correction figures are much lower – only 4% of house of correction committals were for vagrancy. Finally, at the New Prison, Clerkenwell,

indications that magistrates were using powers to charge people with being vagrants, or with idle and disorderly behaviour from an early date. In fact, throughout the early modern period this had been the case. For example, in 1732, the mayor of London issued the following proclamation:

> This Court taking Notice, that divers Poor Vagrant Children are suffered to skulk in the Night-time, and lie upon Bulks, Stalls, and other Places in the Public Streets of this City, whereby many of them perish by the extremity of the Weather, and other Inconveniences ensue. Therefore to prevent the same for the Future, This Court doth desire the several Aldermen of this City to call before them the several Constables and Beadles within their respective Wards, and to give them strictly in charge, that if they or any of them shall find any poor Vagrant-Child, or Children, or others, lurking in the Publick Streets of this City in the Night-time, that they immediately apprehend such, and secure him, her or them, in their Watch-house, or some other convenient Place, until they convey them before some Justice of the Peace for this City and Liberty thereof, that they may be examined and sent to Places of their Legal Settlements, or otherwise disposed of according to Law.[54]

Obviously, whilst the 1824 Vagrancy Act undoubtedly broadened the definition of the offence, substantial numbers of children were already being imprisoned on charges of vagrancy. In the 1817 Police Committee, the principal clerk to the Lord Mayor, Francis Hobler, was examined concerning the extent of magisterial power, and was asked:

> Have the magistrates any authority at present to inquire into petty offenses which are daily committed by children, and to commit those juvenile depredators to hard labour for any given time? – They have not, *strictly speaking* [my italics].[55]

Hobler continued to state his support for the concept of summary jurisdiction by the magistrate. His ambiguity implies that these arguments were long familiar, and perhaps that some of the practices, at least informally, were also familiar:

> the Lord Mayor frequently orders boys to solitary confinement; and though he has no power to confine them a certain time, yet he often exercises that parental authority at the request of parents, by putting the boys into the house of

only 20% of all age committals were charged with misdemeanours or being idle and disorderly, but this would be explained partly by the fact that this was largely a remand prison, holding prisoners awaiting trial or those in want of sureties: *SC Police, with an Additional Report, Minutes of Evidence and Appendix*, PP, 1818, viii. 284–92.
[54] *Mayors proclamation* (28 Nov. 1732), cited in Sanders, *Juvenile offenders*, 40. For discussion of vagrancy and the Vagrant Acts in the early modern period see A. L. Beier, *Masterless men: the vagrancy problem in England, 1560–1640*, London 1985; Sharpe, *Crime in early modern England*, 99–103; P. Slack, *Poverty and policy in Tudor and Stuart England*, London 1988, 91–112.
[55] *SC Police*, PP, 1817, vii. 494.

correction by way of remand; the hearing the irons and bolts and fastenings, and the chains (if he has any feelings left,) frequently produces the best effects, and he comes up quite penitent and full of promises for future behaviour.[56]

In this instance the mayor, with the parents' agreement, placed children in the house of correction, without formal trial by jury, in the hope of redeeming them through a 'short, sharp, shock'.[57] The evidence suggests that magistrates may already have had a summary role in the treatment of young offenders.

Yet the drive for summary jurisdiction was not wholly universal; dissenting opinions were still voiced within the elite. In 1837 the Revd John Ousby, chaplain of the house of correction at Coldbath Fields, was examined by the Select Committee on Metropolitan Police Officers. Asked about the increase in juvenile offenders, Ousby attributed it to 'the close inspection of the police, and the summary jurisdiction of the magistrates'. Moreover, he felt that the summary conviction of vagrants contributed significantly to the increase in crime: 'I think if those persons were not summarily sent to prison, but were sent to be tried before a jury, that many of them would not be convicted; that many of them who are now sent would not be sent to prison.' The combination of over-zealous magistrates and police, led to the committal and ultimate ruin of many children who were, Ousby felt, comparatively innocent:

> I believe a great many of them are innocent; I have got some cases here which will enable the Committee to judge . . . Thomas Smith says he is 17 years of age, and that his father is a journeyman baker, that he was imprisoned with William Cross two months also, having been in company with him gathering bones, rags, &c., in Islington, and that they were imprisoned for trespassing. He had never been imprisoned before.

The minister described how William Cross, Thomas Smith and John White were arrested picking up bones and rags, and then committed to the house of correction by the magistrate. The point Ousby was making was that the eagerness to remove children from the streets on what were often trifling offences contributed to the problem of juvenile delinquency, rendered it self-perpetuating:

> When a boy is taken into custody, though he is innocent, he loses his character, and it is with the greatest difficulty possible he can ever come into society again; he then falls into crime as a matter of necessity; he becomes a continual

---

[56] Ibid. 495.
[57] Magistrates could also refer a few juveniles to the private sector; for example, to the Marine Society, the Refuge for the Destitute, or the Philanthropic Society.

criminal, and we do not lose sight of him until he either dies or commits some crime that will subject him to transportation.[58]

This chapter has explored the diversity and breadth of explanation which surfaced during the early nineteenth century. Whilst it can be shown that there was a statistical rise in juvenile crime indictments, knowledge of the actual extent of juvenile crime is probably unrealisable. Yet, if it is impossible to say how 'real' the rise in crime was, clearly for most contemporaries the 'reality' was a problem which they felt they had to cope with, and respond to. Like most societies when faced with what is perceived as a 'crime-wave' their search for explanation passed through a number of stages.[59] First they sought answers from society, the social explanation; from parents, processes of socialisation, popular entertainments. Secondly they shifted explanations to the institutions of crime; the 'underworld' and the justice system, the criminal explanation. Inevitably this brought them to treatment and punishment. The boundaries and sites were sought in summary trial and jurisdiction, and, as we will see in later chapters, in prison, transportation and reformation. The following chapters will continue to look at explanations for crime, and then at the character and nature of crime, but from a different perspective. Thus elite perceptions of juvenile crime will be balanced by descriptions of environment and offending from the perspective of the perpetrators of the 'crime-wave' themselves.

[58] *Report from the Select Committee on Metropolitan Police Officers*, PP, 1837, xii. 166–73, evidence of Revd John Ousby.
[59] S. Cohen, *Folk devils and moral panics: the creation of the mods and rockers*, London 1972; Pearson, *Hooligans*.

2

Processes: Home and Street-Life

'I have been three years on the town stealing anything I can lay my hands upon – I used to gamble all I got – play heads and tails for a shilling each time – thieves gamble very much – I liked cards best – thieves are playing cards all day long. I usually frequented the Hare and Hounds in St. John's street, Clerkenwell – I generally robbed in company with the same boy . . . and also with Robinson who is now on board this Hulk – we generally had thirty shillings a day between us sometimes a great deal more – I never have worked since I began thieving.' – George Hickman (aged sixteen)

'money never does them any good . . . comes like dirt and goes like dirt'.[1] – Henry Thompson alias Thomas Wade (aged sixteen)

Contemporary analysis of the causes of juvenile crime, and the forms offending took, were often influenced by popular stereotypes of crime and current prejudices.[2] Hence the very poor, who 'infested' the highways and byways of the metropolis, the slums of St Giles, Seven Dials, Saffron Hill, Westminster and Whitechapel, came to be regarded as incapable of innocence.[3] There was a casual assumption that these, the very poor of London, were corrupted from birth. The children from these areas, the product of 'corrupted' and 'hardened' parents, were seemingly 'cradled in iniquity':

There are multitudes of vicious and abandoned parents in the Metropolis, who not only allow their children to go on the same dissolute habits with themselves, but who actually tutor them in crime. The offspring of such persons therefore, may be said to be *cradled in iniquity*. No good can ever be expected from them. They naturally run the career of crime, advancing from one step to another, till they finally attain the greatest heights [my italics]. [4]

Magistrates, police and philanthropists generally accepted this stereotype of slum training in the early nineteenth century. Indeed its potent imagery could still be found in the 1830s in the writing of William Augustus Miles and the fiction of Charles Dickens. In a sense this is a consistent, historical

---

1 PRO, HO 73/16, notebook 1, evidence of G. Hickman; rough notebook iv, evidence of H. Thompson.
2 Parts of this chapter have been used in H. Shore, 'Home, play and street life: causes of, and explanations for, juvenile crime in the early nineteenth century', in A. Fletcher and S. Hussey (eds), *Childhood in question*, Manchester 1999.
3 A typical description of the London slums and their inhabitants can be found in T. Beames, *The rookeries of London: past, present, and prospective*, London 1850.
4 *SC Police*, PP, 1828, vi. 48.

stereotype that will never be completely abandoned. Moreover, for the philanthropists of the period it had a useful appeal, for at its most productive it provoked a curious fascination, indignation and reforming zeal. One early nineteenth-century reform society, The Society for the Diffusion of Information about the Punishment of Death, even went so far as to create their own didactic story of slum training in 1810. They created a generic juvenile criminal, Jack Wild, who was on his way to Botany Bay from Dyot Street, St Giles. His mother a transport, his father a drunkard, this boy was an early charge to society, with his own suggestion for prevention:

> I was born in Dyot Street. I never remember my mother; but my father's companions sometimes spoke of her as one who had been transported for passing bad money; my father used to look gloomy and sorrowful when she was mentioned, and never recovered without a glass of liquor: some people said she died broken-hearted in gaol, but I never heard the truth of it. In our street, he who thieved most cleverly was the most admired, and the only disgrace that could be incurred was the shame of detection. . . . I knew nothing, and was taught nothing but to steal; and I practised my art with an industry which I thought most laudable. . . . There are some hundred boys in London who are all living as I lived; and when I was tried, a gentleman in a great wig talked very kindly to me, and if I knew what his name was I would send this letter to him; he said he would have a school in Dyot Street, where boys might be told what was right; and I think, sir, before they are caught and hanged, it would just be honest to tell them that they are in danger of it, and to tell them what is law, and what is society, and not to let them hear of it for the first time when they are tried.[5]

The reality behind such criminal stereotypes was much more complex. The present and following chapters illustrate the interplay between these elite representations and the experiences and perceptions of juvenile offenders themselves. Evidence derived from juvenile offenders and young inmates interviewed on the *Euraylus* prison hulk at Chatham, and in London prisons in the 1830s, will be used, and with complementary textual sources causation will be reconsidered from the offender's point of view.[6] How did juvenile offenders understand their behaviour? Were they driven by poverty, by bad parenting, or by lack of education or religious training as the debates suggested? The reality of such offending behaviour was usually much more mundane. Opportunity, need, peer pressure and excitement all played a role; few children would have described themselves as 'professional' criminals.

5   J. Wild (pseud.), *Begin. Sir, I am on the point of leaving England for Botany Bay, being convicted of picking pockets, etc* (A Suppositious Letter, 1810).
6   A substantial part of the evidence for this chapter, and for chapters 3, 4, 6 and 7 is drawn from these interviews and accounts. The construction and interpretation of these records is discussed in detail in appendix 1.

Education and religion

Most juvenile offenders had only received a rudimentary education and little formal religious training.[7] Indeed, despite the establishment belief in a compelling link between juvenile delinquency and a lack of religious observance, and the concentration on such matters in contemporary literature, there is little evidence to suggest that religion was a primary concern for delinquent children. Some juvenile offenders had attended Sunday schools, and the Catholic children might have attended church schools, so it could be surmised that these children would at least have the basics of religious training. Certainly the national schools, charity schools, and the schools of the refuges, societies and prisons, relied heavily on religious doctrine as part of a rigorous socialisation. How much of this penetrated through to the children it is impossible to tell, since children may have also been receiving religious education at home. Of course a basic question should be asked about the supposed relationship between lack of religion and delinquency. Religious training was a euphemism for moral training. Criminality was essentially portrayed as immoral. It is unclear whether this process of thought would have occurred in quite the same way to young offenders. The majority of organisations and individuals who invested their time and effort in the problem of juvenile crime came from formidably devout backgrounds. Usually evangelical, often Quaker, notions of morality, states of grace and repentance were central to their understanding and response to criminality. Even the most pragmatic 'child-saver', was informed strongly by a Christian credo. It is probably safe to say that for many children institutionalised 'care', be it the workhouse or the prison, provided their most sustained contact with religious training. Eighteen-year-old Thomas Berry, interviewed in prison, c. 1836, told his interviewer: 'I can read a chapter out of the testament and write my own name.'[8] Such rudiments were typical.

Whilst education attainment was also inconsistent many children had a degree of literacy, although this was admittedly often very limited. Of 150 children indicted for felony in Middlesex in the years 1839, 1844 and 1848 only 5 per cent could read and write well, 66 per cent imperfectly, and 29 per cent not at all.[9] The figures for boys imprisoned at Parkhurst prison between December 1838 and November 1848 were better: 16 per cent could not read and write, 21 per cent could read only, 35 per cent imperfectly, and 28 per cent could do both well.[10] However these improved literacy rates might

7 For a discussion of childhood autobiography and education see J. Burnett, *Destiny obscure: autobiographies of childhood, education, and family from the 1820s to the 1920s*, London 1982, which also gives insights into employment, family life and religious training. To complement this see also D. Vincent, *Bread, knowledge, and freedom: a study of nineteenth-century working-class autobiography*, London 1982.
8 PRO, HO 73/2 pt 2, loose papers, interview with Thomas Berry.
9 PRO, HO 26/45/50/54.
10 PRO, HO 24/15, Parkhurst prison register.

reflect the efficacy of the educational provision in the prison. Whilst many children seem to have spent at least some time at a national school, or a Sunday school, these periods were often brief and punctuated by truancy or by employment. Of the 162 male prisoners aged under sixteen committed to Newgate between August 1834 and August 1835, 102 had been at national or charity schools, thirty-seven at private schools (schools or academies set-up by private groups or individuals), and twenty-three at no school whatso-ever.[11] The erratic nature of educational provision was confirmed by com-ments from a group of juvenile prisoners interviewed on the *Euryalus* c. 1836. Thus fifteen-year-old John Campbell had been to a national school 'for a short time'; John Anderson, also fifteen, had been to a national school and could 'read but cannot write'; Peter Conolly, aged sixteen, 'has never been to school and cannot read nor write'; fourteen-year-old Dennis Walker had 'been to a national school as well as a workhouse – cannot write'; William Cook, aged fifteen, 'was at the German national school, cannot write'.[12]

Whilst most of these boys had had some degree of schooling, it is clear that the extent and effect of their education was limited. Contemporary observers were divided about the effectiveness of the national schools. On the one hand, for example, the members of the Prison Discipline Society saw the edu-cation of the poor as a preventative measure and urged the establishment of infant schools:

> It would be difficult duly to establish the effects on Society, and, amongst many other, the certain diminution of private vice and public delinquency, which, under the divine blessing, must follow the general adoption and steady prosecution of such a system of infant training.[13]

On the other hand, it was argued by a number of commentators that national schools actually increased the tendency to delinquency, creating opportuni-ties for unruly behaviour, petty crime and corruption by other children. Matthew Wood, alderman of the City of London, told the 1828 Select Com-mittee on Metropolitan Police that 'in his opinion, the circumstance of boys congregating together in the national schools tended to produce crime'. However the agenda behind the criticism of the national and charity schools was often more insidious. Hence John Rawlinson, magistrate at the Maryle-bone office, told the same committee that 'I think the over-education of the

---

11 PRO, HO 73/16, loose papers, Select Committee on Gaols (secret), testimony of William Augustus Miles, p. 10.
12 Ibid. notebook 1, evidence of John Campbell and John Anderson; notebook 2, evi-dence of Peter Conolly; notebook 3, evidence of Dennis Walker and William Cook. For broader commentary on literacy and education see L. Stone, 'Literacy and education in England, 1640–1900', *Past and Present* xlii (1969), 69–139, and D. Vincent, *Literacy and popular culture: England, 1750–1914*, Cambridge 1989.
13 *Third report of the Society for the Improvement of Prison Discipline*, London 1821–22, 46; *Sixth report of the Society for the Improvement of Prison Discipline*, London 1824, 347 (pp. 345–9 for report from infant school society).

lower class of people has done harm. I do not mean to say that it is not desirable that children should be educated, but if they are to be educated, and afterwards have no employment, you have merely given them the expertness to become thieves.' This sentiment was echoed by fellow magistrate William Bodkin:

> The facility afforded for obtaining instruction, and the consequent degree of intelligence that pervades the lower ranks of society, has caused, with respect to those boys, a sort of premature manhood, and that, whether for good or evil, a boy at ten or twelve years old, is now much more able to do either the one or the other, than he would have been at the same age some years ago.[14]

Thus education had to be clearly circumscribed. Too much education led to precociousness and engendered a situation where children were difficult to control. For the children themselves the issue was less one of control and more of the opportunities education could offer, particularly the benefits it offered for employment and apprenticeship.[15]

Work

The getting and keeping of work was an eternal problem for many people. Education and leisure came second to the need for sustenance, funds for which could only be provided by employment. Patterns of employment were seasonal, and under-employment prevailed. Much work was casual and poorly paid. The scarcity of employment and lack of opportunity was remarked on by the Marlborough Street magistrate Mr Dyer:

> I think the difficulty of finding employment for young persons of the lower classes is another cause of the increase of crime. The ordinary trades exercised in the Metropolis do not afford a sufficient demand for boys in the shape of apprentices. Some others are provided for as pot-boys, errand-boys, and in other menial situations; but there still remains a considerable surplus who have no honest means of getting a livelihood.[16]

Perhaps unsurprisingly, a number of juvenile offenders commented on the relative lucrativeness of thieving. Yet even those children most thoroughly embedded in criminal activity seem to have spent at least some of their time

14 *SC Police* PP, 1828, vi. 88–9, 57, 68, evidence of Mr Alderman Wood, MP, John Rawlinson esq. and W. H. Bodkin esq. respectively.
15 For broader literature on education and social control see R. Colls, 'Oh happy English children! Coal, class and education in the north east', *Past and Present* lxxiii (1976), 75–99; J. M. Goldstrom, 'The content of education and the socialization of the working-class child, 1830–60', in P. McCann (ed.), *Popular education and socialisation in the nineteenth century*, London 1977, 93–109; P. McCann, 'Popular education, socialisation, and social control: Spitalfields, 1812–24', in his *Popular education*, 1–40.
16 *SC Police*, PP, 1828, vi. 48.

in work, or looking for work, rather belying the supposed sufficiency of a criminal 'career'. Consistent occupational information on juvenile offenders is rare. The generic category of labourer tended to be used most often, although occasionally a boy was entered into the records as an apprentice, a girl as a servant. Most records of the criminal justice system were also inconsistent in recording occupation, generally referring to juveniles in generic forms. The registers of Parkhurst did give more specific occupations than the universal 'labourer',[17] but nevertheless, over half of the Middlesex boys imprisoned there were so described: 81 per cent were described as having a trade, 66 per cent of them labourers. The only other occupations followed by significant numbers were, shoemakers (5 per cent), errand-boys (4 per cent), tailors (3 per cent) and paper-stainers (1 per cent). Several of the boys followed skilled or semi-skilled trades such as harness-making, watch-gilding, willow-weaving, ivory-turning and printing. However, the degree of skill a boy would have possessed is debatable; there is no evidence to indicate whether he would have been an apprentice or simply a general dogsbody. Moreover, although 81 per cent of the boys were described as having a trade, there is no indication whether or not these boys were actually employed at the time of their committal. An occupational breakdown of twenty-five juvenile thieves recorded by William Augustus Miles in Liverpool in May 1837 included three errand boys, two each of carpenters, masons, smiths and watchmakers, a cooper, a labourer, a rope-maker, a shoemaker, a stableboy and a tailor. The most numerous 'real or pretended calling or trade' was the criminal activity apparently followed by the eight habitual thieves.[18]

Clearly a number of juvenile thieves did have recognisable occupations or trades. However, as already suggested, their status is unclear. The general impression is that they were learning a trade, but that they were not on the same footing as an apprentice. Fourteen-year-old William Haynes, found guilty of larceny at the Central Criminal court in November 1838, had been for five years in the employment of John Brazier, timber merchant and general dealer in building materials of Soho. William had fulfilled a number of tasks to do with the business, including the carrying around of various monies and payments. He worked at the premises from six in the morning to eight-o-clock in the evening, with an hour for lunch. He also attended Mr Brazier on Sunday morning to clean knives and boots. John Goode, aged fourteen, was convicted in 1835 of robbing Emma Ann Randall in Goldsmiths Row, Hackney. Goode's employer James Dean, a chimney-sweep, stressed the responsibility of the position held by John:

> That the said John Goode has during these last eight years been employed by your petitioner to sweep chimneys in the houses of a great many highly

---

[17] PRO, HO 24/15, Parkhurst prison register. This is a sample of the 596 Middlesex prisoners who entered the prison between December 1838 and November 1848.
[18] PRO, HO 73/16, loose papers relating to rural police.

respectable individuals, where property of every description has been deposited, and that during the above named period your Petitioner has never had a single complaint made with respect to the said John Goode's integrity. . . . That the said John Goode has, for these last four years, also been employed by your petitioner to collect monies and pay debts, due to, and owing by your Petitioner, and has uniformly acted with the greatest integrity.[19]

Few children were described as being in formal apprenticeships. Few parents could afford to put their child under apprenticeship – they were as much at the mercy of unemployment as were their children. Moreover, apprenticeship as an institution was in decline by the early nineteenth century, particularly after 1814 when parliament repealed the requirement for seven-year apprenticeships in skilled trades.[20] Where apprenticeship continued, the age of binding varied, chimney-sweeping apprenticed boys at a very early age to take advantage of their smallness. Before 1834, when an act laid down ten as the minimum age of apprenticeship, eight had been the normal age at commencement.[21] However, for most artisan trades the age of apprenticeship was usually around fourteen, the age at which many juvenile offenders were already making their first forays into the criminal justice system.

Clearly, some children combined thieving and employment. For example, domestic service was often portrayed as a situation filled with opportunity for pilfering and theft. Certainly plenty of juvenile offenders did steal from their employers. Whilst some thefts from service or from the work-place could be loosely described as legitimate or customary perks, petty pilfering could be viewed seriously by employers.[22] Clive Emsley has pointed out that the cases that came to court really represented a very small proportion of the offences which probably occurred.[23] Many employers would have summarily dismissed servants in these cases rather than go to the trouble of a prosecution. However plenty of employers did take their servants to court and these accounts give some insight into the nature of such employment. In 1809 fourteen-year-old Mary Fisher was found guilty of stealing six pounds of flour, two biscuits and five rolls from Henry Hutchins, a baker in High Holborn. She had worked for him as a servant for twelve months. In 1806 Thomas Smith, aged thirteen, stole a £50 banknote from his employer Thomas Person, a wholesale upholsterer. Thomas was employed as a labourer in the warehouse, packing up goods amongst other things. Fifteen-year-old John

[19] PRO, HO 17/52/pt 1, Hz/17, petition of William Haines; HO/84, petition of John Goode.

[20] Horn, Children's work, 20–1. For more general commentaries on working-class children's employment see C. Nardinelli, Child labor and the industrial revolution, Bloomington, Indiana 1990; Pinchbeck and Hewitt, Children in English society.

[21] Horn, Children's Work, 28.

[22] For further discussion on the redefinition of perquisites as pilfering see P. Linebaugh, The London hanged: crime and civil society in the eighteenth century, London 1991, 404–7, 429, 434.

[23] Emsley, Crime and society, 117–18.

Cooper stole various items from the White Swan public house in Bunhill Row where he was employed as a servant in 1802. Thomas Holly, aged fifteen, had only been in service a month when he was brought home in 1802 by police officers who stopped him after his suspicious behaviour at a pawn-broker's. Thomas was an errand-boy to the prosecutors Henry and Abraham Moses.[24] Of course child employees were particularly vulnerable; some children, for instance, might have been wrongly accused because they were the nearest to hand at the time and less likely to be believed than an older and possibly more 'respectable' servant or employee. Other children offended as a protest against ill-treatment from their masters, as in the case of George Webster, aged thirteen, who was found guilty of larceny by the servant at the May sessions of 1835. An orphan, Webster believed that he was about to be dismissed, and so had resolved to rob his master. He stole a box, which had inside it nine sovereigns, fifty-five shillings, and thirteen sixpences which belonged to his master, George Weaver, a Clerkenwell cheese-monger.[25]

The vulnerability of the child in the work-place was compounded by the difficulties of obtaining long-term employment. Boys like John Goode and William Haynes were probably unusual in that they had been in consistent employment for a number of years.[26] For many children chronic underemployment might mean only a day or two of work a week. The experience of seventeen-year-old Thomas Edwards was probably typical: interviewed in prison, he stated that 'I have worked for a Broom Hawker, but could not get employment for more than two-and-a-half days per week.'[27] Work was often seasonal and transient. Fruit-picking and hop-picking, seasonal fairs and markets, hawking and tramping around the county for work, were all strategies frequently adopted.[28] Nineteen-year-old George Wilkinson 'used to travel the County with hardware'; Peter Conolly, aged sixteen, travelled over the country hawking.[29] Children, like many working-class people, used a

24 *OBSP*, seventh session, 1809, no. 711, p. 438; first session, 1806, no. 56, pp. 38–9; second session, 1802, no. 112, p. 88; first session, 1802, no. 73, pp. 50–1.

25 Ibid. seventh session, 1835, no. 1265, p. 134.

26 Hugh Cunningham has commented on the dearth of employment for children in the early nineteenth century. He points out that the child labour market, as such, was highly localised given the immobility of children. Moreover the increasing proportion of young people in the population resulted in more supply and less demand: 'The employment and unemployment of children in England, c. 1680–1851', *Past and Present* cxxvi (1990), 115–50, esp. pp. 146–50.

27 PRO, HO 73/2 pt 2, loose papers, interview with Thomas Edwards.

28 Underlining this, Margaret May's thesis makes the point that the employment made available to children was usually the least secure, most seasonably variable, and poorest paid. Hence juveniles were at the bottom of the job hierarchy and therefore particularly prone to accusations of 'idleness': 'A child's punishment for a child's crime: the reformatory and industrial schools movement in Britain, c. 1780–1860', unpubl. PhD diss. London 1981, 26–31, esp. p. 29.

29 PRO, HO 73/2 pt 2, loose papers, interview with George Wilkinson; HO 73/16, note-book 2, evidence of Peter Conolly.

variety of occupational strategies in order to achieve some standard of living. It is tempting to view thieving as just another of these strategies.

Play and street-life

The children's own explanations for their descent into offending were remarkably consistent – poverty, usually linked to unemployment; temptations, particularly leisure and entertainment; and the example of other children, some adults and, very occasionally, parents. Not surprisingly there was no mention of lack of religious training; religious morality was much more an issue for those social commentators whose actions and behaviour was heavily informed by Christian ideology. Virtue and godliness were fairly meaningless concepts in the world-view of the average juvenile offender. Practical and functional skills and attitudes were far more valuable in the culture of poverty that many of these children inhabited. Other allegiances, relationships and ideologies took the place that would perhaps have been filled by the Church and by God.[30] As would be expected, peer pressure played a considerable role, particularly in the context of adolescence and street-life. Adolescent male pastimes were significant in both contemporary understanding of juvenile crime causation as well as in the children's own narratives of lifestyle.[31] Gambling and gang behaviour were generally linked together. Boys gathered together to gamble – thieving, it was said, was the natural consequence. In 1817 Samuel Furzon, the constable of St Giles and St George's, Bloomsbury, complained about the gangs of young boys who could be found gambling in the streets. Apparently as many as fifty or sixty boys gathered together for this purpose. Furzman believed that this was an inevitable source of pickpockets and thieves.[32] In the same year Mr Charles Lush recommended that more parochial constables be employed in 'dispersing the vicious young boys and girls, who now so frequently associate together from eight to nine, and ten o'clock in the evening . . . committing acts of pilfering and depredation'.[33]

The evidence of adolescent boys themselves did little to undermine the contemporary perception that gambling, wenching, and visiting penny-gaffs

[30] The 'spiritual neglect' of the people was confirmed by the religious census of 1851. On Sunday 30 Mar. 1851 no more than 54% of the population of England and Wales aged over 10 attended church: G. Best, *Mid-Victorian Britain, 1851–75*, London 1971, repr. London 1985, 196–9.
[31] For a broader examination of these themes see H. Shore, 'The trouble with boys: gender and the "invention" of the juvenile offender in the early-nineteenth century', in M. Arnot and C. Usborne (eds), *Gender and crime in modern Europe*, London 1999.
[32] *SC Police*, PP, 1817, viii. 360–1, evidence of Samuel Furzon.
[33] Ibid. 524, evidence of Mr Charles Lamb. This reference to girls in the context of street-life is quite unusual. On the whole such references are confined to the police committees of 1816 and 1817 which voiced a general concern over unruly youth and street-life.

were major pastimes. Sixteen-year-old William Pembroke, interviewed in prison *c*. 1836, credited his decline into delinquency to 'a particular propensity for tossing and gambling', and to 'drinking, tossing, or larking in public houses'.[34] Experiences of gambling corresponded with the general catalogue of what was seen by authority as anti-social behaviour, but by boys, as very enjoyable. Another boy interviewed in the same cohort as William Pembroke referred to his 'irresistible desire for skittle grounds', yet another wanted 'to frequent theatres and to associate with loose females'.[35] For the boys on the *Euryalus* drinking, gambling and girls had been a common pastime in their former lives: Hewitt 'used to lush hard'; Walker said of gambling, 'they [the boys] think nothing of that – used to toss for 2/6 – the most was a crown'; Thompson spent his ill-gotten earnings drinking and gambling.[36]

What is clear from these narratives is that a mixture of motives preceded the movement into criminality. Whilst a few pleaded outright poverty, it was more usual for the children to have some employment, however minor. The indication is that the immediate gratuities of thieving outweighed the merits of honest living. Nevertheless, these descriptions of adolescent street-life were fundamentally actions of unruly male youths, rather than specifically of juvenile criminals: hanging around, playing skittles, pitching and tossing, attending the penny gaffs and theatres, and pursuing the opposite sex. Moreover, theft, the commission of crime, was not necessarily seen by the boys as a separate category into which they progressed. Whilst there were obviously various degrees of involvement in theft (remembering that the child became a juvenile criminal by the process of being caught), the boys often described their criminality as part of a general pattern of delinquency. This could just as well be termed 'adolescent behaviour', and was characterised by a free and easy attitude, by an aura of excitement and larking about.[37] The boys themselves used hedonistic language and phrases to refer to their lives. In the 1830s (*c*. 1836) Thompson remarked of the delinquent life-style, 'When they once begin they cannot leave it off – because they think it is a very easy life.' This view was confirmed by a twenty-year-old interviewed in 1835 by W. A. Miles: 'It is no wonder boys never reform if they have been in

---

34 PRO, HO 73/2/pt. 2, loose papers, interview with William Pembroke.
35 Ibid. loose papers, interviews with Thomas Keefe, aged 19, and Philip Hall alias Lovell, aged 19.
36 PRO, HO 73/16, rough notebooks.
37 Modern biographical investigations of adolescents and delinquent youths confirm this impression. The boys in Peter Willmott's 1966 study of youth and delinquency constantly refer to 'larking about'. One boy discussed his gang: 'When you're in a group, you get kind of excited. . . . You get carried away'; another boy said of thieving, 'We used to thieve now and again, same as anyone else, but I don't think we was bad – it was just a normal thing we used to do': *Adolescent boys of east London*, London 1966, 40, 145. See also R. Graef, *Living dangerously: young offenders in their own words*, London 1993.

the least successful; for look ye here, Sir, the charm of it is, it comes so easy and it goes just as light, it is better than hard work.'[38]

As John Springhall has suggested, descriptions of unruly adolescent behaviour tended to coalesce much more strongly in the later nineteenth century with the apparent emergence of gang subcultures.[39] While gangs were mentioned in the early nineteenth century, they were rarely described as having the degree of homogeneity and unity that seemed to occur in accounts from the later nineteenth and early twentieth centuries.[40] Partly, this reflects the changing response to boy delinquency. Thus there was an emergence in the later nineteenth century of community-based youth organisations and institutions catering for troublesome adolescents, which were more aware of the existence of, and thus able to identify, local gangs. However, some continuities can be traced and a few identifiable gangs of boys and young men were mentioned earlier. In 1816, for example, magistrate William Fielding was asked about the 'enormous associations in the Metropolis that went by the name of the "Cutter lads" '.[41] Throughout this period references were made to the 'swell-mob' – boys and young men in their late teens and early twenties. A boy called Hewitt, awaiting transportation on the *Euryalus* in the mid 1830s, told an interviewer that the swell-mob would often visit lodging-houses in order to recruit 'go-alongs', for thieving expeditions: 'boys are delighted [they] think it an honour to go with a swell-mob'.[42] Generally, such affiliations tended to be associated with older youths. Nevertheless, these gangs were explicitly male, and contemporary commentators saw them as providing an example of the male juvenile's progression into crime. Another boy on the *Euryalus* (c. 1836), William Johnson, described the appearance of the swell-mob members, in their 'flash-dress', with 'curled hair, blue frock coat to the knees, blue trowsers tight to the knees . . . velvet collar waistcoat, low fancy worked shoes . . . hat, generally on one side . . . [as they] go about with a cigar in their mouth'.[43] The swell-mob epitomised the rewards of a life of crime: a boy who had gained membership of the swell-mob, had arrived. Walker described how boys gambled with the swell-mob, and learnt from them, an association of which they were 'rather proud'.[44]

38 PRO, HO 73/16, rough notebook iv, evidence of H. Thompson; Select Committee on Gaols (secret), evidence of William Augustus Miles, p. 6.
39 J. Springhall, *Coming of age: adolescence in Britain, 1860–1960*, London 1986, 138–52.
40 For historical discussions see J. P. Bean, *The Sheffield gang wars*, Sheffield 1981; A. Davies, 'Youth gangs, masculinity and violence in late Victorian Manchester and Salford', *Journal of Social History* xxxii (1998), 349–69; P. Jenkins and G. W. Potter, 'Before the Krays: organised crime in London, 1920–60', *Criminal Justice History: An International Annual* ix (1988), 209–30; R. Sindall, *Street violence in the nineteenth century: media panic or real danger?*, Leicester 1990.
41 *SC Police*, PP, 1816, i. 129.
42 PRO, HO 73/16, rough notebooks iii, evidence of Hewitt.
43 Ibid. no. 119, evidence of W. Johnson.
44 Ibid. no. 112, evidence of Walker.

What should be recognised is the period of adolescence as a time of extreme vulnerability to delinquency. This was vulnerability bolstered by environmental factors such as poverty, homelessness and parental neglect. Most juvenile offenders described their criminality in terms of a conflict between the sorts of peer pressure and youthful behaviour already mentioned, against a background of poverty and disruptive home and work environment.

Home

A thirteen-year-old boy from Stepney, Samuel Holmes, described his enticement into crime:

> used to play about in the street, father tried to keep me at home – has stripped me, taken away my cloathes and tied me to a bed post – because the boys used to come round the house at night and whistle and entice me to go out thieving again with them – they once got some cloathes, got in at a window in the back parlour where I was tied up naked, dressed me in them and I went away with them.

A similar story was told by Francis Boucher, the fifteen-year-old son of a Westminster brothel-keeper:

> Attributes his present situation to the influence of bad boys – who always enticed him to run away, Father used to pay men to bring him back, then he always beat him – severity of his father forced him to run away – Boys used to come about the house to get me out – when father went to the club boys always came for me – used to watch father out of the house because he used to beat any he could catch – boys were at last afraid to be seen in his company near home because if his father could get hold of any boy who might be in his company he was sure to get thumped.

The resort of parents to force to stop their child from offending was not limited to boys. Seventeen-year-old Caroline Gadberry was the daughter of a City officer. Caroline had started shop-lifting with other girls, telling her parents that she was working late at her employment at a harness-maker in Mile End New Town. She lived a transitory life: in and out of court and penal institutions, fencing goods at Field Lane and Petticoat Lane, attending penny theatres and dances, and sometimes back with her parents. 'During this time she would sometimes visit her parents who would take her clothes from her to endeavour to keep her at home: but she has a great many times run away from them.'[45]

These narratives underline the continual tug-of-war between brutality and desperation on the part of the parents and guardians. It has already been

---

[45] Ibid. notebook 1, evidence of Samuel Holmes; notebook 3, evidence of Francis Boucher; HO 73/2 pt 2, loose papers, interview with Caroline Gadberry, reputed thief.

pointed out that parents were, to a large part, held responsible for the delinquencies of their children. Moreover at times they were accused of taking an
active role in the corruption of their offspring. Yet it is more likely that
parental neglect was the culprit, rather than active parental corruption.
Neglect was often unintended, a result of continuously trying to balance the
scales between poverty and survival. Parents were also subject to the same
vagaries of unemployment and under-employment as their children. A
number of factors undermined the sort of support the family traditionally
ought to sustain. Unemployment, death and disease, poor housing, parental
imprisonment: all played their part in undermining the relationship of
control between parent and child. However these reasons contributed to
juvenile offending, they did not necessarily cause it, since offenders with a
relatively stable and 'respectable' background certainly existed.

Most juvenile offenders did come from working families. Their fathers
were employed as bricklayers, labourers, shoemakers, chimney-sweeps,
porters and costermongers; their mothers as servants, laundresses, dress-
makers and needlewomen.[46] Reading the sources it is possible to construct a
story where families suffered temporary or permanent unemployment, where
the deaths of fathers left widowed mothers, or where the father or mother was
in prison or transported. For example, a seventeen-year-old who was on the
verge of being sent to the Cape of Good Hope through the auspices of Henry
Wilson's School of Industry in Woolwich had lost his father to transportation, on account of his stealing nails to make his son a rabbit hutch. A
fourteen-year-old boy had lost his father to imprisonment. His father had
been a watchman but had lost his job with the establishment of the metropolitan police: 'he used to travel twice a week, twenty-four miles each day, to
gather a bundle of chestnut leaves to decorate the fruit stalls in Covent
Garden Market. On one of these occasions he was taken before a magistrate
for trespassing in a wood . . . and committed to . . . Gaol.'[47] Families were
cleft apart by death, leaving mothers or fathers to struggle with often large
families. Nine-year-old Nicholas White, one of the boys on board the *Euryalus* c. 1836, had lost his father six years before. As his mother, Mary White,
pointed out in petitioning the Home Secretary: 'My Lord I have been a poor
widow six years and get my livelihood by honest industry. I am obliged to be
out from morning till night and it was during my being at work that my poor
child got in company with some evil disposed lads.'[48] Similarly Mary Bennet,
the mother of fifteen-year-old James Bennet, pleaded on behalf of her son

---

[46] These occupations come from tables in appendix 10 of SC *Gaols*, PP, 1835, 4th, 5th
Reports, xii. 5–25. They are taken from the Bridewell and the several prisons and houses of
correction in the metropolis. The compiler noted the many occupations held by parents:
'with respect to the occupation of the father, I beg leave to observe that in very many
Instan.., the fathers are not journeymen or mechanics, but only assistants or labourers in
the workshops or manufactories'.

[47] Ibid. 11, 10

[48] PRO, HO 17/27, Cs/30, petition of Nicholas White.

who had been sentenced to transportation for life: 'Your petitioner being reduced to want by the death of her husband and by many heavy misfortunes could not engage counsel to defend her unhappy child.' Mary had been hit by a double blow since James had been caught and convicted in the company of another boy, her elder son:

> That accomplice to the further grief of your petitioner is her own elder son – for him she is told she may not ask mercy – she crushes her own heart and is silent in his behalf – but again humbly implores your majesty to commute the severe punishment of her younger boy.[49]

Bereavement and subsequent marriage were common themes in the early nineteenth century; several children pointed to poor relationships with step-parents as a contributory factor to their delinquency. In 1835 information on parentage was compiled by William Augustus Miles from various metropolitan Bridewells and houses of correction. Of 148 children aged under eighteen, 34 per cent had both parents living, 19 per cent a father living, and 26 per cent a mother living. Only 9 per cent had a step-parent (it is not known whether this includes common-law wives and husbands), and 10 per cent were orphans. Finally one child lived with a step-father only, and two children had been deserted by their parents.[50] This points tentatively to bereavement or desertion as a factor rather than step-parenthood. Certainly, as evidenced by Mary Bennet and Mary White, the death of a parent could have a damaging effect on a family's financial situation. Moreover, the lack of discipline and care which might be occasioned by the loss of a parent was underlined by the emotional blow of bereavement.

Whilst most juvenile offenders came from working-class families, there was obviously a wide variety of experience. Moreover, since most discussion of parental experience came either from contemporary commentators or from the children themselves, the construction of family stories/backgrounds has a very distant perspective. In the criminal petitions the voice of the parent can be heard; however, even here information and truthfulness may be being used strategically on behalf of the child. Three main constructions of family experience/background tend to occur. Firstly, a picture of a slightly dysfunctional family, probably a fairly normal circumstance, where drunkenness or illness or long-term unemployment had probably led to neglect of the children. Secondly, the respectable family, which perhaps again had fallen on hard times, whose child had bowed to peer pressure, or been corrupted by some outside force or another. Thirdly, there was the truly dysfunctional family, much less common, but the model often favoured in contemporary rhetoric – the father and/or mother who actively encouraged their children

[49] PRO, HO 17/130, petition of James Bennet.
[50] *SC Gaols*, PP, 1835, 4th, 5th Reports, xii, appendix 10, pp. 5–25.

to thieve; or the parents who abused their children; or the parents who neglected their children's welfare in favour of their own entertainments.

The most marked debilitating factor for many working-class families appears to have been drunkenness. There are, however, enormous problems with any assessment of juvenile crime, parental culpability and drink. Given the puritanical leanings of so many contemporary commentators and philanthropists, petitioners were keen to present an agenda of morality and abstinence as opposed to criminality and drunkenness. It is therefore debatable how factually reliable such accounts were. Of the thirty-two boys Miles interviewed c. 1836, seventeen professed to either one or both of their parents or guardians being drunkards; the other fifteen described parents in reduced but respectable situations:

has a mother living who is a tailoress she is a drunkard – John Anderson – fifteen

father and mother living, both weavers and both drunkards – James Jones – twelve

father is a currier and his mother is a washerwoman – both sober – Phillip Maine – fourteen

Has no mother and his father is a waterman and a drunkard – Samuel Holmes – thirteen

His father ran away and his mother is a clog maker – she drinks very hard – took to it when she lost her husband – James Edwards – fourteen

Parents Irish and very industrious people, connected with a public institution – George Fitzgerald.[51]

These statements indicate a wide but troubled variety of experience. Clearly drink was a factor, and one that was constantly seized upon by commentators throughout the century. From the earliest nineteenth-century police select committees, through Mayhew, to Rowntree and Booth at the end of the century, causal connections were made between drink and crime.[52] However, it is likely that drunkenness was often the result of indigence rather than simply bacchanalian pleasures. Many families of juvenile delinquents seem to have been engaged in a fight between destitution and respectability in the struggle to keep their heads above water from day to day. Moreover most

---

[51] PRO, HO 73/16, notebooks 1–3.
[52] Emsley, Crime and society, 54, 56, 61; F. M. L. Thompson, The rise of respectable society: a social history of Victorian Britain, 1830–1900, London 1988, 319, 329–30. Incidentally, Miles lost his place as superintendent of the Sydney police in New South Wales on account of a charge of being drunk on duty: David Philips, 'The royal bastard as policeman? William Augustus Miles and the Sydney police, 1841–48', in D. Philips and S. Davies (eds), A nation of rogues? Crime, law and punishment in colonial Australia, Melbourne 1994, 36–72.

people recognised that respectability was a major currency and the main selling point for those parents intent on saving their children from the colonies.

Respectability

> I have seen the parents of the lad, (William Gadbury) who are highly respectable, his sister also moves in a very respectable sphere in Spitalfields (a widow) he is not known by the Police to have been in custody before, or charged with any previous offence.[53]

Clearly, parents who wanted, or felt able, to plead on behalf of their children, knew that the best way of doing this was to plead their own and their child's respectability. Although reduced circumstances were acceptable, a certain gentility permeated such petitions. Most petitions took the form of a covering letter from the parent, or occasionally the employer, with an annexed list of signatures and occasionally supporting statements from neighbours, tradesmen, local clergy and the like. For example, in William Gadbury's case in 1835, an unusual amount of time was spent canvassing good opinions of William and his family. Inspector Norman of H Division took it upon himself to make local inquiry about William:

> Mr Joseph Pullen 40 Old Castle Street (a person of considerable property and respectability in the Parish of St. Leonards, Shorditch) states, He has known the Boy from his infancy, he does not recollect his ever being in custody before, that his parents are most respectable, his father is owner of from 40 to 50 houses in that Parish.[54]

Not surprisingly William's case was being investigated with rare enthusiasm; not surprisingly, unlike the majority of his contemporaries, William got his sentence reduced to imprisonment in the Penitentiary.

Nevertheless, similar devices pleading respectability and enlisting local favour were employed by most petitioners, although most petitioners had to rely on the words of the local grocer or butcher, rather than of considerable property-owners. For example, when fourteen-year-old John Chaplin was sentenced to transportation after being convicted at the Old Bailey at the November session in 1834, his parents Edward and Bridget Chaplin of Bunhill Row, petitioned a number of their neighbours and acquaintances in John's support:

> Chas. Lewico, 25, Sidney Street, Goswell road, in whose service he was for 4 months (in the year 1834) and always conducted himself with propriety

---

53 PRO, HO 17/124, Yr/1, petition of William Gadby (or Gadbury), letter from William Norman, inspector.
54 Ibid.

Robert Joyce, Master of the London Society Protestant Charity School, North
Street, Moorfields, where he was a scholar 3 years, of good behaviour and
industrious habits

... Wild 78 Chiswell St has known his mother some years and believes her to
be an Honest and Industrious woman.

Joseph Knight Bricklayer 109 Bratterman [?] Street the lad worked with him
for some months and conducted himself honestly and industriously

John Butlin 16 Goswell Street has known his father and mother these 12 years
to be industrious people.[55]

Most parents determined to seek intercession on behalf of their child used
strategies of deference, of appeals to mercy, of religious righteousness, and of
respectability. Few were successful. Promises of good behaviour, of employment, suggestions of alternatives such as custody in the penitentiary or a
sojourn in the Refuge for the Destitute had little impact on a policy that
actively sought to transport juvenile offenders – a policy that was underpinned by a belief in the efficacy of separation and colonial remodelling. Certainly it is probable that a number of these children had been brought up by
poor but respectable parents, and had probably gone astray in a short time,
due to peer pressure, or to detrimental familial or employment circumstances.

However there were also children who were repeat offenders, whose
parents of course had every right to plead on their behalf and use the same
strategies of respectability and deference as any other parent. The petition of
Thomas Pamphillon (aged thirteen), convicted of entering and stealing from
the dwelling-house in October 1834, used the usual devices of disconsolate
parents, good character, previous good behaviour, and the alternative of the
Refuge for the Destitute. An accompanying letter from Henry Cutler of
Austin Friars, provided assurances to good character from the Revd Cotton
and Mr and Mrs Cope during Thomas's period of remand in Newgate, and
statements to the effect that the boy's father, Thomas Pamphillon (sen.), was
a 'very hard working industrious man, a shoemaker by trade, and a widower'.
However, a petition of the same year, on behalf of fourteen-year-old Jesse
Daniels, told a very different story.[56]

Jesse Daniels and another boy, seventeen-year-old William Delaforce,
were tried in July 1834 for the theft of a waistcoat and a pair of trousers from
the dwelling-house of Mr Thorp of Chapman Gardens in the Hackney Road.
At the time of the trial only the waistcoat had been found, pledged at the
shop of Mr John Kelday, a pawnbroker in the Hackney Road. The waistcoat
had been pledged by one Thomas Pamphillon. Later the trousers were
pledged in the name of John Thorp. This was on the 22 May 1834, two days

[55] PRO, HO 17/120, Xt/3, petition of John Chaplin.
[56] PRO, HO 17/100 pt 1, petition of Thomas Pamphillon; HO 17/110, vt/23, petition of
Jesse Daniels.

before the alleged robbery, which took place on the 24 May 1834. The trousers had been pledged at the shop of Joseph Harris, pawnbroker, who had also been offered, but refused, the waistcoat. Evidence then was offered to show that Thomas Pamphillon (on whose evidence Jesse and William had been convicted) had pledged the articles prior to the apparent robbery on the 24 May. Moreover Thomas Pamphillon had since been convicted himself of stealing a watch and other articles from the same person who prosecuted Jesse Daniels and William Delaforce:

> Viz Mr Thorp of Chapman Gardens Hackney Road, whose house is next door to where the boy Thomas Pamphillon resided, the key of which, it is found will open Mr Thorp's door.

Accompanying the petition – which consisted of letters from both Jesse's father, James, and his mother, Ann – was a letter from the pawnbroker, John Kelday, supporting the accusations against Thomas Pamphillon. Moreover Ann Daniels referred to a further letter written by Jesse Daniels while in custody (this letter wasn't found amongst the papers). Jesse, apparently unaware that his parents were petitioning on his behalf, had written to his parents to tell them that Pamphillon, also in custody, had acknowledged his guilt, that he 'took the things, and pawned them'. Ann Daniels finished her plea in fiery form:

> I have not the least doubt but you have too high a sense of justice, knowingly to let the innocent suffer for the guilty, I ask not for a mitigation of punishment, my boy has done nothing wrong, and therefore *deserves no punishment*, but an irreparable injury has been done to him, I ask as a British subject for *Justice only*, and therefore most humbly solicit you to lay my application as soon as possible before the Secretary of State, in order that an investigation of the case may forthwith take place, so that my much injured child may be liberated from the ignominious punishment he has for so many months injustly endured.[57]

Despite Ann Daniels' efforts, the petition achieved no favourable result for Jesse.

There is little real evidence for parental corruption of the type characterised by contemporary rhetoric. Certainly there is evidence for parental brutality, such as that described by Samuel Holmes, Francis Boucher and Caroline Gadberry, although in these cases force was employed in a belief that it was for the child's own good. There were occasional cases of children being tried with parents, often in a partnership of theft and receivership. However for most parents neglect of their children was unintended, a result of living in debilitating environments, with insecure employment and finances, and often little energy and time to spend on their children. Most

[57] Ibid.

likely there were some vicious, malicious parents seeking to get rid of their children by transporting them or imprisoning them. But these were probably few and far between. One such was the father of fifteen-year-old Henry Wells, who was under sentence of transportation in 1834.[58] Henry was convicted at the October session for stealing from his father a gown which had been the property of his late mother. The mother had died in May, leaving six children to a parent 'whose example, unkindness, and neglect, although they may not extenuate, account in great measure for the misconduct of his child'. The father had quickly remarried and was determined to be rid of the children from his first marriage. According to Henry he had stolen the gown on the basis of a wish expressed by his mother, who wanted her clothes destroyed in order to stop them coming into the possession of the woman who was to become Henry's stepmother. The author of the letter supporting the boy, Louisa Skeene of 23 Paddington Green, was keen to emphasise his misfortune and the role of his errant parent. Accompanying the letter was a note from William Potter of South Row, Carnaby Market. Potter had employed Henry for two and a half years without complaint. Moreover:

> On the Monday, before he had his trial I went to engage him to come and live with me – again. I saw his father and he declared he would transport him if possible and threatened to turn the elder brother out of doors as he would not support him.[59]

Another less-than-sympathetic parent was Mr Neal of Archery Ground Cottage, Junction Road, in Paddington, who advertised in the *Daily Police Report* of 12 June 1837, detailed descriptions of his sons Thomas and James, aged seventeen and fourteen, who had stolen 14s. from him.[60] These stories also possessed broader contexts than parental cruelty and neglect. The father of Henry Wells obviously looked to his own survival, with a new wife and the possibility of a new family to support. The motivation of Mr Neal is untraceable: it is impossible to know whether this was an appeal of care or of cruelty. Finally, most of the parents of these children were poor and harried, caught in the conflict of provision and care of their families and trying to control and prevent the petty delinquencies of their vulnerable, adolescent children.

This chapter has considered the causes of juvenile crime through the experience and understanding of criminal children. Whilst the previous chapter discussed elite perceptions of juvenile crime, this chapter has concentrated on education, work, play and home, arguing that the experience of many juvenile offenders was not untypical of the experience of most working children. Limited education, instruction through street-life and pastimes, vulnerability in employment, and familial disruption were all familiar pressures in the lives of working-class youths in the early nineteenth century.

58 PRO, HO 17/110, vt/4, petition of Henry Wells.
59 Ibid.
60 PRO, MEPO4/27, daily police report, no. 2936, Monday 12 June 1837.

Where the experience of the children who became offenders differed was that these factors precipitated their entrance into the criminal justice system. Circumstances meant that these factors became significant. Hence, whilst the behaviour and environments described were common to many children, who such children were, where they offended, and when they offended marked the real precipitance into criminality. In the 1852 Committee on Criminal and Destitute Juveniles, there was some recognition of these factors. Captain William. J. Williams, inspector of prisons for the Home district concurred when the following question was put to him:

> Do you not, however, think that children under our present system are often treated criminally for faults of so slight a character, that if they were committed by children in any more fortunate state of society, those children would never be considered as criminals at all?

Williams answered, 'Many offences are condoned, in the middle and even in the upper classes, of which we know nothing.'[61] The following chapter will move from looking at causation to examining the nature and character of offending behaviour. Consideration will be paid to the crimes that delinquent children committed, and the means by which they committed them. Accordingly, it will examine the combinations of circumstances that eventually led to their incorporation within the criminal justice system.

---

61 SC Criminal Juveniles, PP, 1852, vii. 21, evidence of Captain W. J. Williams.

3

Processes: Offending

'Parsons and Holland were very punctual in attendance at the Churches where they always robbed. They took three watches – one was pawned for 15/- the other two for £1 a piece. Parsons is very clever at "easing a yokel of a Thimble".'[1]

Contemporary opinion was divided about the causes of juvenile crime. Ambiguity and confusion characterised their understanding and interpretation of the lives of criminal children. For many, to view such children as 'cradled in iniquity' was perhaps an easier formula than to search for explanations for crime based on poverty and debilitating environments. Similarly, when commentators moved to describing the crimes that children committed, the figure of the pickpocket, or the small juvenile burglar, sneaking in at a window pointed out by his adult accomplice, was perhaps an easier quarry than the vast, petty, menial, thievery and pilfering that was committed by many children. This chapter to some extent reflects that contemporary fascination with extreme stereotypes of juvenile criminals in giving undue emphasis to pickpocketing, burglary and crimes of violence. This is partly a product of the inadequacy of the records for summary proceedings. However it is also clear that contemporary stereotypes of child criminality rested strongly on observations of the children who committed so-called 'serious crime'. The juvenile pickpocket was possibly the most resonant of stereotypes formulated by contemporary opinion. The construction of the pickpocket allowed for a broad rhetoric of masculine, professionalised, hardened and precocious behaviour. Needless to say, the average juvenile offender bore little resemblance to this delinquent figure, while indictments and convictions of juveniles for violent crime were actually few and far between. In fact, contemporary discussions of juvenile crime rarely considered the issues of adolescent violence which were to become so familiar in twentieth-century understandings of juvenile behaviour. However the responses to those cases that do exist, whilst extreme, are deeply revealing of contemporary opinion on the role of youth, the roots of criminality, and debates over criminal responsibility.

Many children did not reach the point of indictment; their thefts were considered too petty for the superior courts, and they were dealt with by a short period of detention, after being charged summarily under the wide web

---

1 PRO, HO 73/2/pt 2, Holland's journey.

of legislation designed to cover such offences – for example the Vagrancy Act or the Malicious Trespass Act. No accounts remain of these children, although some more experienced offenders refer back to imprisonment for such offences. These children are largely untraceable, passing through the workhouses, houses of correction, the magistrates' court, apprehended by the police and the watch. Naturally, the accounts from juvenile offenders that do exist tend to reflect children who had been much more effectively criminalised, such as those appearing at the Old Bailey, or at general sessions at Clerkenwell and Westminster, those awaiting transportation on the *Euryalus* hulk, or in Newgate, Tothill Fields and, later, Parkhurst. Even so, the overwhelming majority of young offenders were indicted for larceny. In the years covered by the dataset of the Middlesex criminal registers, of the children aged sixteen and under indicted, never fewer than 85 per cent of children were for some sort of larceny. These ranged from the familiar petty larceny and larceny from the person to larcenies with particular conditions. For example, larceny by a servant, larceny from a dwelling-house, from a warehouse, and from a navigable river. If few juveniles were indicted for the more serious capital crimes such as burglary, robbery and the theft of livestock, even fewer were indicted for crimes against the person: murder, manslaughter, rape and other sexual crimes. Indeed, of a sample of 16,515, only 120 of those indicted for crimes against the person were aged under twenty; of these twenty-four were aged sixteen and under.[2] This quantitative framework is overwhelmingly confirmed by other contemporary sources and by the children's accounts of their own offending behaviour.

Summary crime and petty larceny

The crimes that children committed were, therefore, petty and opportunistic, at times barely deserving the label of criminal offence. It has already been stressed that many children who had some interaction with the criminal justice system experienced summary proceedings. These were children such as fourteen-year-old Thomas McNelly, committed summarily to the magistrate six times between April and December 1836, for respectively breaking several squares of glass in St Saviour's church, sleeping in the open air at St Olave's, stealing 14lbs of coal from a barge, stealing a bag containing brushes, stealing two bundles of wood, and stealing carrots from a barge.[3] The triviality of many charges are underlined in a return of children aged between seven and fourteen to the Coldbath Fields house of correction in the years 1835–7. The general headings underneath which children were grouped were vague and non-specific: 694 were categorised as reputed thieves; 360 as being in unlawful possession of property; 214 as rogues and vagabonds; 464 for other

2   PRO, HO 26/5, 13, 23, 33, 43, 53.
3   SC *Police Officers*, PP, 1837, xii. 43, evidence of James Traill esq.

offences not specified.[4] Most of these 'crimes' related to a very broad interpretation of what was seen as delinquent or anti-social behaviour. Rogues and vagabonds, for example, could include vagrants, unlicensed beggars, itinerant players and gamblers; unlawful possession of property included pilfering goods, receiving stolen goods, cheating and extortion.[5] Generally the value of the goods involved was too small for the offence to constitute a larceny. However, as Robert Shoemaker has pointed out, evidential problems resulted in a number of potentially more serious offences being tried summarily. Thus someone might be caught in the process of going to commit a robbery or burglary, but since nothing was stolen, intention was difficult to prove.[6] There are implications here for considering bias by police employing what were effectively 'stop-and-search' powers.[7] To what extent were children and young people considered legitimate targets of suspicion?

Moreover, the Coldbath Field cohort underlines the fundamental dichotomy in interpretations of recorded crime. Thus, while those inmates charged summarily numbered 1,825, those convicted by jury at the Central Criminal Court numbered 171.[8] Nevertheless it is the children convicted of felony who receive most attention from the historian. Yet the line between casual theft treated summarily and larceny treated at the Old Bailey or Clerkenwell was a thin one, and thieving narratives were punctuated by trivial and generally opportunistic thefts. N. S. Mill, a boy on the *Euryalus* hulk, c. 1836, could 'thieve turnips when hungry'. Another boy, Henry Thompson, started off by robbing orchards. H. Marshall stole his mother's watch.[9] Also on the *Euryalus* was John Campbell, a thief for three years, who 'plundered from shop doors or by taking away any articles exposed and neglected'; Charles Downes, who took 'coats and shoes from shop doors'; Henry Underwood, who 'stole provisions – such as bread and bacon'; and William Cook, who stole meat – 'I was a flesh-hunter when I first took to it, that is I used to steal meat of any sort.'[10] Similar stories were re-played in the more formal records of the criminal justice system. Elizabeth Denham, aged fourteen, was sentenced to death in 1814 for her part in the theft of a shawl valued at £3 2s. In 1802 fifteen-year-old John Cooper, was imprisoned for six months and whipped for the theft of a glass bottle, worth 1d., a pint of brandy, valued at 2s., a razor, valued at 1s., and a key, value 1d. The same year James West-

---

4 Ibid. appendix 15, pp. 223.
5 Shoemaker, *Prosecution*, 168–72.
6 Ibid. 172.
7 A. Sanders, 'From suspect to trial', in M. Maguire, R. Morgan and R. Reiner (eds), *The Oxford handbook of criminology*, Oxford 1994, 773–818, esp. pp. 777–9.
8 *SC Police Officers*, PP, 1837, xii, appendix 15, p. 223.
9 PRO, HO 73/16, rough notebook iii, evidence of N. S. Mill; rough notebook iv, evidence of Henry Thompson, H. Marshall.
10 Ibid. notebook 1, evidence of John Campbell; notebook 2, evidence of Charles Downes and Henry Underwood; notebook 3, evidence of William Cook.

brook, aged twelve, was found guilty of the theft of a Cheshire cheese.[11] The types of goods stolen were typically clothes, textiles and money. Using information drawn from a sample of juvenile offenders in the Middlesex criminal registers for the years 1796, 1804 and 1809, of the 168 cases where goods were mentioned, 44 per cent had been indicted for stealing either clothing or textiles; 17 per cent for miscellaneous goods, ranging from umbrellas, to pewter pots, to a bottle of peppermint; 14 per cent for money, bills of exchange or seals; and 5 per cent each for watches and food-stuffs. Also stolen less liberally were pocket-books, jewellery, lead and iron, livestock and silver.[12] Because of the ordinariness of much petty larceny it was paid little attention by social commentators, or even by reformers. Whilst the petty larceny committed by most juvenile offenders was treated as a general activity of delinquents, the 'serious crime' committed by rather fewer juvenile offenders was given pride of place in accounts of child criminality.

Pickpockets

There is certainly an implication that the gravity of crime committed by an offender tended to reflect the length of their involvement in criminal activity. It is a reasonable assumption that many of the children who appeared at the Old Bailey had had at least some prior contact with the criminal justice system. At this stage offenders were judged as much on their previous experience (where it was known) as on the nature of the crime they were charged with. Hence a number of boys sentenced to transportation for seemingly minor larcenies, may well have been known to the court, or an officer of the court may have produced a certificate of previous conviction. It is rare to find children who had been on the hulks convicted for a first offence, although it was not unknown. Whilst the large core of petty juvenile offenders must always inform historians' understanding of juvenile crime, there were undoubtedly a number of children who got drawn into repeat, and relatively more serious, offending. Picking pockets was generally viewed in this latter category. Although the actual process of picking pockets may not seem as serious as, say, burglary or assault, it tended to be associated with group theft and organisation. There is a danger in viewing larceny from the person exclusively in terms of contemporary stereotypes, the standard portrayal of the early nineteenth-century pickpocket, the Artful Dodger, well and truly embroiled in the criminal 'underworld'; it is probable that a great deal of pickpocketing was rather the result of opportunity than organisation. Yet, there is little doubt that contemporary observers, as well as the administrators

11 *OBSP*, first session, 1814, no. 27, pp. 16–17; second session, 1802, no. 113, p. 88; no. 136, pp. 100–1.
12 PRO, HO 26/5, 13, 23, 33, 43, 53.

of the justice system, viewed it with some seriousness. Indeed until 1808 it was a capital offence.[13]

There was a tendency to view pickpocketing as a progressive stage in the criminal career. Time after time, the portrayal of the youth drawn into pick-pocketing, then burglary, was espoused by contemporary commentators. In 1828 Thomas Wontner drew the following portrait of the pickpocket:

> Next to the housebreaker, the pickpockets are the most troublesome body to deal with; not that they occasion so much loss of property to the public, taken as a body, as the burglar, but they are more numerous, and are more readily ini-tiated into the art and mystery of their calling; in consequence of which they are ever augmenting their numbers. As they are, with very few exceptions, all of the thorough London breed, they have from their earliest recollection a large circle of acquaintances, of their own standing in life, most of them com-ing from the low and populous districts of the metropolis. When any of the boys in a neighbourhood are seen to turn gentlemen, it is natural for all the others to inquire how he has acquired such smart clothes, and can afford to spend so much money. They are soon informed, and immediately resolve, if possible, to participate in the same pleasures.[14]

This extract contains a number of assumptions and beliefs about juvenile pickpockets. Firstly, that they were generally children. Certainly this does have some grounding in fact, simply because a small and agile child was much harder to detect, and catch, than an adult. Moreover, the statistical evidence from the Middlesex criminal registers dataset confirms the tendency for larceny from the person to be a younger person's crime, since 74 per cent of people indicted for larceny from the person were aged twenty-five and under.[15] Secondly, the pickpocket was explicitly characterised as male – and hence displayed a demeanour of assertive, precocious, masculinity. Only 9 per cent of the juveniles indicted for larceny/robbery from the person were females, which seems to suggest that pickpocketing was more likely to be committed by males, or at least by younger males. However, it may be that female pickpockets were less likely to be caught. Although, as one of the boys interviewed by Miles for the 1835 Select Committee on Gaols noted, girls, 'are not dexterous; "they pull it out all of a flare" '.[16] Thirdly, pickpockets were identified with a sense of clannishness, one that was underlined by belonging and progression within the 'criminal classes'. As Thomas Wontner

---

[13] Larceny (pickpockets), 48 Geo.III. c.129 (1808).

[14] T. Wonter, *Old Bailey experience: criminal jurisprudence and the actual working of our penal code of laws: also an essay on prison discipline, to which is added a history of the crimes committed by offenders in the present day*, London 1831, 350–1.

[15] PRO, HO 26/5, 13, 23, 33, 43, 53. Of the less serious larcenies (i.e. not burglary, highway robbery or animal theft), for which juveniles were indicted, 19.7% were for larceny from the person.

[16] W. A. Miles, 'Information and statements made by juvenile delinquents', in PRO, HO 73/16, Select Committee on Gaols (secret), box 3, 8.

had implied, the pickpocket was identified with the rags-to-riches story; he was on his way to the swell-mob.

So how much of this mythology can be substantiated by accounts from pickpockets themselves? William Holland, interviewed in about 1836, was a particularly eloquent contributor to the evidence compiled by William Augustus Miles. In his statement to Miles, he made a number of comments on picking pockets. Holland referred particularly to the way in which older thieves would sometimes guide younger boys in their thieving. He worked mainly with a twenty-three-year-old called William Nelson.[17] Nelson was mentioned by a number of juvenile offenders interviewed on board the *Euryalus*, and seems to have been a notorious offender. An officer of police division C (Mayfair and Soho) knew Nelson well:

> [he] is about twenty-three years old, of excellent address and manners, he has been transported and been many times in prison . . . the officers at Marlborough street say that he makes more than any other of the swell mob.

This officer goes on to describe Nelson as the 'pavement Macheath of the day'.[18] William Holland described the set-up used by such men:

> They watch such shops as Grange's or Farrance's, and observe, when the Gentlemen pay, into which pocket the purse is returned; they take it by turns to follow a person, saying, 'this is my man', or 'that is your man'; the younger boys are beckoned over from the over side of the street, and the robbery is effected in a few minutes.

Holland further commented on technique: 'It is easier to take a purse than a handkerchief out of a coat pocket; it drops into the hand if well managed'; and seasonality: 'Money is flying about like dirt up at the Dials just now; we try for purses, only, this fine weather; come winter again we get back to handkerchiefs.'[19] Cases found in the *Old Bailey sessions papers* demonstrate similar elements to those described by Holland. In 1815 sixteen-year-old Samuel Forster was observed by city constable William Barret:

> I saw the prisoner with a jew. I watched their motions; I saw them attempting several pockets, and at last they came to a gentleman who had seals. The jew was in front of the gentleman, pressing with his head and his hands against his breast, and the prisoner was behind the gentleman, with his arms round his waist, and I saw the jew with a hold of the gentleman's seals, with an intent as I supposed, to draw the watch and give it to the prisoner, whose hand was around the gentleman's waist.

---

17 PRO, HO 26/42, 1836, William Nelson, aged 23, was sentenced to transportation for seven years at the Westminster Sessions on 8 Dec. 1836.
18 Miles, *Poverty*, 137.
19 PRO, HO 73/16, Select Committee on Gaols (secret), 8.

In 1817 fifteen-year-old Joseph Knight was observed in the act of picking pockets by officer Thomas Thompson. Thompson watched Knight and two other boys following the prosecutor in High Holborn till he put his hand in the prosecutor's pocket and took out a handkerchief. In 1833 brothers Francis and Charles Wiltshire, aged twelve and thirteen, were found guilty of picking the pocket of John Schmidt. Schmidt told the court that he 'felt something at my pocket in the narrow part of the court – I put my hand in my pocket and missed my handkerchief, and on turning round, saw the two prisoners immediately behind me'.[20]

These cases contain three scenarios typical of the portrayal of a juvenile underworld: complicity with an adult, other children or a sibling. Certainly, the nature of picking pockets made complicity a sensible precaution, as a companion could create a diversion or slip away with the stolen goods. For instance Richard Taylor cautioned that, 'the one who carries the money ought to be able to swallow it in case he is in danger. I once swallowed ten shillings.'[21] The presence of an adult, like William Nelson, or the man identified as a Jew accompanying Samuel Forster, could also suggest coercion and corruption. Such corruption, according to the 'underworld' narrative, might lead the pickpocket to more financially rewarding burglary and robbery.

Burglary

One of the great fears for contemporaries was that the juveniles of the present would become the burglars of tomorrow, maturing into professional criminals. This progression was seen as inevitable and was a major theme in the arguments for penal reformation and colonial retraining. Burglary was associated with professionalisation and consequently with organised crime. Popular convention considered shop-lifting and picking pockets as an apprenticeship – burglary and robbery career steps. This view was explicitly conveyed in a document included in the Report of the Constabulary Commission of 1839, an account apparently collected from prisoners in Coldbath Fields by Chesterton, the governor. This narrative recounts a young thief's progression from petty-theft, through picking pockets, to burglary:

> The next species of thieving pursued, is that which entitles a thief to be placed at 'the top of the tree' in his profession, and to which they all more or less aspire; many terms are made use of implying the various methods of house-breaking, a slight difference in the method pursued constituting the variety.[22]

20 *OBSP*, first session, 1815, no. 58, p. 35; eighth session, 1817, no. 1553, p. 509; first session, 1832, no. 11, p. 12.
21 PRO, HO 73/2 pt 2, interviews with Robert Holland Crawley and Richard Taylor.
22 *First Report of the Commissioners Appointed to Inquire as to the Best Means of Establishing an Efficient Constabulary Force in the Counties of England and Wales*, PP, 1839, xix, appendix 6, pp. 205–15, at pp. 209–10, for this quotation.

However, the most common form of breaking and entering committed by juvenile offenders was 'starring the glaze'. In the Coldbath Fields narrative the technique is described:

> One or two parties divert attention while another 'stars'. This is either done by a diamond or by inserting a small pen-knife through the putty near the corner of a pane and cracking it; the wet finger carries the crack in any direction; an angle is generally formed. The piece is wrought to and fro, and removed; if necessary, another piece is starred to allow of the free ingress of the hand.[23]

Yet it was often the case that children indicted for burglary had simply put their hand through a broken window and taken whatever was within reach. On a February evening in 1819 fifteen-year-old William Serjeant was spotted by Mary Andrews with his hands inside a pane of glass: 'I saw him with both his hands inside a pane of glass, which was cut, pulling some goods out of the window.' William protested in court that he was only looking in the window when the woman had apprehended him.[24] Likewise, in 1813, three ten-year-old children, John Reece, Elizabeth Clark and Jack Sweeney, were indicted for breaking and entering the premises of Richard Audley at 6.00 o'clock in the evening of 23 November. They had been seen picking the putty from the shop-window, removing the glass and taking three pocket books, a box of dominos, a comb and some other trifles. For this they were sentenced to six months in the house of correction, and whipped in jail.[25]

'Starring the glaze' was considered as 'breaking and entering' by indictment, despite the fact that the offender may not have even entered the premises. For example, fifteen-year-old James Barron was sentenced to death for breaking and entering the dwelling-house of Thomas Barber in March 1797. Yet Barron and his accomplice, William Ambridge, had only been described as having broken the glass of the shop-window and thus removing various items of jewellery. They had not actually bodily entered the shop.[26] Similar ambiguity existed for other offences. For example, whilst 'Larceny in the dwelling-house' was a grand larceny which had originated by statute as a protection against thieving servants and apprentices who stole from their masters, 'breaking and entering the dwelling-house' was a burglary.[27] In practice the distinction between the two seemed to rest on two factors. Firstly, that 'burglary' was committed at night, and secondly that there would generally be evidence of actually 'breaking' into the house. For example, there would be some evidence of a broken window or forced lock, through which the intruder had entered, or they would have been observed breaking and entering. In the case of the larceny, however, the defendant was already in

23 Ibid. 206.
24 OBSP, third session, 1819, no. 331, p. 142.
25 Ibid. first session, 1813, no. 46, p. 47.
26 Ibid. fourth session, 1797, no. 299, p. 295.
27 J. Beattie, Crime and the courts in England, 1660–1800, Oxford 1986, 3–5.

the house, either as a member of the household, or having walked in, as in the case of a shop. Juveniles who were indicted for burglariously breaking and entering tended to commit the crime in groups of two or three, or with slightly older boys. The general idea seems to have been that actual breaking and entering, rather than 'starring', was something towards which older boys progressed. Hence sixteen-year-old William Moore was sentenced to death for his part in a burglary in 1819. Moore and his partner, seventeen-year-old John Smith, had broken into the dwelling-house of Robert Gregory Dendy at Hampton, Middlesex, one night in November, taking twenty-three yards of corduroy, eighteen yards of flannel, twenty yards of woollen cord and two waist-coat pieces. They were apprehended the following day, and both claimed to have been given the textiles by another young man.[28] Similarly, in 1809, Thomas Holmit, alias Lacey Thomas Anderson, along with Joel Ware aged twenty and John Fuller aged twenty-two, was indicted for burglariously breaking and entering into *The Black Dog* in Bethnal Green in the early hours of an April morning. The bar at the front of the house had been broken open with a crow-bar, and the shutters forced open. Unfortunately the wheelbarrow which they had used to remove their booty left tracks in the wet ground which led the prosecutor Richard Jones directly to the house of Joel Ware.[29]

The boundaries of street robbery were also blurred, since a fine distinction was drawn between robbery, assault and some larcenies from the person. Robbery, as opposed to burglary, generally took place in the open, for example on the King's Highway. The distinction between robbery and larceny from the person was in the use of violence. Whilst the popular conception of the robber was the highwayman or the bandit, much robbery was defined as assault on the highway, and putting in fear, with the intention or result of feloniously taking from the person. Juveniles were not generally associated with highway robbery or street robbery, and again impressionistic evidence seems to suggest that this was a crime committed by older youths. Of those offenders indicted for serious larcenies, such as burglary, robbery and live-stock theft, just over half were aged between seventeen and twenty-five (56 per cent), 8 per cent were juveniles, and of those juveniles 61 per cent were aged fifteen and sixteen.[30] For example, in 1792 sixteen-year-old John Norman was indicted for feloniously assaulting Mark Small on the King's Highway, and putting him in fear, and feloniously taking from his person, and against his will, three shirts and other things, value 30s. In this case the charge of highway robbery was dropped; as Small described in his evidence, 'as I was going in that house, he snatched my bag, in which were the three

[28] *OBSP*, first session, 1819, no. 3, pp. 7–8.
[29] Ibid. fifth session, 1809, no. 449, pp. 276–80.
[30] PRO, HO 26/5, 13, 23, 33, 43, 53. However, since 15- and 16-year-olds represented 54.6% of all juveniles, the suggestion is that generally children were more prone to commit crime, or at least be caught, in their mid rather than early teens.

bundles, off my head, hat and all, and then he ran down the street'.[31] The distinction is more apparent if the case of another boy, seventeen-year-old John Davis, is considered. Indicted by the same formula as John Norman, evidence given by the victim, William Stephens, described how 'The prisoner passed by me about as far from me to your lordship; he turned sharp round upon me, and drove his head against my chin, and took the seals from my ribbon.'[32] Davis was found guilty and sentenced to death, though recommended to mercy on account of his youth. Finally, a clear cut case of violent robbery can be found in the following example. In October 1828 three sixteen-year-olds, George Reynolds, Thomas Harris and Richard Crozier, assaulted and robbed Stephen Robinson in Chelsea. Giving evidence, Robinson described the attack:

> it was a fine night, there were lamps in the street; I cannot say whether they were gas or oil; it was Crozier who knocked me down, he struck me on the eye with his fist; when they got me down, they throttled me and bruised me; two of them got on top of my breast, I screamed out, and they throttled me; Crozier took three half-crowns from my trowsers pocket, a sixpence, and 9d. in copper, from my waistcoat pocket; also a pen-knife and pair of new braces from my pocket.[33]

Reynolds, Harris and Crozier were sentenced to death.

Violent crime

Nevertheless it must be emphasised that the prosecution of these sort of cases, involving juveniles, were infrequent. Very few children were indicted or convicted for violent crime in the higher courts. Cases of assault, such as that involving Reynolds, Harris and Crozier, were unusual. It is possible that even at the quarter-session or summary trial, children would not be charged with assault in the same manner as adults. Hence there may well have been a tendency to overlook children's fighting and violence. Juvenile cases of murder and manslaughter are virtually unheard of, and in the rare cases that did exist, there was no accompanying media panic – certainly nothing approaching the reaction to later juvenile murderers.[34] Two cases are, however, worth looking at more closely. The first is the case of John Any Bird Bell.[35] Whilst Bell was actually tried, convicted and executed in Maidstone,

---

31 *OBSP*, second session, 1792, no. 58, pp. 62–5.
32 Ibid. fifth session, 1816, no. 538, pp. 276–7.
33 Ibid. eighth session, 1828, no. 1988, pp. 913–14.
34 See, for example, B. Morrison, *As if*, London 1997; G. Sereny, *The case of Mary Bell: a portrait of a child who murdered*, 2nd edn, with new preface and appendix, London 1995; D. J. Smith, *The sleep of reason: the James Bulger case*, London 1994.
35 Any Bird is a corruption of Henebar.

his case has some significance for the contemporary response to such crime. The second is the case of William Newton Allnut, a Hackney boy, who poisoned his grandfather.

Thirteen-year-old John Any Bird Bell had cut the throat of Richard Taylor, also aged thirteen, in Stroud, in the parish of Chatham. The murder was particularly bloody, and the motive was money. Richard was carrying his father's parish money. Whilst John did the actual killing, his younger brother, James Bell, was involved to some degree, although James later gave evidence. What is interesting about the case is the physical and mental portrayal of John, and the explanation of his crime through the context of his parents. Certainly, the crime should not be underestimated: it was brutal and seemingly done with little compunction. John's own statement and confession was used against him in court. Reading the following extract, it is fairly easy to understand why:

> He did it, he said, at one cut; that the deceased was not long dying. The little boy lost his way in the wood, and lay down to cry; and while the boy was lying down he cut his throat. He took the money from the boy's glove, and gave part to his brother. His brother gave him his knife to cut the boy's throat. The boy squeaked when his throat was cut, as a rabbit squeaks. He only squeaked once. He gave him two cuts.[36]

In a contemporary pamphlet, a great deal of attention was paid to the upbringing of the two brothers. Their father was an agricultural labourer, but spent much of his time grubbing for roots, which their mother then hawked from a donkey and cart in the street. A tension between the parents is apparent in the accounts. Whilst the father claimed to be a regular churchgoer, respectable and hard-working, the mother was portrayed as a force of corruption:

> he had always found them very perverse and untractable, and frequently when he would have corrected them for disobedience, he had been prevented by the mother's interference. It is to be feared that correction was oftener inflicted for neglect of labour, than for the pilfering habits to which the culprit and his brother were notoriously addicted.[37]

The contemporary stereotypes at work are strong here: the boys were corrupted by a parent, and that parent was their mother; discipline was not used appropriately. The background to the murder is described in some detail. Thus it seems that for some time John had been involved in petty delinquencies, such as stealing horse-hair from a stable:

> He was also engaged in several thefts of small articles from shops in the neighbourhood, sometimes breaking the windows for the purpose, and in one

36 *Times*, 30 July 1831, 4, col. b.
37 *A narrative of the facts relative to the murder of Richard Faulkner Taylor*, Rochester 1831, 40–1.

instance daringly throwing down and breaking a glass jar at the very door of the house at which it had been stolen, after emptying its contents. There could be no doubt but that a pursuit of such conduct would ultimately lead to more desperate acts of violence.[38]

The model of progression here is also familiar: the downwards spiral of crime, the convenience of hindsight. John Bell's callousness was also commented on; his Sundays were spent, after the murder, playing on the same road, or on fields close to where the body lay (Richard disappeared on 4 March 1831 and was not found till 11 May). Finally, John's appearance was described:

> The prisoner, for the age which he is stated to be, 14, is remarkably short in stature, but thick set and strong built, with an almost infantine countenance. ... His features are not good, although not expressive of any degree of ferocity or depravity, but there is about the eyes, which are deeply sunk in the head, a strong expression of cunning.[39]

> Bell ... was an athletic boy in robust health, and between fourteen and fifteen years old. ... The culprit was of fair complexion, with the light hair so common amongst the peasantry; his forehead and upper lip projecting, and his eyes were deeply sunk in the head, altogether not an inapt prototype of the 'Idle Apprentice' portrayed in Hogarth's inimitable work.[40]

The story that weaves between the lines of these narratives is typical of discussions of children's violence and delinquencies, and especially so in the case of repeat offenders: parental neglect or misuse (specifically on the part of the mother), an early history of delinquency, evidence of callousness and disregard, a slightly unusual, or unpleasing, physical appearance.[41]

One hundred and sixty-two years after the execution of John Any Bird Bell, the media focused on the upbringing and social lives of twelve-year-olds Robert Thompson and Jon Venables, the boys convicted for the murder of toddler James Bulger. Both boys were said to come from poor family back-

---

[38] Ibid. 41.
[39] *Times*, 30 July 1831, 4, col. b.
[40] *Facts relative to the murder of Richard Faulkner Taylor*, 42.
[41] A grim footnote to the case of John Any Bird Bell is provided by the following reference to the activities of John's younger brother, James Bell, after the murder and execution: 'A disgraceful exhibition was made last week at Strood Fair. An itinerant showman produced for the gratification of his visitors and for the small charge of "only one penny" a wax figure intended to represent the poor boy Taylor, who was recently murdered by John Amy Bird Bell, in a wood near Rochester and employed James Bell, the accomplice and brother of the murderer to explain with the assistance of the figure the whole process of murder. The cold and unfeeling way in which the boy related the particulars filled many persons with horror and indignation; and the showman, on being remonstrated with, said he thought he had the right to earn an "honest penny", that he had hired the lad from his parents for 5s. a day, and they had also consented to his travelling with him about the country to attend various fairs': Theatre Museum, Covent Garden, miscellaneous files/fairs – unknown source (1831). My thanks to Dr Brenda Assael for this reference.

grounds. Thompson's mother was a single parent, with a reputation for violence. Venables's parents were separated, his mother was said to drink. Both boys had histories of truancies and petty theft. Robert Thompson took flowers to the place where James Bulger's body had been found (James was murdered on Friday 12 February 1993, the boys were not arrested until the following Thursday). Finally, both boys were commented on for their physical appearance. Robert Thompson, whilst reasonably good-looking, was undersized and was said, by the more hysterical tabloids, to have particularly sinister eyes. Jon Venables had a squint.[42]

The similarities in such rhetoric point, perhaps, to a continuity in representations of criminal children. What makes juvenile murderers so significant in mapping the contours of such continuities is that they represent the extremity of possible behaviour. Hence, whilst violent crime committed by juveniles was and is very rare, the murderous juvenile is used as a device, as a conduit through which are expressed societal doubts about the role and future of youth. Moreover, through the means of singling out physical description and personal tendencies, such as John Bell's deeply sunk eyes or John Venables's squint, the murderous child is portrayed as 'other', something perverse and degenerate. They are no longer troubled children in need of society's help and understanding, but voluntary and purposeful murderers. The representations of, and responses to, child murderers contain expressions of fear about all youth and adolescence; the role of parents; the pervasiveness of petty delinquencies; the lack of any moral understanding, and so on. Whilst these things are familiar in most representations of juvenile delinquency, child murderers have pushed through the social boundaries that contain and allow for a certain level of delinquent behaviour. These children are a product of society, a creation of their parents, yet they murder by their own volition – becoming 'monsters'. Why they are so frightening, despite being so rare, is because they remind society of the possibility that all unruly, undisciplined, immoral children might become 'other'.

Like the trial and response to John Any Bird Bell, the trial of William Newton Allnut in December 1847 can also be used to pinpoint some significant questions about the understanding of juvenile criminality. Newton Allnut, a twelve-year-old boy from Hackney, was charged with the murder of his grandfather, Samuel Nelme. William had already encountered the court earlier in the autumn on a charge of theft, stealing various articles of jewellery and gold from his grandmother, widow Sarah Nelme.[43] The details of the murder are of less concern than the nature of William's defence, and the court's response to that defence. William was defended by a Mr Ballantine, who clearly sought a verdict of diminished responsibility, on the plea of insanity.[44] Thus, William's mother, Mrs M. L. Allnut, described how the boy

---

[42] For a full discussion of the James Bulger case see Smith, *Sleep of reason*.

[43] *Times*, 11 Nov. 1847, 7, col. a.

[44] It was only four years previously, in 1843, that the landmark case of David M'Naghten,

had suffered various debilities. At a year and a half, he had an almost fatal fall on a ploughshare; in 1844 he had had an attack of ringworm and had suffered from scrofulous disease. 'He had given her a great deal of trouble by his misconduct, and she had frequently been compelled to remonstrate with him.'[45] In the previous January he had fallen on the ice, and his conduct had worsened:

> The prisoner was in every respect quite different to her other child, and he had given her great trouble on account of his bad conduct, and also on account of his health. He used to walk in his sleep, and she frequently heard him call out in his sleep as though something had frightened him.[46]

His father, who had been an alcoholic and an epileptic, had died two years previously, 'in a state of complete madness'. The expert witness, Dr Letheby, when questioned by the court, concurred that a violent blow to the head could cause some brain disorder. Indeed, from his demeanour in prison during remand, William seems to have shown all the signs of incipient schizophrenia. Thus his defence told the court: 'The prisoner was given in charge for stealing a watch, and he said, "Pray, forgive me; I was tempted to do it". I asked who had tempted him, and he replied, "it was no person, but a voice which said, "Do it, do it; you will not be found out".'

Other medical men were called upon to give their opinions of William's state of mind. Most agreed to some degree of incapacity. William himself confessed to the murder after being urged to do so by a dream:

> I dreamed there was God seated on his throne, and Satan was on his left hand, and God called us all up and asked us a question. It was an English word to make French, and those that had confessed all their sins and had left off all their wickedness, he said unto them, 'Come ye into my kingdom which I have prepared for you'. And he said unto those on his left hand, 'Go ye into the furnace of fire prepared for Satan and his angels'. I dreamed I was happy, and you and all my brothers and sisters, but I hope all the disgrace will fall upon me and no one else. I now confess that I have done what I am accused of.[47]

William was eventually found guilty, but recommended to mercy, and later reprieved, on account of his age.[48] When judgement was passed upon him,

established the rules for pleas of insanity in cases of murder. In essence the M'Naghten rules stated that to 'establish a defence on the ground of insanity, it must be clearly proved that at the time of committing the act the accused was under such a defect of reason, from disease of the mind, as not to know the nature and quality of the act he was doing; or if he did know it, that he did not know he was doing what was wrong': Radzinowicz and Hood, *Emergence of penal policy*, 681–5, 683–4.

45 *Times*, 16 Dec. 1847, 7, col. f.
46 Ibid.
47 Ibid.
48 William was transported in 1851. Almost immediately granted a ticket-of-leave, he then went to Western Australia and the Swan River colony. Two years later, in April 1853,

the presiding justice, Mr Baron Rolfe, went to great pains to reject any plea of insanity, and indeed any plea that the boy was not aware of wrongdoing (the principle established by *Doli Incapax*, in reference to offenders aged between seven and fourteen). William's life was spared purely because of his age and 'his want of experience', the court being satisfied that, 'he had knowingly sent his aged grandfather to his account, and had, therefore, not hesitated to declare that he was guilty of the crime of wilful murder'.[49] The determination to portray William as a willing, able and knowing murderer is significant. This was in spite of substantial evidence which pointed to some personality problems, if not actual insanity, and despite his tender age. The court felt itself to be magnanimous in allowing William mercy – but yet did not allow for any real understanding of William's predicament. The cases of John Any Bird Bell, and William Newton Allnut, it might be argued, underline the strong degree of punitiveness inherent in the courts' attitude to juveniles in this period, and the refusal to concede any real understanding of childhood debilities and delinquencies. Only fourteen years after William Newton Allnut was sentenced to death, Peter Barratt and James Bradley, two eight-year-old boys in Stockport, Cheshire, were found guilty of the manslaughter of a two-year-old child. The defence counsel had pointed out to the jury that the boys were 'mere babies themselves, who could not have known the crime they committed'. In summing up, the judge also expressed his opinion 'that it seemed straining the case to charge such young children with the crime of wilful murder'.[50]

Innocence *v.* experience

In the cases of John Any Bird Bell and William Newton Allnut the role of *Doli Incapax* is clear-cut, yet it was also deeply embedded in contemporary attitudes to juvenile property offenders. Thus relative innocence or experience was a central concept in many of the commentaries on juvenile crime in the early nineteenth century. The majority of the children who appear in the interviews from the *Euryalus*, from the metropolitan prisons, and within the evidence from parliamentary select committees and royal commissions, were reasonably experienced offenders. Whilst this may only have been petty offending, they stole regularly, and were undetected far more often than they were detected. Asked about the number of robberies they had committed juvenile offenders admitted to extensive levels of offending:

William Newton Allnutt, aged seventeen, died of consumption: PRO, HO 13/93, remission of William Newton Allnut; HO 18/212/46, petition of William Newton Allnutt; HO 24/15, Parkhurst prison register, 79; *Dictionary of western Australians, 1829–1914*: II, *Bond – 1850–68*, ed. R. Erickson, Nedlands, WA 1979, 7.

49 *Times*, 16 Dec. 1847, 7, col. f.

50 G. Sereny, 'A child murdered by children', *Independent on Sunday*, 23 Apr. 1995, 8–12.

'Do you remember the robberies you or they (friends) committed in any one week?'

'Have picked pockets myself upwards of a hundred times in a week'

'I remember to have stolen 40 handkerchiefs in a week'

'The greatest number have been committed by myself and pals or companions at Vauxhall gardens to see the Balloons &c upwards of ninety handkerchiefs in one week, have been taken by us then'

'I recollect to have committed 24 robberies in one week amounting to £40'

'not exactly, I have stolen in one day out a shop in the Strand 40 silk handkerchiefs, in a day in the streets I have stolen 4 to 20'

'one days work with us was very much like another – we did nothing but pick pockets'

'we have had from a pound to £30 a day or more on the average, but it goes away as fast as we get it, it melts away like snow'.[51]

Such statements should not be taken too literally. Exaggeration and bragging may well have been part of the language these children used both with each other, and with their interviewers. Moreover, it is likely that the compilers of such reports as the Constabulary Commission or the Select Committees on the Metropolitan Police were more interested in those who offended frequently, and who escaped detection equally frequently. After all, these children could cast light on the deficiencies of policing, on the places where they offended, on where they sold their goods, on their companions in crime. Moreover, such boys and young men justified contemporary fears of a criminal class. Even allowing for bluffing and exaggeration, however, the frequency of offending that the children recounted, and the networks of exchange and complicity they described, must have had a frightening impact on the reporters, suggesting the existence of a criminal subculture.

Yet alongside these boys existed those many children who were drawn into the criminal justice system at a relatively inexperienced level, sometimes through ill-luck or through an unsympathetic magistrate. Indeed all the boys interviewed had also at one time been petty offenders. Many children did move out of crime, and others may have put offending behaviour behind them too had it not been for the growing tendency to draw increasing numbers of children into some sort of trial proceeding. Most of the children interviewed seem to have spent an average of two years thieving, or, as they referred to it, 'on the town' or 'on the cross'. Thus John Campbell, aged fifteen, had been a thief for three years; Rowland Bassett, aged sixteen, for a year; George Hickman, aged sixteen, for three years; Phillip Maine, aged fourteen, for two years; Charles Downes, aged fourteen, for about twelve

---

[51] PRO, HO 73/2 pt 2, loose papers, interviews with London boys.

months; Henry Underwood, aged fourteen, for about ten months; John O'Donnell, aged thirteen, two years; Dennis Walker, aged fourteen, six months.[52] Whilst it would be impossible to make any real estimate of the average age for embarking on crime, impressionistic evidence suggests that twelve and thirteen were vulnerable years.

The peak age for indictment of juvenile offenders, as suggested by evidence from the Middlesex criminal registers dataset, was sixteen: of the juveniles indicted, 34 per cent were aged sixteen, 20 per cent aged fifteen, and 19 per cent aged fourteen. The peak age for conviction was also sixteen, since this age group had the lowest percentage of acquittals (among the juveniles indicted). Thus only 19 per cent of sixteen-year-olds were acquitted as opposed to 31 per cent of ten-year-olds.[53] If this information is paired with impressions from the textual evidence, it suggests that children spent some time hovering on the edges of the criminal justice system before encountering the superior courts. The older they became, the more of an inevitability this was. Moreover, it can only be supposed that for many children who reached such a pinnacle at least some months, if not years, had been spent being tried and punished summarily. For example, when questioned on his arrival in Van Diemens Land in 1836, George Reid, a fifteen-year-old from Spitalfields, referred to several periods of imprisonment. Besides the conviction in question, he had been indicted 'once for meat acquitted, once for meat again, 8 or 9 times in prison altogether, 1 and 2 months, 14 and 7 days'. William Cook admitted to two previous convictions and imprisonments for vagrancy, although in his interview with Miles he had confessed to having been at least fifteen times in prison.[54] Many of the boys would have spent short periods in prison, on remand, or had very short spells in prison or the house of correction, of anything between a day or a week. Children would also have been placed temporarily in prison if they were to receive corporal punishment, or while awaiting payment of a fine.

Yet the experienced juvenile offenders described above can easily be matched by children who responded to opportunity, for example the opportunity afforded by employment. Servants, apprentices, shop-boys and pot-boys often stole because they were present at that time and place. Opportunity was a strong factor in much of the petty theft that appeared in front of

---

[52] PRO, HO 73/16, notebooks 1, 2, 3.
[53] These figures are based only on indictments and convictions of juvenile offenders (aged 0–16). If all offenders are considered the peak age was 18. Viewed by the sample years the peak ages were as follows: 1797 = 22; 1807 = 24/26/28; 1817 = 18; 1827 = 18; 1837 = 19; 1847 = 17: PRO, HO 26/5, 13, 23, 33, 43, 53. Research carried out by P. King and J. Noel shows similar results: 'Origins', 21–2. See also Peter King's work on the age structure of male and female property offenders, 1791–3, in 'Female offenders, work and life-cycle change in late eighteenth century London', *Continuity and Change* xi (1996), 61–90, esp. p. 64.
[54] AOT, Con 31/37, George Reid, no. 1145; Con 31/7, William Cook, no. 1986; PRO, HO 73/16, interview with William Cook, notebook 3.

the magistrates, and at the sessions. For example, thirteen-year-old George Webster had stolen a considerable amount of money from his master George Weaver. Webster claimed to be relatively inexperienced and not to have been in prison before. On commission of the crime George absconded, but was caught a few weeks later enjoying his ill-gotten gains on a Woolwich steam boat. Charles Stewart, the local superintendent reported that:

> on the 8th of April I saw the prisoner on board a steam boat going to London – I searched him and found this pencil case on him, and 1l.6s., in money – he was in company with another lad about the same age – the prisoner said he was taking the money to his master, a cap-maker, in Holborn – I said I would take him to his master – he afterwards said he lived with this person in Exmouth street – I took him to Weaver who charged him with this.[55]

If Webster was as unfamiliar with the justice system as he maintained, the sentence of transportation he received seems unnecessarily harsh. However, the crime was a theft of substantial value, and George Webster was an orphan, and as such made exemplary material for colonial remodelling. Unfortunately he was never to attain such citizenship. Transported in 1837, he served three years in the juvenile penal colony at Point Puer, dying early in 1841.[56] Like Webster, Rowland Bassett was also indicted for 'larceny by the servant'. Bassett had previously been in court but had been found not guilty. He had been accused of stealing a fender, but as he remonstrated: 'A lad asked me to carry it, and said he would give me a halfpenny.'[57] The following year he was indicted for stealing a pair of opera glasses from his master James Gardner, the owner of the Finsbury Bazaar. Bassett had been five weeks in the service of Gardner. This time he was found guilty, and sentenced to be transported to Australia for seven years.[58] Whilst he confessed to Miles that he had been thieving for a year, these crimes, or potential crimes, have the mark of an opportunist thief.

There is evidence to suggest that larceny by the servant, or from the employer, was more often a female crime, simply because of the numbers of young women in domestic service. In the Middlesex criminal registers dataset, 16 per cent of female juvenile indictments were for larceny by the servant/from the employer, as opposed to 6 per cent of male juvenile indictments.[59] The case of fifteen-year-old Sarah Powell in 1802 was typical. Sarah stole various articles of clothing and textiles from her master James Little, an upholsterer in Cavendish Square. Temporarily employed as a servant and left

---

55 OBSP, seventh session, 1835, no. 1265, pp. 134–5.
56 AOT, Con 31/48, convict register, no. 2341; RGD 34/2, burials register, no. 164.
57 LMA, CRIM 4/1, 11 Nov. 1834; OBSP, first session, no. 129, p. 107.
58 LMA, CRIM 4/5, no. 80, 2 Dec. 1834; OBSP, fifth session, 1835, no. 704, p. 728.
59 PRO, HO 26/5, 13, 23, 33, 43, 53. A development of this theme can also be found in King, 'Female offenders', 75–83.

alone, in Little's absence, on the day she left Sarah had tried to extract some better quality cloth by hiding it between some sacking.[60] Servants and apprentices did not habitually steal goods of great value, simply because of the inevitability that they would get caught or accused. However the theft of small goods that could remain undetected, or theft as an act when intending to leave employment was more common. On the whole children like Rowland Bassett and George Webster had probably spent little time premeditating their crimes. There was little similarity to the world governed by organisation, hierarchy, exchange and reciprocity that was described by other juvenile offenders. Nevertheless, children who strongly identified with the criminal subculture did not exist in some separate vacuum. Many of them had part-time or casual employment, which they supplemented by their dishonest earnings. It was only a few who seem to have given themselves wholly to their criminal 'careers'.

This chapter has examined the nature of the crimes that juveniles committed, and the processes of offending in which they engaged. Paying close attention to the more extreme manifestations of juvenile crime, it has examined the interaction between children's offending behaviour and the prevalent contemporary representations of juvenile offending. A number of issues can be restated. Firstly, the very trivial nature of much crime committed by juveniles. It is clear, from readings of both thieves' narratives and accounts in the *Old Bailey sessions papers*, that juvenile offenders were often engaged in opportunistic thefts. This contrasts sharply with the view expressed by a number of contemporary commentators, that juvenile criminals operated with a degree of premeditation and organisation. Secondly, the commonly evoked representation of this view was the juvenile pickpocket. Whilst it is possible to argue that pickpockets were engaged in some sort of criminal subculture (if only as a mechanism for selling stolen goods), this does not necessarily give credence to the idea that they regarded such activity as a progression to more serious crime. Certainly it is true that juvenile pickpockets did seem to be more 'experienced' offenders. However, it can equally be argued that such children stole at a given opportune moment, rather than embarking on thieving expeditions. Thirdly, the same ambiguities can be applied to juvenile involvement in more serious crimes such as burglary and robbery. The example of 'starring the glaze' illustrates the degree of interpretation prevalent in the legal descriptions of such crime. Fourthly, the numbers of children involved in violent crime were small. The cases of John Any Bird Bell and William Newton Allnut provided extreme examples. The coverage given to the trial of these boys again indicates the pervasiveness of contemporary representations of juvenile crime: in both cases the domestic environment and former delinquency were seen as highly relevant. The

---

[60] OBSP, seventh session, 1802, no. 612, pp. 404–5.

following chapter will examine the processes of criminality leading to the child's incorporation into the criminal justice system, paying particular attention to the role of adult agency: the receiver of stolen goods, the police and, in the context of trial, the magistrate.

4

Processes: Journeying into the Justice System

'I sometimes used to be without money in the mornings as I often gambled it all away over night and if I asked my landlady Mrs Burke to lend me some – she would call me a lazy idle prig, tell me to go out thieving and she would buy any thing I might bring her – If she can she will get a boy to pawn a silver spoon for a mere nothing (?) telling him it is only common metal and then she will offer him three pence or four pence extra for the ticket – she is a shocking bad one, but all these fences live so upon the boys you would be astonished!' – William Cook (aged fifteen)[1]

In the previous chapter the nature of offending and the forms of criminal activity were considered. Yet when these children appear in the criminal records they have come to the end of a process. Whilst the present chapter will continue to examine the forms of child criminality, it will concentrate upon the child's journey into the justice system: the process that inevitably led 'him' to the police, to court and, ultimately, to acquittal or punishment.[2] It has been established that most of the existing narratives of juvenile crime come from children more strongly engaged with criminal activity. In the criminal networks to which they had access, they seem to have been involved in shifting power relationships with adult agents. Thus they describe confrontations with both the forces of criminality and the forces of law and order on a daily basis. Their interactions with that central figure in their narratives, the fence, or receiver of stolen goods, are mirrored by their relationships with those arbiters of their futures, the police and the magistrate.

A number of children referred to the myriad of connections and associations to which they had recourse. It is debatable how representative such descriptions of criminal life-styles were. However, the way in which these children offended was less different than the frequency with which they offended, the frequency with which they had been apprehended, and the extent to which they interacted with the networks of fences and fellow thieves which existed around the metropolis. For argument's sake it will be assumed that most juvenile offenders did not have much direct contact with these networks. Yet as soon as an offender stole and sold on goods (rather than say, stealing food to eat), he or she was drawn into a relationship of

1 · PRO, HO 73/16, notebook 3, evidence of W. Cook.
2 Parts of this chapter have been used in H. Shore, ' "Cross coves, buzzers and general sorts of prigs": juvenile crime and the criminal "underworld" in the early nineteenth century', *British Journal of Criminology* xxxix (1999), 10–24.

exchange with a fence. 'Fence' is essentially a generic term for the receiver, the pawnbroker, the marine store keeper, or even an older lad, or sister, who acted in a fencing capacity. Arguably descriptions of fences and their function as receivers of stolen goods are relevant to many juvenile offenders. Children could choose from a variety of avenues to off-load their stolen goods. However, there seem to be have been a number of established fences, particularly in certain areas or streets. Certainly, as the following statements show, Dickens's choice of Field Lane was highly relevant, since many children mention fences in that, and in the general area of Saffron Hill:

> 'She principally sold the things she stole to two women called the two sisters in Field Lane, jewessess – they will only give 6s/ for a thing worth 35s/. She has also sold things to Sheen' – Mary Mause – eighteen

> 'They sold their plunder to jews in Field Lane or Petticoat Lane: who would give them 30s/ or 35s/ for goods worth £7' – Caroline Gadberry – seventeen

> 'My companion's mistress pawned it chiefly, some at the pawnbrokers in the Borough & sometimes she would go over to Field Lane' – George Wilkinson – nineteen

> 'Sold handkerchiefs to other thieves frequently – and also to several Jews in Field Lane, one by name Benjamin' – William Pembroke – sixteen

> 'I generally sold my plunder to two sister jewessess in Field Lane – they keep 'a handkerchief shop' and give 2 shillings for a good one' – George Hickman – sixteen

Some lodging-house keepers also apparently doubled as fences, establishing a relationship whereby the child received free or cheap lodgings in return for stolen goods. For example, sixteen-year-old Peter Conolly, 'Used to lodge at Scott's, St. Giles price of his bed was four pence – if he had not the money, Mrs Scott would take a silk handkerchief for security.'[3]

Certain fences were notorious. Ikey Solomons, operating in the 1820s, achieved fame in his own lifetime, and has often been cited as a model for Fagin. Earlier in 1816 the magistrate Sir John Silvester compiled a notebook which gave details of a number of receivers and in some cases the names of the juvenile thieves who apparently supplied them.[4] During the mid 1830s a number of fences were in operation, several of them well-known to the police and magistrates. The fences seem to have wielded a significant amount of power. They usually had some sort of business as a cover for their more nefarious activities, often that of pawnbroker, marine-store keeper, or old-clothes shop-keeper. Presumably there were problems in actually convicting a fence,

---

3   PRO, HO 73/16, notebook 2, evidence of Peter Conolly.
4   J. J. Tobias has refuted the association between Solomons and the fictional Fagin: *Prince of fences: the life and crimes of Ikey Solomons*, London 1974; British Library, MS Egerton 3710, Sir J. Silvester notebook (1816).

since the onus was on the court to prove that the accused was aware that the goods that he or she received were stolen. Moreover, amongst the c. 1836 interviews there were a number of fences alleged to be in collusion with police, or with parish officers. For example, a boy named Walker described the activities of Maria Benjamin, one of two sisters who fenced around the Whitecross Street area. According to this boy Benjamin used her associations with the police to make sure she controlled the bargaining process. Indeed boys had no power to bargain since, 'if the boy sauces her & refuses her price he has him taken up . . . a very tall policeman nicknamed cauliflower is in her service – he lives in Pickford wharf, was himself a cracksman'. The Benjamin sisters seem to have been formidable businesswomen: Walker commented of the other Benjamin sister that '(she) would buy of a baby'.[5] William Cook made similar insinuations about the well-known fence, Pigeony, who oper-ated in the Commercial Road: 'Pigeony keeps a house Whitechapel way and Boys go to him with any thing for sale, the police men say nothing to them.'[6] How reliable these assertions are, as in the allegations of police corruption described below, can only be speculated. Certainly the metropolitan police was at this time in its youth, and the 'police' to whom the boys were referring may well have been parish officers, or remnants of the old Watch, who may have been more amenable to involvement in processes of negotiation with fences.[7] Moreover, these are the children's interpretation of the fences' activities. They may well have seen or imagined relationships that did not exist, at least not in the way in which the children understood them. It may also have made their testimony more exciting if they were able to drop in a mention of corruption, particularly adult corruption. However, it may be that the children were simply telling the truth, describing what they had seen: certainly there is little doubt that the fence had a central role in their lives. As many of boys pointed out, if more energy were to be put into charging and convicting the fences than was put into charging children, crime might well decrease. Essentially the fence supported the market, provided a nexus for exchange. As Henry Thompson astutely commented to Miles: 'it is those "fences" who do us boys the most harm – we are only their workmen after all, and unless they are stopped you cannot stop thieving'.[8] This sentiment was repeated by many of the children interviewed in the mid 1830s.

Moreover, in the narratives of their lives, countless occasions were referred to when a fence had stolen from them, undersold them, threatened them. Fourteen-year-old James Edwards, found guilty of robbery in 1835, sold property to a woman in Wentworth Street who sometimes cheated him 'by

---

[5] PRO, HO 73/16, rough notebook iii, evidence of Walker.
[6] Ibid. notebook 3, evidence of W. Cook.
[7] When the children refer to officers, it is unclear whether they were referring to actual metropolitan police officers or to parochial officers. Certainly the children perceived them as the law.
[8] PRO, HO 73/16, notebook 2, evidence of H. Thompson.

getting the property into her possession and then telling the boy to be off about his business'. Similarly a seventeen-year-old named Robinson remarked on the vulnerability of new thieves, when visiting the two sisters in Field Lane:

> if a new thief goes to them with anything valuable they will try to frighten him out of it, by calling 'Jane, Jane, go for a Police man' but an old hand knows better – all fences cheat the young ones this way at first.[9]

The names of a number of fences occur time and time again in these documents – William Sheen and his father, who ran lodging-houses in the Wentworth Street area of Whitechapel; Pigeony, the Whitechapel fence; the two Jewish sisters, who operated from Field Lane; Mrs Benjamin and her sister Maria; Reuben Martin; Mrs Hummerson; Mrs Scott. The police were aware of the problem fences posed, but were either unwilling, or unable, to do anything very effective about it. As well as acting as fences, such people also had legitimate businesses: Reuben Martin was the publican of the Golden Boot public house in Milton Street (also known as Grub Street); Mrs Hummerson kept a chandler's shop in Orchard Street, Westminster; Pigeony kept a birdshop on the Commercial Road in Whitechapel.[10] These people may well have used fencing as a profitable, if risky, sideline in times of hardship. However, there is also some evidence of fences who were involved in criminal activities for substantial periods of time.

William Sheen, who was well-known as a fence by the mid 1830s at least, had a string of convictions from the late 1820s until the mid 1840s. He was mentioned by a number of the children. Hewitt, interviewed on the *Euryalus* c. 1836, spoke about Sheen and his father: 'Sheen always teaching boys – (this is the one who cut the child's head off) his father lives about three doors off – also buys & dosses – walks about & gets boys to buzz him. Sometimes they do it & flare it . . . & he sends for gin & treats them.'[11] He was referred to by William Augustus Miles as 'a thorough villain'.[12] Yet, during a 'career' spanning twenty years, William Sheen, unlike the many juvenile thieves with whom he dealt, evaded transportation; indeed his most serious sentence was eighteen months imprisonment. In 1827 he was put on trial at the Old Bailey for the murder of his child, but discharged; in 1830 he was involved in a robbery, appeared at Lambeth Street, but was remanded; in 1833 he was possibly indicted for larceny, appearing at Clerkenwell; in 1834 he assaulted his father, appeared at Lambeth Street and was dismissed; in 1835 he was charged with robbery and dismissed from Lambeth Street; in 1836 he appeared at the Middlesex sessions, after he had threatened to rip up the

9 Ibid. notebook 1, evidence of Robinson and Edwards.
10 Reuben Martin, proprietor of the *Golden Boot*, Milton Street, Finsbury: *Robson's London directory, for 1835*, 15th edn, London 1835, 583.
11 PRO, HO 73/16, rough notebooks iii, evidence of Hewitt.
12 Miles, *Poverty*, 101.

bowels of one Thomas Moore and his wife, 'and had declared that he would not be satisfied until he had their lives' – he was entered into recognizances to keep the peace, with sureties to be found within twenty-four hours; in 1837 he was convicted of keeping a brothel at the Middlesex sessions, and sentenced to eighteen months' imprisonment, solitary confinement and recognizances for twelve months; in 1845 he was charged with assaulting and threatening the life of Mr Conrad Beuhler, the landlord of the *City of Norwich* public house in Whitechapel, and ordered to keep the peace for twelve months; in 1847 he was charged with cutting and wounding his common-law wife Mary Anne Sullivan, found guilty of aggravated assault and sentenced to hard labour for twelve months.[13] Given the contemporary preoccupation with juvenile crime and nurseries of crime, the details of his 1835 and 1837 charges are rather interesting. In 1835 he was charged with trying to rob a young man (or boy) who had been lodging at Sheen's house, 'a low brothel of the most infamous description in Wentworth-street'. Sheen apparently attacked the boy when he tried to leave the lodging-house without paying. Robert Taylor denied this and claimed to be leaving because he 'had ultimately become so shocked at the numbers of silk-handkerchiefs that were brought there by juvenile thieves and other improper goings on'.[14] The case was dismissed. Two years later, Sheen was again tried, this time at the instigation of the Society for the Suppression of Juvenile Prostitution. According to the Society:

> As many as 20 boys and ten young girls under the age of sixteen were found in the house on one night recently when the police visited it. They were huddled together without any distinction of sexes: the boys were encouraged in picking pockets, and the wretched girls were made victims of the grossest depravity.[15]

Moreover, Sheen's father and mother were also involved in criminal activities to some degree.[16] His mother, Anne, in particular had a fruitful career as a brothel-owner and fence. Thus in 1840 she was tried at the Old Bailey for receiving:

> it further appeared that the prisoner kept a chandlers Shop in Rose-Lane Spitalfields, and had also two houses in Wentworth Street, Whitechapel, which she kept as brothels for the use of dissolute youth of both sexes. . . . Sergeant Power of the H division stated that when he searched the prisoners house he

---

13 *Times*, 30 May 1827, 3, col. e; 2 June 1827, 4, col. c; 4 June 1827, 5, col. e; 14 July 1827, 3, col. e; 16 July 1827, 3, col. d; 13 Sept. 1830, 4, col. b; 29 Nov. 1834, 4, col. c; 8 Sept. 1835, 4, col. d; *Cleave's Weekly Police Gazette* iii, no. 31, 30 July 1836, front page; *Times*, 28 June 1837, o col. d; 29 June 1837, 3, col. f; 21 May 1845, 8, col. e; 27 July 1847, 7, col. d; 23 Aug. 1847 ᴜ, col. e; PRO, HO 17/111/vy/5, petition of William Sheen.
14 *Times*, 8 Sept. 1835, 4, col. d.
15 Ibid. 28 June 1837, 6, col. d.
16 Sheen is described by children and youths as being in partnership with his father.

found eighteen silk handkerchiefs, marked with different persons names, a large number of silver spoons, watches and other property.[17]

Anne's death in October 1842 was reported by the Prison Discipline Society, who commented on the fact that before her trial in 1840 she had made over her property, which consisted of bank stock and houses 'to a considerable amount', to her favourite son 'Bill', so as to secure it from the sheriff in the event of a conviction.[18] However, at some point, relations between Bill and his mother had obviously soured, since in her will she left him nothing. Instead she left her belongings to her other children, and the rest of the estate to the trust of her friend Conrad Beuhler, with provisions for the education up to apprenticeship of her son John Sheen.[19] So perhaps at the end Anne decided to go straight. This decision, of course, cost Mr Beuhler a violent assault when William, convinced that Beuhler had been the cause of his misfortune, attacked him in his pub. Declaring with an oath that he would instantly go out and rip the witness up, he rushed out of the taproom to the front of the bar, and snatching from his pocket a penknife, opened it, and made a desperate stab at the witness's body. Despite this, the warrant-officer, Rowland, testified to the court, that, 'the prisoner when sober, was a very quiet and inoffensive man, but he was strongly addicted to habits of intemperance, and when he was intoxicated he was violent and ungovernable'.[20] Certainly William's spell of imprisonment after his conviction for keeping a brothel, seems to have done little to quell his temper, or to quell his predilections to criminality. Thus, in the census for 1841, William Sheen can be found with his common-law wife Mary in Keates Street, Whitechapel, occupying, along with several young men and women, what looks suspiciously like a brothel. Presumably Sheen had came out of prison and relocated his operation from Winford Court to Keates Street.[21]

The children's relationships with the fences was double-edged. On the one hand the fence provided the market for the exchange and sale of goods, and in the case of those operating as lodging-house keepers, shelter. On the other, the control they exerted over the children made them an unpopular necessity. The pervasiveness of references to fences confirms their centrality in the networks into which criminal children and youths were drawn. Their implicit power and control over young offenders was matched, however, by the exertions of the police.

17 *Times*, 10 Apr. 1840, 7, col. f; *OBSP*, sixth session, 1840, no. 1132, p. 897.
18 *Times*, 12 Oct. 1842, 5, col. a.
19 LMA, DL/C/404 (842–3), Consistory Court of London, Register of wills and administration, will of Anne Sheen.
20 *Times*, 21 May 1845, 8, col. e.
21 1841 Census, enumeration district 18, fos 14, 20, Keate Street, Spitalfields.

Policing and detection

There is little firm evidence of the manipulations of power and justice. Yet such processes of control are at the root of the criminal justice system. Capture was the earliest stage at which the manipulation of power could occur. Many juvenile offenders were pursued and caught by their victim, or by a witness to the offence, and then taken to the police officer. For example in February 1820 Martha Blakeman pursued nine-year-old Charles Elliott from her haberdasher's shop: 'I saw a boy run out, I followed the boy, and as I ran through the shop I missed five silk handkerchiefs and one cotton one. . . . I followed him into the street, crying Stop thief! And Rickman secured him.' In July 1816 thirteen-year-old Hugh Farrell was caught by Phineas Murphy, from whom he had stole a silver butter-boat and spoon:

> I went out and saw the prisoner in my area; he appeared to me to be endeav-
> ouring to hide the butter-boat which was within two or three inches of his
> hand, among some broken bricks which were in the area; he must have got
> over the rails for the gate was locked; I had the key of the area, and on going
> into it, I found the spoon among the bricks. I took the prisoner, and went
> down to Bow-street, and brought the officers up.[22]

At this stage, the police officer could decide on the appropriate course of action, based mainly on the victim's decision on whether or not to prosecute. Whilst the cases reported in the *Old Bailey session papers* represent cases where a prosecution had been pursued, some victims failed to follow the charge up, in which case it would be dropped. Moreover there was some sug-gestion, from both children and magistrates, that justice was sometimes deliv-ered on the street, by police officers, in the form of a good thrashing. Indeed much of the protest against the increasing numbers of children appearing in front of the courts seemed to hark back to a golden age when the beadle, officer or watch-man could dispense a summary, generally physical, justice.[23] A number of magistrates and officers favoured a swift application of justice. Mr Serjeant Pell explained to the 1828 Select Committee on Metropolitan Police:

> I cannot but think myself that it is not a likely way to bring a lad of seven,
> eight, nine or ten years of age, round to a good course of life, to send him to
> gaol, where he shall be found in company with the most depraved boys which
> human nature can produce; and if I could have the means of having my opin-
> ion carried into effect, I do really think a more domestic and summary process
> against a juvenile offender would be much the best mode of proceeding against

---

[22] OBSP, third session, 1820, no. 368, p. 161; seventh session, 1816, no. 916, p. 425.
[23] For example see the *Eighth report of the Committee of the Society for the Improvement of Prison Discipline and for the Reformation of Juvenile Offenders*, London 1832, 48: 'offenses which were formerly either passed over, or visited with Summary correction, are now made the occasion of commitment to gaol'.

him, to let him be punished on the spot and discharged. . . . Yes, I would have him punished by the constable.[24]

Certainly, the police did put such 'domestic and summary' processes into practice, despite legislative requirements. Like so much law, a certain level of interpretation existed which recognised that it was not always practical or indeed sensible to follow the letter of the law. Hence magistrates might send boys to short periods on remand rather than to trial; and the police might dispense justice on the streets rather than arrest juvenile offenders. Thus eighteen-year-old Andrew Clark (c. 1836) had been 'frequently let off with a thrashing or box on the ear'.[25] According to the thieves' narratives from Coldbath Fields, boys often received punishment on the spot, at times in the form of community-dispensed justice: 'They are sometimes horse-whipped, at other times they have their faces and hands oiled and soot sprinkled over them.'[26]

Confrontation with the police, then, did not automatically lead to committal to trial. Yet clearly, for the juvenile criminal, the police were the most visible representatives of the criminal justice system. Such encounters had to be avoided on a day-to-day basis. Moreover the police, unlike their colleagues in the justice system, occupied the same streets, shopped in the same shops, knew the public houses (if only by reputation), and may well have known the children's families.[27] In many ways the police were in an ambiguous position. Despite the efforts to curtail police corruption after the Vaughan case, and the systematisation of the police with the 1829 act, there was still plenty of distrust. On the one hand the police were substantial contributors to the juvenile justice debate. Indeed, as practitioners of juvenile justice, they were in the front line. On the other hand, as is clear from the interviews conducted by Miles and those conducted for the Constabulary Commission, there were serious doubts about the efficacy of the new police force. Questions 23 and 24 of the Constabulary Commission interviews asked: 'Did any of them [thieves] associate with the Constables?'; 'Did they ever use any means with the Constables to get their escape facilitated?'[28] In fact, according to these interviews, the police and police corruption were a constant source of discussion. This was partly a consequence of the ambivalent position occupied by the police. Unlike the magistrates, officials and reformers, for the police firm distinctions between 'them' and 'us' did not sit so easily. In terms of class many policemen

24 SC Police, PP, 1828, vi. 239, evidence of Mr Serjeant Pell.
25 PRO, HO 73/2 pt 2, loose papers, interview with Andrew Clarke.
26 Constabulary Commission, PP, 1839, xix, appendix 6, p. 206.
27 On the social history of the police see D. Ascoli, The queen's peace: the origins and development of the metropolitan police, 1829–1979, London 1979; T. A. Critchley, A history of police in England and Wales, 2nd edn, London 1978; C. Emsley, The English police: a political and social history, Hemel Hempstead 1991; C. Steedman, Policing the Victorian community: the formation of English provincial police forces, 1856–80, London 1984.
28 PRO, HO 73/2/2, loose papers, Constabulary Commission questionnaire.

were working men, often from Irish backgrounds, speaking the same language as the people with whom they dealt.[29] From the descriptions given by juvenile offenders, speaking the same language could mean a number of things. Mostly it meant a willingness to turn a blind eye – if the price was right. Admittedly the reliability of these interviews calls for caution, as these children might have had every reason for wanting to implicate certain officers. However, certain names do recur suggesting, if not outright corruption, then at least that the relationship between police and criminals was multi-faceted.

Clearly, in these formative years of the police force, corruption was an insidious problem. In 1855 an officer named Charles King, of C division, was charged with larceny and receiving:

> The chief occupation of this cumulative offender for many years has been to train young thieves to the occupation of picking pockets, he himself conducting them to the places where their profession might be most advantageously exercised, pointing out the victims, and covering his pupils in the performance of their tasks.[30]

King was charged at the Central Criminal Court with stealing at St Mary Abbott's, Kensington, a purse containing 17s. The principal witness was a thirteen-year-old criminal:

> I first made the acquaintance of the prisoner about three years ago; I knew he was a policeman. . . . I continued to see him from that time down to the time of the frost in 1853. One day, during that frost, I met the prisoner at a public-house in Pulteney Street; the prisoner said, 'I can take you to a good place to get money', and then named the bridge over the Serpentine. . . . When we got there we met a great many other thieves, boys and men; the prisoner spoke to them, and there was a man there who used to go out with boys to thieve; he is in prison now.[31]

Caroline Gadberry, herself the daughter of a City officer, admitted to frequently paying the police officers. The general inference is that 'protection' was practised by certain corrupt officers, a mendacious form of negotiation: 'she was afraid of the Police: but many were treated & paid by them and would not take them: she has frequently given them 3/s & 5/s: and to more than one'. For Caroline this payment paid off since she was only ever detected 'by the parties robbed', and claimed to have committed at least forty or fifty robberies from shops, without detection.[32] Reading between the lines

---

[29] The first six companies of the metropolitan police force included, amongst others, ex-navy men (101), ex-army men (402), butchers (135), labourers (1,154), blacksmiths (55) and tailors (51): J. Morton, *Bent coppers: a survey of police corruption*, London 1993, 21.
[30] *Annual Register*, Chronicle, 13 Apr. 1855, 61–4.
[31] Ibid. 63.
[32] PRO, HO 73/2/2, loose papers, interview with reputed thief Caroline Gadberry. In May 1836 a Caroline Gadbury was committed for trial at Newgate from Lambeth Street police office, in Whitechapel, where Caroline Gadberry also lived. She was charged with four

of these interviews, it is possible to detect the dispensation of sexual favours as well. Caroline's partner-in-crime, Mary Mause, claimed to be intimate with a young policeman called George, proffering him shillings and brandy and presumably her body. Henry Thompson claimed to have seen a police officer named Ford frequenting the young prostitutes in Union Court in Westminster. According to Thompson, Ford walked a beat around Orchard Street and Pye Street, the area just above and to the east of the site of what is now Westminster Cathedral and was previously the prison: 'Ford has been seen by this boy to go in at 11 Union Court, first floor, front room to Hannah Briant & . . . other girls – & no men in the room – goes & has supper there sometimes – when on duty.'[33]

The payment of protection or bribes to police is mentioned so often, and by so many children, that it seems that there must be more than a grain of truth in such statements. Just using the set of interviews from Tothill Fields, compiled by Lieutenant Tracey, the following picture of profound police corruption emerges:

> Q. twenty-four – 'Did they ever use any means with the Constables to get their escape facilitated?'
>
> 'I know they have by giving the Constable half the booty' – Michael Ready alias William Davies – nineteen.
>
> 'Have frequently known money given to the Constables, particularly the night men and has known as much as fifty shillings, given to Officers to be away from the spot when robbery or House-breaking has been intended' – Andrew Clark – eighteen.
>
> 'I have heard my associates say they have made it all right with the Constables' – Thomas Keefe – nineteen.
>
> 'Yes – I myself have divided the contents of a Purse with one, and given silk handkerchiefs & a snuff box' – Philip Hall alias Lovell – nineteen.
>
> 'I have heard Sankey and others say that they were set at large by Grose after having committed robberies' – David Daly – eighteen.[34]

Whilst many of these accusations seem to be second-hand, there were many children, particularly in the less public interviews, who admitted to having paid to the police. Possibly there was some reluctance to admit to having bribed police officers. George Hickman showed no such reluctance when he told Miles:

others, including a Sarah Gadbury, for the theft of five yards of printed cotton: PRO, MEPO 4/26, May 13 1836.
[33] PRO, HO 73/2/2, loose papers, interview with reputed thief Mary Mause; HO 73/16, rough notebook iv, evidence of Henry Thompson.
[34] PRO, HO 73/2/2, loose papers, interviews from Tothill Fields.

Policemen, especially City Police are so nice – There is one fellow (number given) who behaves very well to us in the City. He never cares about getting a fellow sent to prison for three months because it does him no good, but if he can make an Old Bailey case of it, he takes the Boy up, because he gets his expenses, or something, I believe, for his trouble – He sometimes stops a fellow and takes anything from him which he may have about him and lets him go again.[35]

Generally, the children seem to have disliked the police, spending a considerable time avoiding them, being chased by them, or even on occasions swallowing evidence in the form of coin. Whilst a number of boys and young men gleefully describe their escape from and evasion of the police, the over-riding sentiment is resentment and fear. Escape from the police generally meant running and ducking into alleyways, or any other convenient opening. For example, sixteen-year-old William Pembroke, 'escaped by means of a coach or omnibus, sometimes got into a public house and secreted myself for a time there'; Pembroke described a memorable incident in Oxford Street, when he had escaped from the police 'by drawing my arms from my jacket, and waistcoat, and leaving them behind'. Eighteen-year-old Andrew Clark hid, 'in a place termed the broken down, or new ditch running along distance under ground, & from which there were a variety of places to escape'.[36] Other boys were less lucky; George Wilkinson alias Bevan, aged nineteen, had been convicted twice for picking pockets. The first time:

> the police came after me, but I got away – he however knew me & (came) the next day & took me – the Gentleman (whose pocket he had picked) came to the station house and recognised me, he told the inspector he would come to the Town against me, but finding he could not recover his handkerchief . . . he did not appear.[37]

Indeed, recognition by the police was a major problem. For those boys engaged in habitual theft, recognition by the police was inevitable, as one boy commented: 'Old hands talk more about reforming than young ones; it is new to them, but the old Hands are too well known to make it answer; knows some who have left off thieving because they were too notorious to continue their courses.'[38] Moreover, despite their bravado, children were not insouciant in their attitude to the police. Fear of being recognised, fear of being caught, resonates throughout these accounts. Henry Thompson had learnt the signs of an approaching officer, 'these men go out in different disguises but their boots betray them, turn up at toes – hear him by his walk. . . . Boots

35 PRO, HO 73/16, notebook 1, evidence of George Hickman.
36 PRO, HO 73/2, pt 2, loose papers, evidence of William Pembroke and Andrew Clark.
37 Ibid. evidence of George Wilkinson alias Bevan.
38 PRO, HO 73/16, loose papers, Select Committee on Gaols and Houses of Correction (secret), 9.

made all alike – in the B division they are wide across the instep'.[39] Juvenile offenders were trapped between the police and the fences. Thus to sell their goods they had to use the fences – some of whom subsequently maintained relationships with amenable officers, and used them as a threat so that the children had little choice but do their bidding. How real this threat was is uncertain. To an extent the police played a similar role to the fence; they could be crooked, but also reputable and, like the fence, they wielded considerable power over young thieves. To the juvenile, the police and the fence were like two faces of the same coin: both influenced the direction of their 'careers' for good or ill. Finally, it was the police who formed the link with the criminal justice system, and thus the relationship between the officer and the juvenile offender could follow a number of routes. The officer could take the law into his own hands, and apply immediate corporal punishment; he could follow the corrupt example of an officer like George Vaughan; or he could take the child to the magistrate, and so into the next stage of the criminal justice system.[40]

The child's word in court

Whilst a number of documents attached to the processes of trial survive, such as journalistic accounts, depositions and the indictment, there is little evidence to cast light on the experience of the trial for the offender. This is especially the case for petty criminal offenders, since such proceedings were so frequent and common, and the appearance of children and young people in front of the court was an unremarkable occurrence. Dramatic trials such as those of John Any Bird Bell or William Newton Allnut, on the other hand, were reported in some detail; yet even then the child's voice is rarely heard in the surviving documentation. Although the letters of William Newton Allnut were read extensively at his trial, William was educated and indicted for a crime of violence and was therefore far from a typical juvenile offender. Besides evidence from the accounts in the *Old Bailey sessions papers*, the only source which really captures anything of the child's experience of court are anecdotal extracts occasionally found in newspapers such as *The Times*. These tend to fall into one of two categories: either the cheery and cheeky, or the rhetoric of outrage, usually when a substantial number of children are being tried at the same time, or when a subject such as child prostitution is broached.[41] Juvenile impudence in court was described with great indigna-

---

39 Ibid. rough notebook iv, evidence of Henry Thompson.
40 Whilst records of metropolitan police service do survive, those for the 1830s are inconsistent and only cover a few divisions. This rules out any definite placing of the policemen mentioned. Departmental records relating to the metropolitan police can be found in PRO, MEPO2, MEPO3, MEPO4, MEPO5, MEPO7.
41 Such descriptions of trials are a rich and vastly under-used source. For example, certain

tion, pointing as it did to a lack of respect, and propriety. However, in the newspaper accounts there is a sense of sneaking admiration behind the indignation. Such a confrontation was portrayed by Dickens in his account of the Artful Dodger's final performance at Bow Street:

'I never seen such an out-and-out young wagabond, your worship,' observed the officer with a grin. 'Do you mean to say anything, you young shaver?'

'No,' replied the Dodger, 'not here, for this ain't the shop for justice; besides which, my attorney is a-breakfasting this morning with the Wice President of the House of Commons; but I shall have something to say elsewhere, and so will he, and so will a wery numerous and 'spectable circle of acquaintance as 'll make them beaks wish they'd never been born, or that they'd got their footmen to hang 'em up to their own hatpegs, 'afore they let 'em come out this morning to try it upon me. I'll-

'There! He's fully committed!' interposed the clerk. 'Take him away.'

'Come on,' said the jailer.

'Oh ah! I'll come on,' replied the Dodger, brushing his hat with the palm of his hand. 'Ah! (to the Bench) it's no use your looking frightened; I won't show you no mercy, no a ha'porth of it. You'll pay for this, my fine fellers. I wouldn't be you for something! I wouldn't go free, now, if you was to fall down on you knees and ask me. Here, carry me off to prison! Take me away!'[42]

Whilst this literary account is suffused with melodrama and histrionics, it was not without parallel in real life. In 1830 *The Times* reported an exchange between the Lord Mayor and a young pickpocket at the Mansion House:

The Prisoner – Please your lordship, I was wandering about without anything to eat, and I said to myself when I seed the handkerchief, 'Jack,' says I, 'there's a summut that'll get you a dinner or a lodging.'

The Lord Mayor – Very well, and you were right; it got you a lodging. (A laugh.)

The Prisoner – Why, my lord, I was careless whether I went to the watchus or not, and I tuck the handkerchief.

The Lord Mayor – I am afraid that you are an old hand, and I don't know what to do with you except send you for trial.

The Prisoner – Why, my lord, you can do as you like; I won't make no rash promises.

The Lord Mayor – And I won't let you break any.[43]

---

cases were discussed by the press with great relish. In 1831 two cases were described by *The Times*, the first referring to two child prostitutes (girls aged 11 and 12), who were charged with 'walking the streets for the purpose of prostitution, and with uttering the most abominable language under the Piazzas of Covent garden', the second commenting on a 14-year-old who apparently ran a gang of nearly 40 boys, 'who used to assemble regularly every morning in Hyde-park, and receive orders from their captain to take different routes for the purpose of thieving': ibid. 26 Jan. 1831, 3, col. 3.

[42] Charles Dickens, *Oliver Twist*, London 1837–9, this edn London 1986, 396.

[43] *Times*, 13 Sept. 1830, 4, col. b. Parallels can be drawn between the lack of deference

In some ways, it might be argued that such light-hearted accounts were one way to deal with the tragedy of children in court. Such demeanour, exhibiting a lack of respect, a lack of fear of the authority of the court, led back directly into contemporary stereotypes of juveniles. They were bold, impudent, they were out of control. At the trial of a number of the boys interviewed by Miles on the *Euryalus*, there was a general atmosphere of commotion in court:

> The court was literally crammed with spectators during the passing the sentences, and we regret to say that great confusion prevailed occasionally. Several of the prisoners, the majority of whom were young persons, behaved with so much levity, that the learned recorder was compelled to recall them, and lecture them upon their indecorous and hardened behaviour. He also reminded them that transportation was not a removal to a state of comparative idleness, but a continuous course of constraint, severity and privitation. Some of their friends in the gallery added to the disorder by insolent exclamations towards the learned judge of the grossest kind, and others by vehement screaming and exultations. The court however, exercised great forbearance towards those who disturbed its proceedings.[44]

As suggested above, one source which can be used to reconstruct the experience of the child at trial is the *Old Bailey sessions papers*. In these journalistic accounts of the proceedings of the Old Bailey, the words of criminal children – arguing with witnesses, pleading in defence, given as evidence in prosecution – can occasionally be found. Witness testimony sometimes contained statements that the prisoner had apparently made, used to convey a sense of threat or a knowledge of guilt. In 1820, at the trial of sixteen-year-old pickpocket William Adnum, the watch-man of Great Wild Street, Patrick Carmody, told the court how he had collared Adnum when he saw him running down Pitt's Place (near Drury Lane) late at night. There was a struggle between Adnum and Carmody in the course of which a watch fell out of Adnum's pocket. At the same time the victim appeared on the scene claiming the watch as his own. Carmody continued:

> I was taking him to the watch-house, and when we got to Wild-street he said, 'Let the old fool go to hell, he has got his watch. I will give you something handsome to let me go, as it will be a serious job to me – I want to fly and be off.' He put 6s.6d into my hand, but I kept hold of him and the money, and took him to the watch-house.[45]

In William Adnum's case bribery failed to work. However, in the same year another boy was tried who used the more direct method of a threat of

exhibited by these children and the language of plebian protest described in E. P. Thompson, 'Patricians and plebs', in his *Customs in common*, London 1991, 16–96, esp. pp. 64–83.
44 *Times*, 15 Apr. 1835, 6, cols d, e.
45 *OBSP*, second session, 1820, no. 285, p. 128.

physical violence. Sixteen-year-old William Powers had snatched the watch of William Clapson in the evening of 7 April 1820. He ran away but was stopped by John Over, a Fleet Street butcher. Over took the boy to Clapson:

> The prisoner behaved very bad, and made use of bad language – he told me to be on my guard, for if he was in confinement there were those who would mark me, and he did not care for himself, for he was as well out of the country as in it and he knew we could not rope him for this.[46]

Of course, in these cases the validity of these statements rested much on the position and status of the witness. Obviously nobody was going to take William Adnum's word over that of Patrick Carmody, the watch-man. Similarly in William Powers's case, the men giving evidence against him were automatically superior given their status as adults, and as tradesmen. However there was some room for doubt in the case of William Jones, aged sixteen, convicted of sending a threatening letter with menaces to Robert Colley, a servant at a house in Shoe Lane. According to the evidence William had approached the house where Colley worked looking for work as an errand-boy. Apparently William was very hungry and had been walking about all day – Colley took him in, gave him some food and sent him on his way. Over the next couple of days William turned up at the house a number of times after food and money. Colley said, 'he has annoyed me ever since I relieved him'.[47] Finally William arrived at the house bearing the following letter:

> London, July 1st, 1833.
> Sir – I am veary sorry to trouble you a gain, but you know your situation is that, and i expect you wilt give me some recompence for wat you have don, you recollect you intised me in this house for your own purposes, I consider you acted a unnatural crime, sodomy, and therefore I shal expect you will lend me the sum of two pounds, and if you do refuse it, i will rite a letter to your master, for I am determined to have the money. I remain, with much respect, yours, &c. &c. – I want an answer, and will not go with out it. I have somebody close at and, that has got another letter for your master relating wat you have done.[48]

The trial continued in a form of attack and parry between Robert Colley and William Jones, supplemented by the evidence of the superintendent of the nightly watch, William Marchant. Unsuprisingly, Jones's version of the events differed substantially from Colley's. According to Jones, Colley had propositioned him on a walk down to Blackfriar's Bridge:

> and there he committed what was highly improper; he put my hand into his trousers, and said, he thought it was not safe in the street, but he would let me in for the night if I chose . . . he let down the bedstead out of the wardrobe, and

[46] Ibid. fourth session, 1820, no. 414, p. 300.
[47] Ibid. sixth session, 1833, no. 1114, pp. 609–11.
[48] Ibid. 609.

we went to bed – I awoke about half-past seven o'clock; we got up, I eat the rest of the mutton, and went out; and that night he did similar to what he did before.[49]

Jones continued to defend himself by offering to describe Colley's bedroom. However William Marchant pointed out that everything described by Jones could have been seen by anybody:

> by laying hold of the rails, and see all over the room when he was going to bed; he don't shut the window shutters, because there is a dead wall facing his bed-room; and he says he never shuts his shutters because it should not be dark in the morning; his bed does open with folding doors right opposite the window, anybody can see it by looking in at the window.[50]

Moreover Jones had blustered by asserting that he knew nothing of the letter, that it was handed to him by another young man who asked him to deliver the note. Later he dropped this aspect of his story altogether, denied asking for money, claiming that he only asked for recompense for what had been done to him, 'he said, "What do you want with me;" I said, I wanted some recompense for what he had done; the officer said, Walk in, and I went into the parlour, and the officer said, "You are in custody;" I said very well'.[51] Despite a vigorous defence, William Jones was found guilty and transported for life. Clearly the prosecutors chose to concentrate on the element of pre-meditation that was suggested by the evidence. The truth of the assault on Jones was less important. Overwhelmingly such cases point to the vulnerability of the child in court. William Jones's guilt is less at issue. The case stands out because of the uniqueness of William's spirited defence of himself. For other children, the only defence they could offer was of mitigating circumstances, of promises not to offend again, or promises to reform if sent to the Marine Society or Refuge for the Destitute.

Most children had little to say in their own defence. John Cooper, aged fifteen, found guilty of stealing a glass bottle, a pint of brandy, a razor and a key in January 1802 told the court: 'I bought the brandy at the Rose and Crown, and found the razor in the tap-room, and kept it to cut my toe-nails.'[52] Fifteen-year-old Joseph Mason, convicted of stealing 5lbs of bee's wax privately in a shop in January 1811, protested: 'The bees wax fell down by accident, I catched it between my thighs, I did not intend to steal it.'[53] Peter McEvan, described as a ragged young urchin, was charged at the Marylebone magistrates office in 1836 with stealing eggs from a Hampstead baker, Mr Tomlin. McEvans had been caught with his hand reaching through to the enclosure where the fowls eggs lay. When asked if had anything to say for

---

49 Ibid.
50 Ibid. 610.
51 Ibid. 611.
52 Ibid. second session, 1802, no. 113, p. 88.
53 Ibid. third session, 1811, no. 230, p. 148.

himself, McEvan apparently blubbered 'Vy, I've got nothing to say, no more than I vos coming along, ven a boy chucked my cap through the hole, and I vent to lay hold on it, instead of vich I vos laid hold on. I did'nt vont to steal the heggs, for mother says I ar'nt got no mouth for sich harticles.'[54] The attempt to parody the colloquialisms of the boy's speech, as in the excerpt from *The Times* cited above, perhaps gives some indication of how little credence was given to the evidence of children. Yet children could submit a more formal defence to the court. Ann Lugg the younger (aged fifteen), indicted with her mother, Ann Lugg the elder, in 1833 for the theft of a silver spoon and three handkerchiefs from the dwelling-house of Robert McLellan, submitted a written defence to the court:

> I left my situation through the cook's beating me, and turning me out of the house; I went home to my mother, who returned with me, and insisted on my staying until my mistress came home. . . . My mother came for me on Saturday evening. . . . The cook and my mistress were both in the kitchen. I fetched my box, and my mother emptied it before them, and they said there was nothing there belonging to them. . . . My mistress paid me, and I went home. On the following Tuesday . . . a policeman came and said Mrs McLellan wished to speak with me. I went with him immediately; when she charged me with stealing a table-spoon, which I knew nothing about. . . . The next night the policeman came to my mother's lodgings and asked her to let him see her duplicates, which he had seen before, when he kept two of them. They were two pocket handkerchiefs which Mrs McLellan said I had stolen, and my mother received, which I deny.[55]

Ann, like William Jones, felt that she had been the victim of adult negligence and perfidy. Other children blamed poverty and distress, lack of employment and opportunity for the genesis of their crimes. A second, and final, example of more formal address to the court, encapsulates both the child's word in court and also turns the rhetoric of reformers and commentators on juvenile crime against the court. George Power, aged thirteen, was indicted along with eight-year-old Henry Hughes in 1828, for the theft of a handkerchief from the person of James Thornhill in Jermyn Street. Power, in his defence, handed the court an extract from the *Morning Chronicle* of 24 March 1828. It is worth reproducing this extract in full given its pointed and accusatory content:

> Bow-street – A young man, who said that he had suffered the sentence of the law, for picking a gentleman's pocket in Leicester-square, applied to know how he was to act under the following circumstances: on obtaining his liberty, he determined to amend his life, and retrieve the character he had lost; in pursuance of this design, he had procured an employment, in which he was doing prosperously, until some evil-disposed person disclosed to his master and fellow-workmen, the history of his life. The latter, as might be expected,

54 *Cleave's Weekly Police Gazette* iii, no. 23, 4 June 1836, front page.
55 *OBSP*, first session, 1833, no. 112, pp. 90–1.

refused to remain in the shop with a convicted thief; and the former having his own fears, pleaded that as an excuse for discharging him. He was then, he said, again thrown on the town, and unless he could procure some means of getting bread honestly, a return to his former evil courses, must be the inevitable consequence; and a consequence, it was his anxious desire to avoid. – Jones (the gaoler) Were you not brought here by Boston? APPLICANT. Yes; I was. Jones. I see how it is your Worship; this Boston is an amateur constable, who, with a fellow named Roberts, goes about assuming the character of officers; when he takes young men up, who, afterwards reforming, get employment; he goes to their master, and tells what they have been. SIR RICHARD BIRNIE. I declare I never in my life, heard anything half so villainous. Why is not such a fellow brought here: I now give strict orders, that both he and his colleague shall be watched; really, my poor fellow, your case is lamentable – I myself, will speak to your master on your behalf, and if I do not succeed there I know I shall elsewhere; the lad then left his name and address, and, after thanking his Worship, retired.

Power added, 'The two men in question, are the same as have got me in charge.'[56] Whilst the order of events is a little confusing, it seems that John Boston (the 'amateur' officer) had brought George Power into the magistrate on a number of occasions, including the present one. Boston denied any knowledge of the boy's accusation. Whatever the reality of Power's situation the *Morning Chronicle* extract was a powerful indictment of circumstances which must often have resulted in the basic conflict of reform – the stigmatising of the criminal and the seemingly inexorable slide into reoffending. Criminal trial was irrecoverably tied to imprisonment. Even if the sentence did not result in imprisonment, the indicted person would spend at least some time in one of the city's remand prisons, such as Newgate or Clerkenwell. For children like George Powers the relationship between the court and the prison was one which they would encounter time and time again in the vicious circle of offending and punishment.

This chapter has charted the juvenile's passage from offender through to entry into the criminal justice system, outlining the relationship with both forces of corruption and of law and order. To some extent it might be argued that the 1830s represents a unique period. This was a time when the police were reinventing themselves as a more formal, moral, preventative force. At the same time hangovers of the old police still remained.[57] Thus conflicts between theoretical methods and actual practice were still being worked out; police corruption and collusion still needed to be addressed. The shift from the street to the court marked the criminal child's initiation into the criminal justice system. Whilst this initiation began tentatively at the hands of the

56 Ibid. second session, 1828, no. 940, p. 466.
57 Despite the passage of the Metropolitan Police Act in 1829 (10 Geo. IV c.44), the move from the 'old' to the 'new' police was gradual. The City police were only fully incorporated under the Metropolitan Police Act of 1839 (2 & 3 Vict. c. 47). See Emsley, *Crime and society*, 62–3.

police and magistrate, as soon as the decision was made to commit the child to trial a number of stages were broached, and possible consequences emerged. What this chapter has illustrated is that none of these processes was simple, or clear-cut. For example, the relationship between juvenile criminals and the police officers they encountered could depend very much on a policeman's individual actions and behaviour. Similarly, the theatre of justice played out at trial was occasionally confronted by children who offered their own defences and interpretations of events. Trial could result in a number of outcomes. Dismissal, discharge and acquittal on the one hand could bring an immediate end to a particular case. Then again, short periods of remand, or a referral to a refuge or society, could bring the child into at least temporary contact with institutions of penality. A similar outcome was likely if the child was processed summarily, for example through the Vagrancy Act, or through the Malicious Trespass Act. Alternatively, if the child was indicted, he or she would appear at the general or quarter sessions (in Middlesex this would most likely mean Clerkenwell or Westminster) or at the Old Bailey sessions. A this stage acquittal was still an option. If the child was found guilty, a number of outcomes were again possible, with resolutions such as fines, corporal punishment, imprisonment and transportation. The next chapter will further chronicle the criminal child's journey into the justice system, charting the debates about penal and reformatory solutions to juvenile crime, issues that were attracting increasing attention in the early nineteenth century. Subsequent chapters will consider juvenile offenders' descriptions of their incarceration and experience of custody. Many of the children questioned in the prisons and prison hulks were waiting to be transported. Consequently, juvenile offenders' responses to transportation, colonial emigration and the various strategies of reformation, which were apparently carried out on their behalf, will also be examined.

5

Debates: Punishment

'Strong are often the misgivings of those who, in the discharge of their duty, are compelled to commit these young creatures to an imprisonment and a discipline, which, however admirably calculated for the reformation of adults, they feel, they know, by long years' experience, is quite inefficacious to check juvenile crime; and if so is worse than useless.'[1] – Mary Carpenter

Two major strands ran through the debate about the punishment of juvenile offenders. The first was the interplay between punishment and reformation. Ideally it was felt that a punitive regime should not be wholly abandoned; rather the issue was the degree of application. Whilst it was increasingly clear that custodial punishment alone (without any training or occupation) would only compound juvenile offending, it was felt unwise to show imprisonment to be in any way an attractive option. In his letter to Lord John Russell, William Augustus Miles told the apocryphal story of a poor ragged sweep brought into prison for a trifling offence: 'The warm bath into which he was put much delighted him, but nothing could exceed his astonishment on being told to put on shoes and stockings . . . his joy was complete when they took him to his cell; he turned down the bed-clothes with great delight.' This scenario continued to the following morning, when, confronted by the governor the boy announced, 'Think of it master! Why I'm damn'd if ever I do another stroke of Work!', and was subsequently transported.[2] Whilst attacking the use of prison as a 'soft option', it was recognised that some incentive had to be offered. Generally this was in the form of training, and subsequently colonial emigration. However, how to maintain such incentives and not to risk encouraging other poor children to offend was seen as a major problem. Contemporary commentators argued, even prior to emigration, that transportation could be viewed by some desperate children as a way to elevate themselves from their present situations. Sir Richard Birnie felt that 'a great many of them would like to go, there are such excellent accounts of the climate and country, that I believe they deem it no punishment at all'.[3] Whilst on one level the debate swung between punishment and reformation, on another it anticipated the type of punishment or reformation, and the extent to which the two could coexist. The options available (some already

---

[1] Carpenter, *Reformatory schools*, 38–9.
[2] W. A. Miles, *Letter to Lord John Russell concerning juvenile delinquency, together with suggestions concerning a reformatory establishment*, Shrewsbury 1837, 2.
[3] SC *Police*, PP, 1828, vi. 39, evidence of Sir Richard Birnie.

in use) spanned transportation, corporal punishment, classification and separation, solitary confinement, occupational and educational strategies, and
agricultural training; there was also some argument about whether reformation could be affected at home, although the weight of opinion preferred
some form of transportation.

The second strand to the debate was also based on a dichotomy. This was
the problem of how to differentiate between 'perishing' and 'dangerous' juveniles. Whilst this particular expression was to be most closely associated with
the writings of Mary Carpenter, the traditional rhetoric of 'deserving' and
'undeserving' lay firmly behind it. The paradox of the situation was how to
control the behaviour both of those children already labelled as criminal and
of those who were only on the periphery of the criminal justice system. The
criminalisation of behaviour that resulted from the increasing adoption of
summary jurisdiction effectively drew more children into the system, despite
its aims which were to keep young delinquents out of the superior courts and
away from more serious and 'hardening' punishment. Subsequently, a reduction in juvenile crime did not occur, since rather more children were now
spending time in front of the magistrates, and inside the houses of correction,
Bridewells and prisons. Many of the children who spent time in the voluntary
custodial institutions, such as the Refuge for the Destitute and the Philanthropic Society, were not specifically criminal. Rather they were troubled and
troublesome adolescents. This resulted in a effort to find a scheme which
could incorporate both groups of children – one specifically tailored to juveniles, using the tools of classification and separation already practised by the
Philanthropic Society in the form of its Reform and Manufactory. It is noticeable that little attempt was made to cater for non-criminal (the 'perishing')
children within their communities. Although the heavily criticised ragged
schools did point in this direction, the emphasis was upon custodial solutions.

Voluntary institutions

The work of voluntary organisations, such as the Philanthropic Society and
the Refuge for the Destitute, were early attempts at a more welfare-orientated
approach to juvenile offenders. Leon Radzinowicz saw this as a humanitarian
and progressive movement: 'the earliest of these endeavours sprang from
philanthropic zeal. They sought to take children right out of the traditional
criminal justice system. To use the modern pennological terminology, their
aim was diversion.'[4] Certainly, an early form of diversionary tactic was identifiable. Children on the fringes of delinquency went into these institutions
where they were either reformed and returned to society, or remodelled into
colonial citizens. However, these institutions also welcomed children who

4 Radzinowicz and Hood, *Emergence of penal policy*, 133.

were already involved in the criminal justice system. Hence magistrates could send an offending child to the Philanthropic as a probationary measure. The impact of these institutions in Middlesex, and the rest the country, was fairly limited. Their largely voluntary financial nature meant that their choice of the children they 'rescued' was circumscribed. It allowed them to be selective of which children they took in, placing parameters such as age or criminal background. For example, the Philanthropic Society only ever had a limited effect on the reformation of juveniles (for the first seven years they took 236 children; in 1817 they had 160).[5] The 1817 Police Committee heard the evidence of Mr Thomas Russell, representing the Society:

> Does not it always happen that there are more candidates for admission than admissions? – Of the whole number of applicants, not one in ten; but as many of those are not proper cases for admission, it may be said that not one in seven of real objects brought before the Society's Committee can be admitted for want of funds.[6]

Moreover, John Wontner, keeper of Newgate, commented that:

> I have turned my thought to it, (how should boys be provided for) but I have had great difficulty in coming to a conclusion what was best to be done, because the societies that are formed for criminal boys who are destitute, if they are under a certain age, often object to taking them, for instance, the Refuge for the Destitute and the Philanthropic Society, will but very seldom receive them after they have committed a theft.[7]

Whilst these institutions received strong public approbation and grants from private individuals, there was no move to bring them into the public sector. Indeed, it was not until the 1830s and the onset of the reformatories that such organisations could come under the remit of government (and then most made way for the official reformatories and industrial schools). There were some small grants available from government. For example in 1835 the Refuge for the Destitute received £3,000, although previously they had received the larger sums of £5,000 and £4,000. As early as the 1810s and 1820s the stewards of the Philanthropic Society and the Refuge for the Destitute were being asked about their costs, presumably with a view to comparing them with those of the official prison population. These organisations relied

---

5 *Report on State of the Philanthropic Society*, abstract 04; SC *Police*, PP, 1817, vii. 441.
6 Ibid. 442.
7 SC *Police*, PP, 1828, vi. 53, evidence of Mr John Wontner. This may be unfair since it is clear that the Philanthropic Society did take some criminal boys (see, for example, SC *Criminal Juveniles*, PP, 1852, vii, appendix 1, pp. 389–405, for accounts of boys recommended for reformatory training at the Philanthropic school). However, there is some suggestion that the Society concentrated on boys most likely to be 'reformable'. The Refuge for the Destitute was established in the Hackney Road in 1804; it later joined forces with the Society for the Improvement of Prison Discipline and for the Reformation of Juvenile Offenders.

strongly on the considerable financial endowments settled upon them by their founders, together with donations from private individuals and associations.[8]

The aims of the voluntary institutions varied according to the type of inmates and means of support they attracted. The Philanthropic Society, established in 1788, aimed to teach industry and morality to delinquent children and those who had been thrown off-course by the criminality of their parents. It aimed to supply instruction in 'useful occupations to enable them to gain an honest livelihood and become beneficial members of society'.[9] It also helped some children into apprenticeships. Typical inmates were: 'Roger, John, and Michael Connor. – Their father is now under sentence of death in Newgate. – Their mother lives in Carrier-Street; a place where few but persons of the most abandoned character reside', and 'Samuel Grub. – His mother is a miserable wretch, living in Hog Yard; Liquor-Pond-Street, and was bringing her child up to vagrancy and ruin.'[10] The Children's Friend Society, formed in 1830, aspired to prevent juvenile vagrancy, providing employment through agricultural training, manual employment and religious instruction.[11] Subsequently it hoped to place them in suitable situations at home or in the colonies. Whilst the Society was restricted to taking destitute children (unlike the Philanthropic Society and the Refuge for the Destitute which did receive young criminals directed to them from the courts) these were children from the same backgrounds and situation, the difference being that they had resisted crime or thus far escaped the criminal justice system. The Refuge for the Destitute worked along similar lines to the other institutions, although they also took adults. However the Refuge placed its inmates in local apprenticeships or domestic situations.

There seems to have been a much stronger female juvenile presence in these voluntary organisations than in the official custodial institutions. Three initiatives in particular existed for delinquent girls, other than those like the Magdalen which were aimed more specifically at prostitutes: the Female Refuge, which was the sister of the Refuge for the Destitute; the

8 For example, the Refuge for the Destitute also received funds from Maidstone prison, Guildford prison, the Sheriffs fund, the Prison Discipline Society and the City Bridewell Committee; the Philanthropic Society relied on voluntary input, legacies, dividends from shares and, like the Refuge, the labour of the inmates. The Children's Friend Society (otherwise Brenton's Academy at Hackney Wick) existed on similar means, laying emphasis on personal recommendation and sponsorship: SC Police, PP, 1828, vi. 163, 184; SC Gaols, PP, 1835, 4th, 5th Reports, xii. 523, evidence of Thomas Russell, and appendix 3, pp. 397–404, account and plan of the Children's Friend Society.
9 'The memorial of certain persons calling themselves the Philanthropic Society', cited in Carlebach, Caring for children, 10. This description of the aims of the Society is reproduced from a petition presented to William Pitt in 1795, in an attempt to generate finances.
10 The Philanthropic Society, instituted September, 1788, for the prevention of crimes and the reform of the criminal poor . . ., London 1789, 15–16.
11 This Society was originally named the 'Society for the Suppression of Juvenile Vagrancy', later changing its name to the Children's Friend Society.

School of Reform, Chelsea, 'for viciously disposed and neglected Female Children'; and the sister to Brenton's academy, the Royal Victoria Asylum at Chiswick.[12] There is some indication that girls were likely to be placed in these institutions prior to trial or via the magistrate at a fairly informal level.[13] Certainly the Refuge saw themselves as having a strong role in the care and reformation of young females:

> the committal and re-committal of females to the metropolitan and suburban houses of correction, amounts to about 7,000 annually: and when this fact is taken into consideration, together with those of the privitations, and, too often excessive occupation, by which so large a portion of our female population is predisposed and incited to crime and vice; the duty of affording an asylum to the penitent must be strongly felt, as well as the interest of society acknowledged, in withdrawing them from plunder.[14]

This informal admission of females to these institutions may be one of the reasons why the public debates were so heavily male-orientated, particularly as the majority of accounts and impressions were gleaned from the courts, prisons and hulks. The School of Discipline took in children from prison but also, 'before they have been committed to prison; when they have been before the Magistrates for the first time they have sent them to us, preferring that to sending them to prison'.[15] They also received girls who had proved too much for parents and charity schools. The Female Refuge worked a similar scheme, taking in girls recommended by magistrates, chaplains, members of the committee and sometimes by their parents. The Royal Victoria Asylum relied heavily on private recommendation and funding, although they did receive girls from the workhouses and girls who were the children of criminal parents; they had no power to receive children found guilty of stealing. The approach to the girls seems, from the little information available, to be comparable to that adopted towards the boys:[16] domestic service rather than apprenticeship and, for all but the girls of the Female Refuge, colonial emigration.

The role of these institutions as prototypes should be stressed. Thus the

---

[12] SC Gaols, PP, 1835, 4th, 5th Reports, xii, appendix 16, p. 547. The Philanthropic Society closed its doors to girls in 1845. In any event, the female population of the Society had generally consisted of the children of offenders rather than offenders themselves.

[13] See the Hackney Borough Archives, Rose Lipman Library, Refuge for the Destitute, minutes 1819–47. These include lists of children, describing their offences as well as their route of admission. It is clear that many of the girls came through a route other than trial.

[14] Ibid. Refuge for the Destitute, opening address, 1849.

[15] SC Gaols, PP, 1835, 4th, 5th Reports, xii. 483, evidence of Mrs Shaw.

[16] Material on specifically female juvenile offenders is scattered and thin. However, the reports of the 1835 Select Committee on Gaols do have some evidence from the various female establishments. See, for example, SC Gaols, PP, 1835, 4th, 5th Reports, xii. 483–8, evidence of Mrs Shaw, secretary to the Chelsea School of Discipline; ibid. appendixes 3, 16, pp. 397–412, 547–50; ibid. 1st Report, xi. 97–9, evidence of Mrs Rebecca Bourhill, head of the Royal Victoria Asylum.

principles of reform and manufacture were to be clearly embodied in the reformatory and industrial schools. The division between 'deserving' and 'undeserving' or 'perishing' and 'dangerous', or 'semi-delinquent' and 'delinquent', was maintained with industrial schools aimed at the reception of neglected, vagrant children – children at risk of becoming 'hardened'. In 1851, at the Birmingham conference on juvenile delinquency, a national conference assembled on the initiative of Mary Carpenter and Matthew Davenport Hill, the following resolutions were adopted:

> 4th. – That for those Children who are not attending any School and have subjected themselves to police interference, by vagrancy, mendicity, or petty infringements of the law, legislative enactments are urgently required, in order to aid or establish Industrial Feeding Schools, at which the attendance of such Children shall be enforced by Magistrates.

> 5th. – That legislative enactments are also required in order to establish Correctional and Reformatory Schools for those Children who have been convicted of felony, or such misdemeanours as involve dishonesty; and to confer upon magistrates power to commit Juvenile Offenders to such Schools instead of Prison.[17]

Certainly this conference crystallised many of the concepts that had been expressed over the previous decades. The main philosophy was the combination of a work ethic with religious training and limited education. The institutions also imbued their inmates with the striving for advancement. At the Philanthropic, criminal boys automatically went to the Reform, whereas the sons of convicts, or the semi-delinquent, went straight to the Manufactory. Essentially the Reform was a prison, 'they are on no account permitted to go out of the Reform, where there is ample space for air and exercise: their relatives are allowed to see them once in every three months, but no other persons are admitted'. If a boy behaved well he could move up to the Manufactory, where he could learn a trade, printing, book-binding, shoe-making or rope-making for example. 'The boys of the Manufactory are not always confined within walls, but are occasionally allowed to go out, and are treated like other apprentices.'[18] This was a system that combined firm discipline and control with incentive and example. However, not all the boys responded to the ethical stance of self-improvement. When the Revd Sydney Turner arrived in 1841 he was critical of the present system, feeling that whilst it could work for boys who had some aptitude, it held little appeal or incentive for the 'incorrigible'.[19]

---

17 *Report of the proceedings of a conference on the subject of preventive and reformatory schools, held at Birmingham, on the 9th and 10th December*, London 1851, repr. in *SC Criminal Juveniles*, PP, 1852, vii, appendix 6, p. 443. The Revd Sydney Turner of the Philanthropic Society was also present on the committee of this conference.
18 *SC Gaols*, PP, 1835, 4th, 5th Reports, xii, appendix 15, pp. 536–47.
19 Carlebach, *Caring for children*, 15–25. *Revd Sydney Turner* (1814–79); 1838, curate at

Neither the Refuge for the Destitute nor Brenton's Juvenile Asylum were segregated on the same lines as the Philanthropic Society. In principle they adhered to the dualism of moral education and occupation. At the Hackney Wick Asylum there was some attempt to classify. Thus children were divided into either 'A', 'B' or 'C', depending on their 'moral conduct and industrious habits'.[20] However, even at the Philanthropic the success of the regime was limited. In the early years of the Society a number of children absconded: according to a report of 1796, fifty-one of 176 boys, and five of sixty girls had absconded.[21] A noted reoffender, John Leary, had run away from the Philanthropic where he had been placed after a previous crime.[22] Despite the involvement of philanthropy, and the attempt to create a caring environment, these institutions were effectively custodial institutions. Thus the superintendent of the Refuge of the Destitute, Mr James Ross, told the 1828 Select Committee on Metropolitan Police that 'The place is quite secure, surrounded with walls.'[23] There seems to have been a general consensus that a strong degree of control and custody had to prevail. Yet these organisations distanced themselves from the existing prison system, using semantics to emphasise the difference – refuge, asylum, school.

During the early decades of the nineteenth century there was an increasing professionalisation of the agencies in the field. The Prison Discipline Society, which involved many well-known philanthropists, metamorphosed into something approaching a professional pressure group, anticipating the formation of the Howard League at the end of the nineteenth century. The society pushed hard for the legislation that would result in the 1823 and 1824 Gaol Acts, and had conducted extensive research into continental and American penal institutions and the problems of prison administration and labour.[24] The Revd Sydney Turner too sought out the example of foreign institutions. In 1846 he visited the Colonie Agricole at Mettray, in France. Both he, and later Mary Carpenter, were impressed by Mettray and other foreign institutions like the Rauhe Haus in Germany. These organisations had trained staff and featured family groups, encouragement rather than force, outdoor activities, and the sanction and financial patronage of government.[25] These schemes offered an alternative to prison: and yet a substantial

Christ Church, Southwark; 1841, resident chaplain and reader of the Philanthropic Society School; 1857, inspector of reformatory schools; 1861, inspectorate extended to industrial schools; 1875, dean of Ripon. (Source – Royal Philanthropic Society.)

20 SC Gaols, PP, 1835, 4th, 5th Reports, xii, appendix 3, pp. 397–412.
21 Cited in Carlebach, Caring for children, 10–11.
22 SC Police, PP, 1817, vii. 542, evidence of Hon. H. G. Bennet; OBSP, first session, 1814, no. 24, pp. 13–15.
23 SC Police, PP, 1828, xii. 181, evidence of Mr James Ross.
24 Gaol Acts, 4 Geo. 4 c.64 (1823); 5 Geo. 4 c.85. (1824). William Crawford, of course, went on to be the first inspector of prisons along with Whitworth Russell.
25 Carlebach, Caring for children, 20–3.

overlap and many continuities existed between the voluntary organisations and the prison sector.

Prison reform and penal policy

The transition from unreformed, unregulated prisons to something like a coherent penal policy was fraught with both practical difficulties and a more theoretical resistance. The issue of imprisonment had been on the agenda for some time, most notably in Howard's *The state of prisons* (1777). However, the debate did not really gather force until the 1800s, under the impetus of the increasing adoption of custodial sentences. The twin cornerstones of the development of prisons in the nineteenth century were the extent of the application of punishment and reformation. The early parliamentary debate thus struggled to find the proper balance between these two positions. Part of the problem lay in the fact that the majority of prisons were ill-kept and badly regulated. Many adhered to archaic systems of management which acted as a stumbling-block to any attempts at uniformity.[26] Thus, while the prison system was not organised on a national basis until 1877, the government had involved itself increasingly in its management since the beginning of the century.[27] Whilst the parliamentary debate can be traced through the various 'crime' select committees, a considerable number of independent philanthropists and researchers also found their way into the prisons. These people, generally of a religious disposition and from the propertied classes, were clearly shocked by some of what they saw. And it was the image of children in prison that aroused the greatest condemnation.

The philanthropists realised from quite early on that separation for juvenile offenders meant something quite definite and irreproachable. Hence the institutions set up by private initiative pre-dated the post-Parkhurst reformatories and industrial schools. During the 1820s, '30s and '40s, these 'experts' submitted a myriad of evidence to show the beneficial effects of separate juvenile provision not only on the crime rates, but also on the public purse. Fairly early on, prison 'professionals' realised the counter-productive effects of incarcerating children. The 1818 Select Committee on Metropolitan Police concentrated most of its energies on the state of the prisons, particularly on their systems of classification. The three major prisons to be investigated, Clerkenwell, Coldbath Fields and Tothill Fields were roundly condemned. Of Tothill Fields, the committee concluded that, 'this prison, like many other, contributes most materially to promote and augment that deplorable increase of crime which exists throughout the metropolis'. This was compounded by the acknowledgement that (at Clerkenwell), "till some plan be adopted to

---

[26] This was a particular problem in the local and borough prisons. See, for example, W. J. Forsythe, *A system of discipline: Exeter borough prison, 1819–63*, Exeter 1983.
[27] Prison Act, 40 & 41 Vict., c.21 (1877).

separate the old from the young offenders, and to classify prisoners according to their degree of guilt, these places of confinement can be considered as nothing else but nurseries of crime'. Coldbath Fields, which had been the great penitentiary experiment of the 1790s and early 1800s, had 'failed entirely'.[28]

James Bevans's design for a juvenile penitentiary had been presented to parliament the previous year. The plan, influenced by many of the soon-to-become luminaries of the penal movement, provided for the structured punishment, reformation and employment of juveniles. The men of the 1815 Committee had gone so far as to survey, cost and decide upon a location, yet the plan disappeared without a trace. The penitentiary would have proved more expensive than Newgate, but cheaper than the Refuge for the Destitute.[29] Moreover, as Hoare suggested to the committee, the existing prison system contributed to the increase of crime:

> I consider that the indiscriminate confinement practised in most of our prisons, where the child committed for trial or some small offence, is locked up in the same yard, and obliged constantly to associate with the hardened offender and convicted felon, is the most certain method that can be devised of increasing the number of delinquents.[30]

Even in the previous century Hewling Luson, had called for the government to 'Let these children . . . be taken under the protection of the public, and placed in some asylum, where similar maintenance, employment, and instruction, may be provided for them.'[31] In 1828 the Select Committee on Metropolitan Police concluded that a separate juvenile prison should be provided, but that the cost of such an undertaking, would probably postpone its construction. In this case the alternative was to be a juvenile convict ship (the *Euryalus*, already in existence and ineffective), or the provision of a juvenile ward in the Penitentiary. The question is, why the effective separation of juveniles (i.e. in separate establishments) was not realised until the 1838 Parkhurst scheme, and what the results of this inactivity were.

In 1847 64 per cent of convicted criminals in Middlesex were in some sort of custody (other than transportation); in addition were those on remand, and those sentenced to imprisonment through summary jurisdiction. Of that 64 per cent, just under two-thirds were juveniles and young adults aged

---

28 *SC Police*, PP, 1818, viii. 7, 9, 13.
29 *SC Police*, PP, 1817, vii. 524–52, evidence of Samuel Hoare esq. and Mr James Bevans. The cost of Newgate to the City was said to be £9 *per annum* per prisoner; the cost of this projected penitentiary would be £12 *per annum*, while the Refuge for the Destitute cost £30. This difference was accounted for by discharge clothes and apprenticeship and, whilst the Refuge received some funding from government, this was a small amount.
30 *SC Police*, PP, 1817, vii. 529, evidence of Samuel Hoare.
31 Hewling Luson, *Inferior politics: or, considerations on the wretchedness and prolificacy of the POOR . . . on the defects in the present system of parochial and penal laws . . .*, London 1786, 110.

twenty-five and under.[32] The prison population then, was an especially youthful one. The number of indicted juveniles in prison had been negligible in the 1790s. It was only after the war, and coinciding with the expansion of the debate on prison as a secondary punishment, that numbers started to grow. By 1847 they represented 18 per cent of the prison population. In other words, by that time 76 per cent of all juvenile indictments resulted in a custodial sentence. While the numbers of seventeen to twenty-five-year-olds in prison had more than doubled in the period, the number of juveniles had quadrupled.[33] Of course, this may merely have been a reflection of the fact that indictments and prosecutions of juveniles had risen anyway (and the growing youthful population of Middlesex also had an impact). However, there seems little doubt that after 1815 imprisonment was increasingly being used as a remedy for juvenile offending, with a corresponding decrease in the level of acquittals. The implication was that the impact of reformation, which was a specifically custodial tool, fell squarely on young people. This, along with the changes in the perception of criminal behaviour, had resulted in many more juveniles entering custody, and reoffending and recommittal came sharply into focus.

By the end of the period, juvenile offenders stood the least chance of acquittal. Where they were not being reformed through colonial endeavour, they were in prison at home, being prepared for the outside world. But why did this absorption of juveniles into the penal system persist when so much evidence was presented to show that customary imprisonment of juveniles did not work? Partly, there was an ideological shift. Whilst the attitude to juveniles seemed to be on the one hand more sympathetic, stressing the need to remove them from the more lurid aspects of the criminal justice system, those that kept offending were portrayed as 'hardened' criminals, the products of a depraved background. Much emphasis was placed on the lack of fear or care about their situation exhibited by juveniles in custody. This was particularly seen to be the case with regard to transportation, which seemingly held little dread:

> I have often heard them, when sentence of transportation has been passed . . . return thanks for it, and seem overjoyed by the sentence . . . the very last party that went off I happened to see them; when they were put into the caravan they shouted and huzzaed, and were very joyous; and several of them called out to the keepers, who were then in the yard, 'Aye, the first fine Sunday we have we will have a glorious kangeroo hunt at the Bay.'[34]

In the years between 1820 and 1840 there was a growing sense of the 'career criminal'. Edward Gibbon Wakefield spoke in such terms of the boys he had seen during his sojourn in Newgate:

[32] PRO, HO 26/5, 13, 23, 33, 43, 53.
[33] Ibid.
[34] SC Police, PP, 1818, viii. 1, evidence of Revd H. S. Cotton, Ordinary of Newgate.

Let twenty boys, selected by the Newgate Schoolmaster, be from time to time discharged from prison, and every one of them shall straight proceed to one of these pest-houses, shall leave it with money in his pocket, and, if watched, shall be seen to pursue the sort of career which I have described. . . . I know the fact to be, that the greater number of the smallest boys discharged from Newgate for want of prosecution or evidence, or after undergoing a sentence of whipping, do instantly proceed to places of this description, as to their home; and at one time I knew the names and addresses of more than twenty persons who lived by this villainous trade.[35]

Quite how Wakefield came across this information is unclear. Like many of the contributors to the deluge of commentaries on juvenile crime, his information was highly subjective, and influenced by an increasingly paranoiac view of juvenile crime. This was very much the characterisation that was to be immortalised by Dickens in the 1830s. Dickens's descriptions of juvenile thieves show them imbued with a precocious masculinity: boys are pictured as 'smoking long clay pipes, and drinking spirits with the air of middle-aged men'.[36] The lack of childishness which both Dickens and his more official contemporaries describe in juveniles is alarming.[37] In 1835, seventeen years after submitting evidence to the police select committee, Horace Salisbury Cotton again played witness, succinctly painting the image of the 'hordes' and 'swarms' of criminals: 'I have repeatedly observed, talking of common thieves, that they are born in a Crowd; they live in a Crowd; and they absolutely die in a Crowd.'[38]

In the discourse of the 1810s there was some allusion to preventative policing, and to the possibility of diverting juveniles from crime. Whilst consideration of such schemes continued, for example in the suppression of gambling, lodging-houses, theatres and the encouragement of education, the emphasis was clearly on removal from what was understood as the source of juvenile corruption. The decades before the Reformatory and Industrial School acts witnessed an uneasy campaign of tug-of-war. It was clear that something needed to be done, yet the one viable course, the temporary incarceration of children, seemed to aggravate the situation. The result of this was the conflict between the advocates of punishment strategies such as corporal punishment, solitary confinement, training, education and emigration, and those who felt that many juveniles should not be imprisoned, that the fault lay less with the offenders and more with a society that made them into criminals. Needless to say, the latter viewpoint was heard but rarely.[39]

---

35 E. G. Wakefield, *Facts relating to the punishment of death in the metropolis*, London 1831, 202.

36 Dickens, *Oliver Twist*, 105.

37 For a broader view of the anxieties over childhood in this period, particularly in the context of child labour, see H. Cunningham, *Children and childhood in western society since 1500*, London 1995, 138–45; Horn, *Children's work*, 50–62; Nardinelli, *Child labor*.

38 *SC Gaols*, PP, 1835, 4th, 5th Reports, xii. 520, evidence of Revd H. S. Cotton.

39 See *SC Police*, PP, 1828, vi. 134–44, evidence of Mr Serjeant Scriven, for a much

Solitary confinement

Solitary confinement was more than a punishment. Like so many penal strategies it aimed to stem the corruption and contagion which seemed inevitable in the atmosphere of the unreformed prisons: 'Some boasting of their former Robberies, some cursing and swearing, some telling of obscene Stories, and some singing vile songs.'[40] It was intended that the separation of prisoners into solitary confinement and/or the use of the silent system would prevent the contamination of the novice by the 'hardened' prisoner. It would also – in theory at least – make the inmates more malleable and easier to control.[41] These systems were generally combined with some sort of arduous task, one that involved little or no mental stimulation, such as oakum picking. The needs of morality were served by the strong emphasis on the Scriptures. Religiosity was always a central reformatory tool, but the combination of religious text, with silence and/or separation struck an exacting blow to the inmate. In a Foucauldian manner, these were attacks on the spiritual body, the mind, while still taming the physical body through limited exercise and claustrophobic environments.[42] Whilst classification systems had been in use (often unsuccessfully) for some years, it was not until the Holford Committee and Gaol Acts of the 1820s that classification really came into being.[43] Generally it was felt that classification and separation should go together. William Crawford, after visiting American penitentiaries noted that:

> In some parts of America that silence, even when enforced very strictly, is not effectual . . . still it is found that men will return; and that Fact had led to a very strong impression that nothing short of Solitude will have the Effect of deterring Men from the commission of crime. Still, next to solitude I should say that silence is extremely valuable.[44]

The Revd Whitworth Russell felt that silence would be particularly compatible with the use of schools, since it would make the prisoners more grateful

---

broader critique of the many factors which encouraged delinquency; SC *Police Officers*, PP, 1837, xii, 166–73, evidence of Revd John Ousby, for a critique directed specifically at summary processes of trial and punishment; SC *Gaols*, PP, 1835, 4th, 5th Reports, xii. 508–15, esp. p. 514, evidence of W. A. Miles, esq., for a direct critique of social policy.

[40] SC *Gaols*, PP, 1835, 1st Report, xi, 307, evidence of Mr W. W. Cope. This quotation came from a statement that was read by the committee to Mr Cope, governor of Newgate. It apparently came from a 15-year-old inmate. Cope himself denied all allegations.

[41] See U. Henriques, 'The rise and decline of the separate system of prison discipline', *Past and Present* liv (1972), 61–93.

[42] For discussion of the changing nature of punishment regimes see Foucault, *Discipline and punish*.

[43] For discussion of earlier systems of classification see S. McConville, *A history of English prison administration*, I: *1750–1877*, London 1981, 3, 16, 18, 91.

[44] SC *Gaols*, PP, 1835, 1st Report, xi. 4, evidence of William Crawford esq.

for instruction, where some communication would be allowed. Silence, Russell stated, served:

> Not only to prevent the more experienced thieves from contaminating others; but for giving prisoners more opportunities of reflection, depriving them of those means they now have of solacing themselves with companions of similar tastes and habits, and driving away serious thought, and also with a view of deterring others from entering a situation where they will be subject to so serious a privation.[45]

Clearly, these strategies aimed to fulfil the main condition of penal reform, that prison should be a reformatory experience, but not an appealing one.

However, from quite early on there were suggestions that silence and solitary confinement were inappropriate for children. Whitworth Russell conceded: 'I do not think the system of separation and silence of which I have been speaking is at all suited to children of that age; I think a very different system of prison discipline should be enforced in respect to very young persons.'[46] Certainly by the mid century several commentators were arguing against the application of silence and solitary confinement to juveniles. Mary Carpenter felt the system to be injurious to the spirit of the child:

> The child is then placed in a condition perfectly discordant with his nature. The exercise of his buoyant animal spirits is severely visited as a prison offence: he must not even raise his voice in those loud and joyous sounds which seem a necessity of his nature; all exercise of his social feelings is cut off, no voice of tenderness is heard, and the spirited boy who will be softened to tears by the gentle reproof of his teacher, vents his energy in ingenious attempts at mischief in the prison cell.[47]

Carpenter also used evidence from Whitworth Russell, and the experience of Wakefield gaol, where the system was discontinued in respect of juveniles, since they suffered from 'debility and contraction of the joints; premonitory symptoms of sluggishness and feeble-mindedness appeared, and there was evident danger to their minds'.[48]

Whilst the more sensitive reformers abhorred the effects of solitary confinement on juvenile offenders, many were happy to recommend corporal punishment.[49] There was a widespread feeling that the birch, rod or cat was an effective tool for juveniles. Sir Richard Birnie recommended 'a little

---

45 Ibid. 37, evidence of Revd W. Russell.
46 Ibid. 62.
47 Carpenter, *Reformatory schools*, 298.
48 Ibid. 296.
49 However, most of the voluntary institutions shied away from the use of corporal punishment. The Children's Friend Society and the Refuge for the Destitute would not flog their inmates; instead they used a combination of limited solitary confinement and withdrawal of privileges. There was some use of corporal punishment at the Philanthropic, although this seems to have been used only in the most extreme circumstances: SC *Gaols*, PP, 1835,

flogging at a certain age'; Mr Alderman Brown felt that 'for very young offenders, probably corporal punishment might be useful'; John Sibley, governor of the Brixton house of correction, noted that 'One or two whippings may be inflicted with good effect . . . it should, however, be wholly confined to boys.' The general impression, though, was that corporal punishment should be used less as a torture, and more as a short sharp shock. Indeed, Birnie and John Wontner, both men of some experience, felt that very young boys should be punished summarily, that is flogged and discharged without imprisonment.[50]

Punishment at its most basic was a raw feature of daily living on the hulks. In these institutions it was impossible to enforce the systems of control that were being applied to the model penitentiaries at Millbank and Pentonville. In 1835 Thomas Dexter gave evidence to the Select Committee on Gaols. Dexter was an adult prisoner who had been sentenced to transportation. He had worked in the juvenile convict hospital at Chatham, and saw boys from the *Euryalus* hulk. When asked about the reformatory effects of such discipline on the *Euryalus*, Dexter replied negatively: 'I should certainly say not. . . . I have made the observation that was it a child of mine I would rather see him dead at my feet than see him sent to that place.' Dexter also described the lack of discipline which allowed gang subcultures to emerge on the ship. The main gang was called the Nobs: 'I have seen them myself take a Broomstick and strike a boy over the arm, almost to break his arm, and the other dare not say a single word to him.'[51] The hulks represented the worst abuses of the unreformed prison system. Massive, rotting men-of-war, destined for the breakers' yard, they became the object of public approbation and attack. In 1835 the Prison Discipline Society recommended that the 'Hulks be entirely abolished'.[52] Earlier, in 1833, Thomas Wontner had launched an attack on the *Euryalus*:

If there be any regular and established schools for teaching crime, the ship *Euryalus* is the place. From this college (the thieves themselves call it so) comes the chief of the housebreakers. The want of room to accommodate so many, occasions their being placed in wards, where thirty or forty sleep together; and as they are, for young ones, of the very worst description of offenders, the consequence may easily be imagined . . . the whole system of their management and treatment calls for a revision. This, however, cannot be done, without the construction of a place sufficiently large for their reception. Separate compartments for sleeping are absolutely necessary in further-

---

4th, 5th Reports, xii, appendix 3, p. 399; SC *Police*, PP, 1828, vi. 183, evidence of Mr James Ross.
[50] Ibid. 38, 45, 66, 53, evidence of Sir Richard Birnie, Mr Alderman Brown and Mr John Wontner respectively; SC *Gaols*, PP, 1835, 1st Report, xi. 163, evidence of Lieutenant John Silby, RN.
[51] Ibid. 2nd Report, xi. 321, 323, evidence of Thomas Dexter.
[52] Ibid. 4th, 5th Reports, xii. 470, evidence of Samuel Hoare.

ance of their moral improvement, and the desuetude of the cat-o-nine tails, which does more harm than any other part of the system in the treatment of these boys.[53]

The hulks were the subject of one of the earliest attempts at classification and separation.[54] In 1818 Thomas Price, the chaplain of the *Retribution* hulk, suggested the possibility of a hulk especially fitted out for juveniles.[55] This proposal was carried out in 1824, when the adult prisoners were cleared off the *Bellerophon* at Sheerness, to make way for boy convicts, but little attempt at classification on the ship itself was made: rather than place the more aggressive boys together, they were placed in bays with smaller and weaker boys.[56] The stay on the *Bellerophon* was short, since at the end of 1825 the boys were transferred to the *Euryalus*, at Chatham. This ship, unlike the *Bellerophon*, was said to be designed particularly with juveniles in mind. Thomas Price was transferred to the *Euryalus* as chaplain, and showed an unprecedented level of application and integrity in his work. He constantly fought with the authorities, particularly with Capper, the head of the hulk establishment. Price recognised that the mere separation of juveniles from adults was not effective, that the boys had to be 'separated and classed according to age and character',[57] and throughout 1827-8 he continued to complain about the lack of classification, and the incompetence shown in the running of the ship. Not surprisingly he was dismissed in 1828 and replaced with a more compliant chaplain, H. J. Dawes.

The debate between Price and his colleagues was mirrored onshore, in parliament. The majority view was that classification and separation of prisoners were absolutely unavoidable. However, despite the suggestions made by the Prison Discipline Society, and the example already shown by the Philanthropic Society, the attempts to separate and classify juveniles took place within the established prisons and houses of correction. In 1828 questionnaires were completed by several metropolitan prison keepers. The reports that accompanied the questions shed a grave light on the real state of classification in the prisons. For example, the Newgate subcommittee reported the prison's 'very inadequate accommodation', noting that the numbers allowed

53 Wontner, *Old Bailey experience*, 360-1.

54 Separation in this context meaning the physical separation of juvenile from adult prisoners, as opposed to the separation imposed by solitary confinement.

55 'Copy of Report of the Chaplain of the Retribution Convict Ship to J. H. Capper esq.', in *Papers Relating to the Convict Establishment*, PP, 1818, xvi. 207, 214-15. For material on the hulk establishment see C. Bateson, *The convict ships, 1787-1868*, Glasgow 1959; C. Campbell, *The intolerable hulks: British shipboard confinement, 1776-1857*, Bowie, MD 1993; W. Branch Johnson, *The English prison hulks*, London 1957.

56 Campbell, *Intolerable hulks*, 130.

57 Ibid. 132. According to John Henry Capper in the 1831 Select Committee on Secondary Punishments, the boys were divided into twenty classes, although given the continued criticism of the *Euryalus* it is unlikely that this system met with much success: *Report from the Select Committee on Secondary Punishments*, PP, 1831, vii. 52.

for were often exceeded, and that 'the necessary result is, that the wards are much too crowded, and the classification is consequently not only very imperfect, but is hardly attempted to be carried into effect'. Some effort was made to keep the boys separate, but 'Education is not much attended to.'[58] The main point, made by many of the reports, was that the design of the prisons meant that most attempts at classification were ineffectual. Peel's Gaol Act of 1823 recommended a five-fold method of classification, which many institutions found difficult to put into practice. The system was based on classification by offence rather than character, and by 1832 the Select Committee on Secondary Punishments could conclude of classification that:

> the result has been far from satisfactory. By the Gaol Act, 4 Geo. 4, C.64, no provision was made for dividing prisoners before or after trial into more than two classes. The larger prisons, especially those in and near the Metropolis, usually contain several hundred prisoners, whose periods of confinement before trial, vary from a few days to several months. It is hardly necessary to remark, that any classification, with the inadequate means provided by the Gaol Act, must be inefficacious . . . it must associate the most hardened offenders with those who may be guiltless of crime.[59]

In the context of juvenile offenders, the problem of enforcing classification was compounded by the attitude of the boys. Unlike their adult counterparts, who would probably have lost an established job, had families to support, and accommodation to keep, many of the boys had fewer responsibilities. Whilst many had some sort of work, they were at that stage of life when the full impact of obligation and liability was yet to take its toll. The unreformed prisons may have deprived them of their liberty, but it was not thought by their rulers to be an extreme hardship:

> the punishment of prison is no punishment to them; I do not mean that they would not rather be out of the prison than in it, but they are so well able to bear the punishment, and the prison allowance of food is so good, and their spirits so buoyant, that the consequences are most deplorable.[60]

Increasingly, the charge of contamination was laid less on adults, and more on the different classes of juvenile criminal. At its most elementary, this was the difference between the 'hardened' juvenile and the relatively inexperienced child. This was also the conceptual development which was eventually to be crystallised by Mary Carpenter's designation of 'dangerous' and 'perishing' juveniles. Thus the criminal justice system was embracing children from a number of situations, many drawn in through the criminalisation of delinquent and semi-delinquent behaviour, others habitual incumbents of the

[58] SC Police, PP, 1828, vi, appendix D, p. 307.
[59] Report from the Select Committee on Secondary Punishments, PP, 1832, vii. 5.
[60] SC Secondary Punishments, PP, 1831, vii. 33, evidence of Mr George Laval Chesterton, governor of the Coldbath Fields house of correction.

system. Henry Wilson, a friend of William Augustus Miles, and the superintendent of a school of industry in Woolwich, outlined his scheme of classification to the 1835 committee. Wilson's classification stressed an approach to all delinquent children, 'with a view of assisting in considering the Means of preventing early crime'. Like the members of the Philanthropic Society, the Prison Discipline Society and so many other commentators, Wilson advocated a separate provision for juveniles, with further classification within that provision – 'A place of occupation and one of restraint'. He also recommended that this be followed by colonial emigration, and indeed, had sent all his own boys to the Cape of Good Hope.[61]

Transportation and colonial emigration

The idea of sending children off to a new start in the colonies was in many ways a thinly veiled extension of transportation. However, as in the fraught relationship between punishment and reformation debated in parliament, these two forms of emigration shared an equally symbiotic relationship. Firstly, transportation was a punishment. However, there was more than a whiff of reformatory idealism in the air, especially in the case of young offenders. There was some feeling that once a boy had worked his assignment for a while, and had got his ticket-of-leave, then he too could strike out on his own. Similarly, compulsory emigration could easily be seen as a punishment. This depended very much on the place that a child was assigned to, some children being treated as little more than slave labour. Transportation to Australia had been operating since the late eighteenth century, carrying a markedly young population to the colony.[62] Emigration, as opposed to penal transportation, had been mooted by various officials and commentators in the early nineteenth century. In 1816 William Fielding suggested sending juvenile offenders to the West Indies or Cape of Good Hope.[63] In 1828 the police magistrate, H. M. Dyer, also recommended voluntary emigration for 'those who are detected in offences, and yet have not advanced so far as to bring themselves, under the existing law, within the pale of transportation'.[64] It seemed to be gradually dawning on people that sending a child abroad with a minimum of support, training and education, was not going to be terribly effective. Yet transportation was more than a policy of removal. Whether through altruism or self-interest, there was a growing feeling that it should provide a new start, a chance to break free from the environment and companions that, it was

---

61 SC *Gaols*, PP, 1835, 4th, 5th Reports, xii. 448, 452–3, evidence of Mr Henry Wilson.
62 L. L. Robson, *The convict settlers of Australia: an enquiry into the origins and character of the convicts transported to New South Wales and Van Diemens Land, 1787–1852*, Melbourne 1965, 182, 187.
63 SC *Police*, PP, 1816, v. 127, evidence of William Fielding esq.
64 SC *Police*, PP, 1828, vi. 2, evidence of H. M. Dyer esq.

believed, were a strong inducement to crime. However, enough of the old school still existed, wanting to maintain the punishment element of transportation, wanting to ensure that it had some deterrent effect.

Young people were understandably the focus of the reformatory rhetoric: they were not so far gone in crime that they could not be 'saved'. As Mrs Rebecca Bourhill of the Royal Victoria Asylum noted: 'The Committee abroad prefer them young before their habits are fully formed.'[65] If the concept of colonial emigration took away the stigma of penal transportation, it also provided 'useful' occupations, agricultural training, manual work outdoors, and the rudiments of a didactically moral education. Before Parkhurst, the main institutions to provide a path to colonial emigration were those of Captain Brenton, the organisations of the Children's Friend Society.[66] The Brenton Juvenile Asylum was situated on the edge of Hackney Marshes, on Hackney Wick. Land, of course, was seen as a premium requirement for colonial training, and indeed such institutions became known as agricultural colonies, or farm schools.[67] The female branch, the Royal Victoria Asylum, trained its girls for domestic service, alternating their training as kitchenmaids, chambermaids, laundresses and dairymaids.[68] The Society was extensively publicised, and letters published from contented children, well on their way to becoming stalwart colonial emigrés, frontier boys and girls, men and women.[69] One boy wrote to his parents in May 1834, from the Cape:

> I arrived in this Country in Safety, and am engaged to a Gentleman named Mr——, to learn to be a Farmer. I have no Reason but to respect my Master and Mistress; they find me in Plenty of Clothes and Food; and at this Place —— stops, and is well. My Brother stops near Cape Town, and I hear he is well. . . . My Mistress teaches me to write, and we have Prayers most nights. I like the Place, and wish you were both here.[70]

This enlightened trade was soon to come into some disrepute. Increasingly there were suspicions that Brenton was operating nothing more than a glorified slave trade. Accusations were made of severe punishments in the colo-

---

65 SC *Goals*, PP, 1835, 1st Report, xi. 99, evidence of Mrs Rebecca Bourhill.
66 Edward Pelham Brenton (1774–1839), naval captain, published on the naval history of Britain in 1823: *DNB*; G. Blackburn, *The Children's Friend Society: juvenile emigrants to western Australia, South Africa and Canada, 1834–42*, Northbridge, WA 1994; E. Bradlow, 'The Children's Friend Society at the Cape of Good Hope', *Victorian Studies* xxvii (1984), 155–77; E. Hadley, 'Natives in a strange land: the philanthropic discourse of juvenile emigration in mid-nineteenth century England', *Victorian Studies* xxxiii (1990), 411–37.
67 E. P. Brenton Esq., *Observations on the training and education of children in Great Britain*, London 1834, pp. xv–xvi, xiii.
68 SC *Gaols*, PP, 1835, vi. 97, evidence of Mrs Rebecca Bourhill.
69 For example, 'Report of meeting at British coffee house, Cockspur Street for the formation (The Society for the Suppression of Juvenile Vagrancy" ', *Times*, 19 Nov. 1830, 3, col. e; 'Report of meeting held 10 Jan. re sending boys to the Cape', ibid. 11 Jan. 1833, 3, col. d.
70 SC *Gaols*, PP, 1835, 4th, 5th Reports, xii, appendix 3, p. 412, account and plan of the Children's Friend Society.

nies, and that Brenton was running a 'kidnappers Society'. There was also some uneasiness that children were losing their native tongue and culture, since many were sent to Dutch farmers, and worked amongst black slaves.[71] Moreover, as Edna Bradlow has noted, there was more than a whiff of commercial self-interest and confederation: 'it was intended primarily to rid England of unwanted population while simultaneously providing Cape employers with a satisfactory substitute for the servile, unskilled labour supply which they were shortly to lose as the four years of slave apprenticeship drew to a close'.[72] This, of course, was the eternal conflict within philanthropy, for philanthropists were generally businessmen, and were skilled in making money. It is impossible to assess the true motivation behind compulsory emigration, and while there is undoubted truth in Bradlow's comment, there were also men and women who were misguided, or who closed their eyes to any unpleasantness. Children were effectively removed from all that was familiar. In the case of the Brenton children they were not even 'hardened' offenders, for whom some sort of emigration might be a last resort. When Sir George Napier, governor of Cape Colony, pursued an inquiry into the children of the Cape, the voices of such children reveal little enthusiasm: 'I am about 15 years old; my mother is living in England: cannot read or write; never go to church; am employed as a farm labourer and herding cattle: had a letter from my mother some time back and my master answered it for me; I wish to get back to her.'[73]

The move towards colonial emigration was to some extent based on a collective belief that boys were not averse to transportation, that in fact they looked forward to it, their only qualms being the leave-taking of family and friends. The concept itself was not in fact a problem. On the other hand the process that the boys followed prior to transportation was. The hulks, despite Capper's reassurances, epitomised the great dread of 'contagion' and 'contamination'. In 1835 W. A. Miles received information from the juvenile penal settlement in Van Diemen's Land, Point Puer, indicating that the boys' sojourn on the *Euryalus* had aggravated their criminal tendencies: 'however criminal they might have been before their Commitments, he seriously believes that previous to their Imprisonment in that accursed Hulk . . . they were comparatively innocent'.[74] Transportation, whether it was by government or cloaked in humanity by philanthropy, was for England's rulers a fine concept. It pleased the traditionalists who wanted young thieves out of sight and out of mind, but not on the gallows; it pleased the advocates of both *laissez-faire* and of intervention. For the former, there was no need to interfere in the affairs of businessmen and employers at home, the colonies could be

---

71 Radzinowicz and Hood, *Emergence of penal policy*, 137–8; Bradlow, 'Children's Friend Society', 6–8.
72 Ibid. 168.
73 Cited in P. Bean and J. Melville, *Lost children of the empire*, London 1989, 31.
74 *SC Gaols*, PP, 1835, 4th, 5th Reports, xii. 508, evidence of Mr William Augustus Miles.

left to sort themselves out; for the interventionists, it allowed decision-making and action, control and a paternalist role limited by geographical separation.

Despite the obvious benefits, to the elite, of transportation and emigration, ultimately a solution was desired that would incorporate all the many strategies employed for the treatment of juvenile offenders. In the late 1830s and in the 1840s many commentators believed that Parkhurst prison would provide this solution.[75] In 1838 'An Act for Establishing a Prison for Young Offenders' was passed by parliament, and in December that year the first prisoner was received into Parkurst Juvenile Penitentiary.[76] The regime and aims of Parkhurst combined both custodial reformatory strategies and colonial emigration. In so doing the creators of the Parkhurst regime sought to take the best features of the experiments and debates which had characterised the preceding decades. Thus the prison offered moral, religious and industrial training, followed by transportation. Originally the prison had sent boys to New Zealand as 'free emigrants' – much closer to the ideal spirit of colonial emigration. However, after 1841, the prison moved away from the sort of zeal and empathy associated with the philanthropic movement, and started to resemble much more a punitive, disciplined institution. The regime became increasingly deterrent, boys were more closely supervised, and the nature of transportation would depend on a boy's behaviour in prison. Good behaviour would result in a ticket-of-leave on arrival in Australia, poor behaviour would result in a passage to the juvenile penal colony at Point Puer.[77] By the late 1840s Parkhurst had completely moved away from its reformatory beginnings. It was now reserved for boys of fourteen and upwards, who had committed serious crime.[78] Essentially it had become a prison for young convicts, the forerunner of today's young offenders' institutions. The reformatory experiment, in the shape of Parkhurst at least, had failed. The responsibility for the continuance of the ethos of reformation would lie in the province of the new industrial and reformatory schools from the mid century. The level of failure at Parkhurst was made clear by a rather lyrical Mary Carpenter in 1851:

> It attempts to fashion children into machines instead of self-acting beings, to make them obedient prisoners within certain iron limits, not men who have been taught how to use their liberty without abusing it; without this knowledge, and the power of employing it, we have seen that the best instruction, the Word of God itself, but little avails its possessor. Such a system must fail; for the boy whose heart has never been purified and softened by any good

---

[75] The establishment and regime of Parkhurst prison has been dealt with extensively in the following: Carlebach, *Caring for children*, 25–46; McConville, *English prison administration*, 204–10; Radzinowicz and Hood, *Emergence of penal policy*, 148–55.

[76] 1 & 2 Vict. c.82 (1838).

[77] Radzinowicz and Hood, *Emergence of penal policy*, 152.

[78] Ibid. 153.

home influence, who has always done 'what is right in his own eyes,' will never give a willing obedience where his power can have no free exercise, where there is no softening power of love to subdue him, where he can never hear from woman what should have been the entreating tones of a mother, where he regards with profound suspicion the appointed agents of his reformation.[79]

This chapter has sketched the outlines of the reformatory movement in both ideal and practice. Throughout the early nineteenth century this debate and the working out of the practical application of reformatory strategies was characterised by the continual conflict between punishment and a more benevolent, correctional approach to the treatment of juvenile offenders. To the children themselves such a paradox was to mean a number of things. As the following two chapters will show, whether in the form of the Refuge, the prison, transportation or colonial emigration it still meant imprisonment, discipline and separation from all that was familiar.

[79] Carpenter, *Reformatory schools*, 321–2.

6

Treatment: from the Court to the Prison

'A School would be of no use; its here we learn, this is the best school; a prison teaches best, and trains a young one, who is sure to learn a trick or two from the older ones.'[1]

Most delinquent children, whether or not they were eventually convicted of a felony, experienced some sort of punishment; this generally meant some form of incarceration. Besides imprisonment as a specific punishment, a sentence of transportation would bring the child into contact with the prison, whether on remand in Newgate, in the condemned cell, waiting with adult felons, or on the juvenile hulk, the *Euraylus*. The impact of such sentencing, and the experience of prison, are central to an understanding of the various punitive and reformatory strategies that children encountered. Whilst in the previous chapter the ideologies which lay behind, and helped form, such strategies were examined, the present chapter will focus more centrally on experience. Children who were the recipients of punitive rationales such as the systems of silence and separation were voluble in their feelings and preferences about prison regimes. Moreover, within the categories of juvenile offender confined in prison were both those on remand and those sentenced to death. Whilst remand prisoners still stood some chance of acquittal, the evidence suggests that increasingly, for London juveniles in the early nineteenth century, this was not the case. One of the great concerns of penal reformers was the proximity of such children to 'hardened' prisoners, both juvenile and adult; this conflict was mirrored by the arrangements made for those receiving the death penalty. Thus the incongruity of placing children for whom the death sentence was nominal, with adults whose lives had every possibility of ending in the execution ground outside Newgate prison was not lost on contemporary commentators.

Acquittal

Many indicted people, both adults and juveniles, were acquitted of the offence of which they were accused. In fact just under a third of all indictments sampled from the Middlesex criminal registers resulted in such verdicts.[2] This could happen at different stages of the criminal justice process

1 PRO, HO 73/16, Select Committee on Gaols (secret), 7.
2 However, in this case acquittal includes verdicts of 'no prosecution', where the prosecutor had failed to appear; and 'no bill' where the case had been dismissed by the Grand Jury.

from when the formal indictment was served. Besides somebody being found 'not guilty', there were various technical points which could undermine an indictment. If there was a problem with the way in which the indictment was written, the judge could direct the jury to acquit. For example John Beattie cites a case in the eighteenth century where a man who was accused of stealing from a William Blake was found not guilty, since the goods actually belonged to Blake's brother Matthew.[3] Other situations could lead to acquittal, for example if the judge felt that a confession had been forced; if the accused had turned king's evidence but had still been indicted; and in the case of women, if it was felt that they had acted under their husbands' direction. Other prisoners were acquitted as part of the trial process, when evidence was found to be flimsy, or if personal rivalries were involved (implying false accusations).[4]

In the context of juvenile offenders, it might be thought that the age of the accused would influence the chance of a favourable trial outcome. It did, but not in a positive way. On the contrary, juveniles stood a much lower chance of receiving a verdict of acquittal than adults. Thus, in the sample data 22 per cent of juveniles received a verdict of acquittal, or their charges were dropped. Yet 28 per cent of young adults aged between seventeen and twenty-five, and 33 per cent of those aged thirty-five and under were acquitted (the highest rates of acquittal or 'not found' verdicts were in the cases where the defendant's age was missing). Since juvenile indictments were increasing over the period, the paucity of juvenile acquittal is important. The point becomes rather clearer if we consider the different age groups as a proportion of those acquitted. Hence, juveniles represented 12 per cent of the whole Middlesex sample, but only 9 per cent as a proportion of those who were acquitted. The pattern is similar for those between seventeen and twenty-five, who represented 42 per cent of the whole sample, and 39 per cent of acquittals. However, for all other age groups the percentage they represent as a proportion of those acquitted is higher than the proportion they represent in the whole sample. This indicates that younger people were less likely to be acquitted, and juveniles were the least likely to be acquitted. It is clear that despite the growing debate over custodial arrangements, the courts felt the need to punish juveniles. This was partly a response to the growing public concern over juvenile crime, which meant that the courts had to be

---

[3] Beattie, *Crime and the courts*, 412. Another striking case of an indictment being undermined is in the case of William Sheen (see chapter 4). In June 1827 Sheen was acquitted of murdering his child, despite evidence that seemed to indicate that he had in fact done the deed. Because of confusion over the name of the baby (who had been born illegitimate), the indictment was found to be bad, and the court ordered a fresh indictment to be made. However, at the second trial in July, Sheen pleaded *autre fois acquit*, effectively arguing that he had already been acquitted of the crime since the child named in the second indictment was the same child named in the first: OBSP, fifth session, 1827, no. 1026, pp. 395-7; sixth session, 1827, no. 1381, pp. 533–4.

[4] Beattie, *Crime and the courts*, 410–19.

seen to be taking juvenile crime seriously and applying appropriate punishment. But this wasn't purely a punitive exercise, for despite the recognised problems with the prison system, custody was clearly seen to be the best vehicle for reformation. Thus the emphasis was on separation from their previous 'corrupting' environments and transference into an institution where the process of rescuing and reforming the criminal child could begin. The contradiction in this was the wide gap between the reformatory expectations of those involved in the management of juvenile offenders and the reality of conditions inside custodial institutions. Moreover, despite the emphasis in the debates on keeping juveniles out of prison, reformatory ambitions clearly over-rode consideration of prevention, or what was later called 'diversion'.

The impact, during the early nineteenth century, of access to secondary punishments had a knock-on effect for the levels of acquittals in Middlesex generally. In 1797 43 per cent of offenders had been acquitted; by 1847 this figure had almost halved to 22 per cent. By 1847 the percentage of juveniles acquitted had decreased by nearly two-thirds (from 40 per cent in 1797 to 14 per cent in 1847).[5] The crucial factor in the reduction of acquittal verdicts seems to have been the growth of penal sentences. The broader application of forms of imprisonment, leading ultimately to penal servitude, meant that offenders might be given a short sentence for a minor offence, rather than fines or corporal punishment being used. Fines only ever formed a very small proportion of sentences for felony; indeed large numbers of offenders were not in a position to pay a fine, which presumably affected sentencing policy. Hence fines were paid by those who could afford them. The alternative for the working population was imprisonment, usually in the house of correction, and/or a whipping. Whipping was administered less over time, and was reserved almost solely for juveniles by the end of the period. Improvements in police techniques may also have affected the levels of acquittal: charges were substantiated by more reliable investigation and handling of evidence. Complementing this was the fact that victims were more willing and able to prosecute.[6] Overall, then, the evidence suggests an inter-relationship between the growth of secondary punishments and the rise in juvenile crime indictments. The increasing use of imprisonment also affected the application of the death sentence.

---

[5] PRO, HO 26/5, 13, 23, 33, 43, 53. There is some indication that acquittals may have increased during the war period, since offenders could join the armed forces as an alternative to a prison sentence.
[6] See pp. 21, 27–8 above.

Death

It is a historical orthodoxy that in the eighteenth and early nineteenth centuries there was a gap between the number of death sentences handed out and the actual number of executions.[7] This was particularly the case with children, despite which the image of the child and the gibbet is still an over-used one in popular histories. B. E. F. Knell has argued with great conviction the fallacy of this image.[8] His article explores the end result of sentencing policy in the eighteenth and early nineteenth centuries. By following the trail of evidence from the original sentences of death, Knell found that between 1801 and 1836, of the 103 children aged under fourteen who were sentenced to capital punishment at the Old Bailey, none was executed. Moreover he demonstrated that of the five cases that are most quoted to illustrate the application of capital punishment to juveniles, only one (John Any Bird Bell who was tried in Kent) was actually executed. It is probable that the situation was the same in the eighteenth century (although the picture may be different for youths over fourteen), the case of William York in 1748 at least pointing to an active consideration of the defendant's age.[9] Only 7 per cent of offenders in the Middlesex criminal registers sample sentenced to death were juveniles. In contrast 53 per cent were aged between seventeen and twenty-five, and in three-quarters (77 per cent) of all capital verdicts the convicted were aged between seventeen and thirty-five. Whilst the number of juveniles sentenced to death was small, it still represented 41 children. Of these four were girls. Three of the girls were aged sixteen, but one was aged eleven. Despite the fact that in these cases a death sentence did not result in actual execution, there would most certainly have been an impact on the child's mental processes, experiencing the pomp and ceremony of the court dispensing death, and probably spending time in the condemned cell. In 1804 Charlotte Wright, one such eleven-year-old girl, was sentenced to death for stealing some money from the dwelling-house of John Bligh in Knightsbridge. Charlotte had been with the Bligh family for eighteen weeks before she was caught leaving the house with a french franc worth a little over 4s. and a £5 bank note.[10] While most of those juveniles sentenced to death were indicted for serious crime, some appear for relatively trivial offences. Reading between the lines undermines the seriousness of some cases. In February 1814, for example, Moses Solomon, Joseph Burrell and John Morris were found guilty and sentenced to death for 'burglariously

---

7 D. Hay, 'Property, authority and the criminal trial', in D. Hay and others, *Albion's fatal tree: crime and society in eighteenth-century England*, London 1975, this edn, 1988, 17–63.
8 B. E. F. Knell, 'Capital punishment: its administration in relation to juvenile offenders in the nineteenth century and its possible administration in the eighteenth', *British Journal of Criminology, Delinquency and Deviant Behaviour* v (1965), 198–207, esp. pp. 200–3.
9 See p. 9, n. 25 above.
10 *OBSP*, sixth session, 1804, no. 400, p. 341.

breaking and entering the dwelling-house of Richard Atkinson . . . stealing therein a pair of shoes, value eight shillings'. The boys, Solomon and Burrell aged nine, and Morris eight, had in fact broken the window and taken the shoes out.[11] It is clear that this case was treated more seriously because the boys had been witnessed attempting another window previously.[12] Likewise Knell supplied details of ten children aged ten and under, sentenced to death at the Old Bailey, including John Barney and Charles Elliott, both nine years old, for shoplifting.[13] Possibly children capitally convicted of lesser crimes were repeat offenders, or else some other factor made their crime particularly heinous in the eyes of their prosecutors.

Amongst criminal justice professionals, and boys alike, it was accepted that the death sentence was effectively a sentence of transportation. Horace Salisbury Cotton, the Newgate chaplain, frequently expressed exasperation over the nonchalant attitude exhibited by inmates towards the death sentence. The boys, in particular, undermined the gravity of the situation in the condemned cell, since they knew very well that they would not be executed:

> visited the condemned men – found very few serious or properly impressed with a sense of their situation. . . . One of the men complained to me of the numbers confined together and of the impossibility of maintaining a serious frame of mind, he stated that by far the greater part of those under sentence felt confident from the nature of their cases, that they shall not be executed and therefore conducted themselves with great levity and unconcern to the grief and hindrance of those who really expected to suffer the extreme punishment of the law.

Whilst increasingly it was general practice not to place children in the condemned cells, visiting the condemned rooms on 24 May 1824, Cotton none the less found nine boys there aged between fourteen and seventeen years.[14] Such youthful disrespect was discussed by a number of contemporary commentators. For example, William Augustus Miles and Edward Gibbon Wakefield felt that it was ridiculous to place boys in the condemned cell when it was clear that the sentence would not be implemented.[15] Furthermore it was felt that youngsters sentenced to death played on the 'status' and 'credibility' it seemed to afford them in an unhealthy manner. Miles claimed to have 'observed the boys in Newgate, who have been sentenced to death (although the boy, as well as the judge and every person present, knew that he would not be hung in pursuance of that sentence) conduct themselves as boys of a superior class to the transport lads'.[16] Thus it was argued that, since virtually

---

11 Ibid. third session, 1814, no. 208, p. 126.
12 See p. 27 above.
13 Knell, 'Capital punishment', 206.
14 CLRO, 209 c/13, Newgate prison visitors' book, Sept. 1823–Nov. 1825 (kept by Revd H. S. Cotton), 4 Oct. 1823, 24 May 1824.
15 Miles, *Poverty*, 93; Wakefield, *Punishment of death*, 228–35.
16 Miles, *Poverty*, 93.

no juveniles were executed, the capital penalty had little role as a deterrent or exemplary punishment. It undermined the law, it unsettled the less fortunate adult condemned, and it encouraged bravado amongst the boys:

> A boy named Rogers, who had been confined in the school-yard before trial, was sentenced to death, and, contrary to the usual practice with boys of his age, was, immediately after sentence, removed from the school to the cells. I saw him arrive in the school to fetch his clothes, coming from the bar, where sentence of death had just then been passed on him. He told the schoolmaster with great glee, that he was ordered to the cells; and when the other boys crowded round him to learn why he was to be removed, he answered their questions in a triumphant tone, and showed, by his whole manner as well, that he enjoyed the importance conferred on him, by being placed amongst those of whom no one can say which of them will, or will not, be executed.[17]

For both boy and men prisoners, one way of dealing with the proximity of death was to turn it into the ultimate resistance, a tableau where the prisoner, imbued with qualities of masculinity, could become the hero, a renegade to the last. Of course, part of the chaplain's brief was to elicit a proper sense of remorse from the condemned prisoners prior to execution. The battle then, between the prisoner and authority, was for the soul. Adult felons on their way to the scaffold, many of them little more than callow youths themselves, would be exhorted by their fellow inmates to 'diehard my boy', 'remember yourself', 'act like a man'. In 1818 J. A. Newman, an ex-keeper of Newgate, described how a boy named Cox had, at nineteen, eventually come to be executed. Cox 'had received many addresses from the court, and he used jokingly to call the Recorder his god-father; he came to be executed at last; and the night before he was executed he amused himself by engraving on a plain half-penny, the picture of a man hanging, and W.C. on the other side'.[18] However, the reality for a number of young men was approached with far less levity. Whilst age was some protection, this was removed swiftly once the child reached his late teens. Using the sample from the Middlesex criminal registers, it is clear that once the prisoner was over sixteen the chances of being sentenced to death increased sharply. Of those prisoners receiving the death sentence, forty-one or 6 per cent were juveniles aged sixteen and under, while 334 or fifty-three per cent were aged between seventeen and twenty-five.[19] Because of the number of respites from the death sentence, it is difficult without substantial investigation to gauge the number and age structure of offenders where execution was actually carried out. However, tables derived from Edward Gibbon Wakefield's work on punishment give some idea of the numbers that were actually being executed.[20] These tables show

17 Wakefield, *Punishment of death*, 233.
18 *SC Police*, PP, 1818, viii. 181–2.
19 PRO, HO 26/5, 13, 23, 33, 43, 53.
20 Wakefield, *Punishment of death*, 208–18.

the number of people charged with capital crime, and those who were punished by death, in Middlesex and the City of London, from 1 May 1827 to 30
April 1830. Fifty-five people were executed in that period, thirteen of whom
were aged between seventeen and twenty-five, seven of these under twenty.
All were male; the three eighteen-year-olds were executed for highway
robbery; the seventeen-year-old for housebreaking; and the nineteen-year-
olds for housebreaking, highway robbery and forgery.[21] It is hard to imagine
these young men as other than boys – boys such as Joseph Harwood, who
when visited in the condemned cell by Cotton was described as 'a youth of
eighteen . . . dreadfully distressed'. Harwood had been convicted of highway
robbery, with circumstances of cruelty. He spent the days leading up to his
execution veering between distress and sickness, spending two days in the
infirmary. Cotton visited him frequently, and was relieved to see his distress
turn to resignation: 'This morning Joseph Harwood after receiving the Sacra-
ment, was executed pursuant to his sentence . . . he evinced very great contri-
tion and I trust was well prepared for his fate.'[22] For John Any Bird Bell, his
last moments in 1831 were filled with remorse and warning: ' "Pray for a Poor
boy! Pray for me! . . . Lord have mercy upon us; pray good Lord have mercy
upon us. All you people take warning by me – take warning." '[23]

Imprisonment

Institutional punishment, in one form or another, was an important tool in
the armoury of juvenile justice. Imprisonment invariably meant incorporation within the criminal justice system, however temporarily. Even those
children who entered custody for a very short period, or on remand, encountered similar experiences to those children who entered prison as a prelude to
transportation. It has already been pointed out that despite the Gaols Acts of
the 1820s most systems of classification and attempts at separating remand
prisoners were ineffective. Precisely how many children spent time in prison,
for how long and how many times, is impossible to gauge. Besides the official
prisons and houses of correction, reformatories and industrial schools, children experienced 'informal' institutionalisation in the houses and refuges of
the voluntary institutions and in the state workhouses. Moreover, whilst
many children were officially sentenced to some manner of imprisonment, a
great many more were sent summarily to a house of correction, or to the Philanthropic Society. For example, amongst the petitions for London children
sentenced in 1838, 22 per cent had been sent to the Children's Friend

---

[21] Ibid. 208, 210, 211, 214, tables 1, 3, 4, 7.
[22] CLRO, 209 c/13, Newgate prison visitors' book, 25 Sept.–25 Nov. 1824. The case of
Joseph Harwood is discussed in some detail in Gatrell, *Hanging tree*, 40–5.
[23] *Facts relative to the murder of Richard Faulkner Taylor*, 40.

Society.[24] This was one of the most prolific of the child emigration societies, and the overwhelming number of parents petitioning on behalf of a child were interceding to prevent transportation. Thus a vast number of children, whether their sentence was self-contained or a stage on the road to the colonies, spent time in prison. The chances were that if a child had reached the prison hulks he or she (usually he) had a prior record of imprisonment. Out of thirty-two boys interviewed by William Augustus Miles on the *Euryalus* twenty confessed to having been in prison before; only three boys actually stated that they had never been in prison.[25] Just under half (45 per cent) of the juvenile offenders in the Middlesex criminal registers sample who were found guilty, were punished by imprisonment, a figure which does not take account of children on remand, children placed in prison whilst they waited for corporal punishment, and children waiting to be transported. Whilst the use of custodial sentences was increasing generally over the period, it was only after the early years of the nineteenth century that significant numbers of juvenile offenders officially received a sentence of imprisonment. In 1817 juveniles formed 6 per cent of the whole prison population, in 1847 this had trebled to 18 per cent.[26] Whilst these percentages are not staggeringly high, it should be noted that the 18 per cent in 1847 represented as many as 76 per cent of all convicted juveniles in that year. Hence the proportion of juvenile prisoners increased over time, as did the proportion of those between seventeen and twenty-five. Since indictments of those aged twenty-five and below were increasing over the period, the implication is that a supply-and-demand relationship was created: the escalating prosecution of young people prompted a growth in custodial sentences, but also in the building of prisons.[27] Alternatively, it could as well be argued that the increasing tendency to imprison offenders, and the increasing means to do so, drove up juvenile indictments. In other words, because more custodial institutions were being built, and because the building and organisation of these institutions encompassed reformatory programmes, prosecutors were more willing to draw juveniles into the justice system. The larcenies for which children were imprisoned were often trifling affairs. For example in 1802 James Westbrook, aged twelve, was indicted along with another boy, Nathanial Inch, for stealing a Cheshire cheese, valued at 8s. Westbrook was found guilty and sentenced to a six month's stretch in prison and a public whipping.[28] Again in 1802 three boys, Thomas Parker (aged fifteen), Thomas Brown (aged twelve) and James Brown (aged sixteen) were charged with stealing four napkins and a tablecloth from the wash-house of George Scales, in Homerton. All the

24 PRO, HO 19/8, petitions archive register, 1838–9.
25 PRO, HO 73/16, notebooks 1, 2, 3.
26 PRO, HO 26/5, 13, 23, 33, 43, 53.
27 For similar insights into the relationship between the growing use of custodial sentences and criminalisation of juvenile crime see May, 'A child's punishment'.
28 OBSP, 1802, second session, no. 136, pp. 100–1.

boys were sentenced to six months in the house of correction.[29] These children were imprisoned for committing felonies. A substantial number of children were committed to the Bridewells, houses of correction or to the Philanthropic Society, for less than felony. The juvenile prisoners at the Tothill Fields Bridewell in 1828 had been committed to the prison on remand or by summary conviction. Seventy children under sixteen were in the Bridewell in March 1828. For half of these the offence is recorded. Twelve were on remand awaiting trial for felony, eleven had been committed for being disorderly (for girls it is possible that this might refer to prostitution), eight for vagrancy, two for being a reputed thief, and two for attempted felony. Similarly, in the Philanthropic Society between March 1832 and March 1835 sixty-four 'objects' had been received, aged between nine and twelve. Thirty-two of these children were resident with the Society because of their parents' death, transportation or execution. The other thirty-two were resident on various charges or because they had been labelled as delinquent. For example:

> Aged eleven, had been Twice charged before a Magistrate with stealing various Articles, and otherwise frequently guilty of Acts of Delinquency.

> Aged eleven, convicted of Felony at the Middlesex Sessions. A very depraved Character.

> Aged ten, a destitute Orphan, certified by a Magistrate to have been One Month in the House of Correction, and of very vicious Habits.

> Aged ten, certified by several respectable Persons, Magistrates and others, as continually guilty of Thieving and other bad conduct.[30]

As pointed out in the previous chapter the need for juvenile-specific institutions had been a concern throughout the period. Indeed the pressure group, the Prison Discipline Society, was established with the removal of children from adult prisons as a major campaigning point. Yet, within the ideologies and strategies of such groups as the Philanthropic Society and the Children's Friend Society, there were inherent contradictions. These essentially boiled down to a number of conflicts in the strands of thought of those involved in the criminal justice system. Firstly, everyone agreed that it was wrong to imprison children and adults together; secondly, most agreed that some sort of vocational training and limited education should be made available to juvenile patrons. However, the conflict lay in problems between the greater and lesser evil. Whilst it was right to move youths from the corruption of criminal adults, it was not necessarily right to allow them back to their parents. In order to be redeemed such children had to make a break with

---

[29] Ibid. eighth session, no. 826, pp. 522–3.
[30] SC Police, PP, 1828, vi, appendix D, pp. 3–8; SC Gaols, PP, 1835, 4th, 5th Reports, xii, appendix 15, p. 537.

their past, to allow themselves to be remodelled into more able and more successful subjects, whether at home or abroad. The stress on uniformity meant that many of the institutions were indistinguishable from the state prisons and reformatories. Certainly the children may have received a better standard of care, more tailored to the child, but the child's experience of institutionalisation, of separation from what was familiar, of possible emotional neglect, was universal within the network of institutions.[31]

For juvenile offenders, their perception of prison, and the manner in which they coped, seems to have depended largely on the shifting tides of discipline and reformatory practice during these years. Like all prisoners, children used a number of strategies to cope with the punishment, isolation and lack of individualism inherent in prison life. For male juvenile prisoners particularly, one way of coping was to use the prison experience as a way of underlining their status as burgeoning criminals and emphasising both their masculinity and comradeship with other juveniles and older prisoners. For instance in 1817 an apparently notorious recidivist, fourteen-year-old John Leary, was described by Spitalfields philanthropist Peter Bedford. Bedford found him in Newgate 'standing in one corner of the room with his arms akimbo, looking as bold as any lion'. It was noted that Leary refused to go into the schoolroom, preferring to stay in the prison yard with the men.[32] As contemporary commentators recognised, repeated periods of custody did little to reform children, and indeed had the main effect of hardening them. Naturally most imprisoned children developed ways of dealing with custody. Much depended on the running of the prison. Despite the provisions of Peel's Gaol Acts, many of the prisons had found it difficult to put disciplinary and reformatory regimes into operation. Neither the manpower nor the raw materials (rooms, books, furniture) were always available to fill the gap between theory and practice. Some of the newer institutions were more readily able to effect these regimes, although they were looked on much less favourably by the juvenile inmates themselves. Sixteen-year-old George Hickman had been in Coldbath Fields house of correction four times, New prison Clerkenwell twice, Newgate twice, and Brixton twice. He 'prefers Newgate, in every respect except sleeping because they can see their friends, can play, talk and

---

31 Much of the discussion of children's institutional experiences has focused on the reformatory school period, hence generally the later nineteenth century. Moreover, because of the greater access to information on female criminality offered by the records of such institutions, work has generally emphasised female rather than male juveniles. However, a reasonably balanced account can be drawn from the following works: Cale, 'Girls and the perception of sexual danger'; R. Harris and N. Timms, *Secure accommodation in child care: between hospital and prison or thereabouts?*, London 1993; Mahood and Littlewood, 'The "vicious" girl and the "street-corner" boy'; T. Ploszajska, 'Moral landscapes and manipulated spaces: gender, class and space in Victorian reformatory schools', *Journal of Historical Geography* xx (1994), 413–29.

32 William Beck, *Friends, ancient and modern*, London 1908, 26–7; SC Police, PP, 1817, vii. 542.

do as they like'. Thirteen-year-old Samuel Holmes had been in Coldbath Fields three times and Tothill Fields once. He preferred the latter 'because boys are under less restraint – they steal one another's bread'. Sixteen-year-old Henry Thompson also favoured Tothill Fields, 'because the food is better and the work is less'.[33] In 1818 Tothill Fields prison had been roundly condemned by the committee appointed to inquire into the state of the prison for the Select Committee on Metropolitan Police. In summing up the committee said that:

> they are of opinion that it is unbecoming and unseemly, in a civilised and Christian country, to have in the heart of its metropolis a prison, which should annually contain within its walls 2,652 persons of both sexes, of whom it could be said by the chaplain, that the punishment of imprisonment made them much worse and corrupted, and debased their characters in a higher degree than they were before their commitment.[34]

Nearly fifty years later, reports on the prison were still as damning. In their 1862 survey of the metropolitan prisons and houses of correction, Henry Mayhew and John Binny commented on the state of Tothill Fields, as well as the seemingly static criminal justice system:

> We have before spoken of convict nurseries – of baby-felons, born and suckled in prison; and now we have to speak of felon-academies, where the young offender is duly trained and educated for the Hulks. True, the place is called a house of correction; but, rightly viewed, it is simply a criminal preparatory school, where students are qualified for matriculating at Millbank or Pentonville.[35]

The contrast between the perceived archaic and corrupt regimes at Tothill Fields and Newgate and the new, punitive, disciplined regime in practice at Millbank was very much at issue during the 1830s. For the 1835 Select Committee on Gaols, a number of prisoners held at Millbank Penitentiary were questioned about their previous spells of imprisonment in less 'enlightened' institutions. One boy, a fifteen-year-old who had previously been in remand at Newgate and then spent time on the *Euryalus*, was particularly unimpressed by the disorderly regime at Newgate, alluding to the lack of classification and separation:

> was one week in Newgate before trial, in what is called the Chapel Yard; there were upwards of thirty prisoners in it, some of them tried and some untried, five or six of them had been convicted before, and one of them no less than four times; there were persons for different offences, some for housebreaking,

33 PRO, HO 73/16, notebooks 1, 2, evidence of George Hickman, Samuel Holmes and Henry Thompson.
34 *SC Police*, PP, 1818, iii. 6.
35 H. Mayhew and J. Binny, *The criminal prisons of London and scenes of prison life*, London 1862, repr. London 1968, 406.

some for highway robbery, some for stealing poultry, ten or eleven for passing bad money, (they were called 'Smashers') and several for picking pockets.[36]

The lack of order in Newgate, according to this boy, was formidable, and was colluded in by the wardsmen (long-stay prisoners). In his experience, the north side of the prison which housed the more permanent prisoners, where he was sent to await removal to the *Euryalus*, was even more subject to disorderly behaviour: 'the conversation in the North Side was worse, if possible, than in the Chapel Yard; there was a Wardsman there also, full as bad as any of them'.[37] This boy also commented on the ease with which prisoners were able to procure extra food and drink, via the wardsmen, depending on their financial situation: 'once received from his friends 3lbs. of Pork Chops, a Plumb Pudding between 3 and 4lbs. Weight, and a Plumb Cake after Twelfth Day; had occasionally Milk and Beer'.[38]

Not surprisingly, considering the endeavours of his inquirers, the model, disciplined, orderly regime profited much in comparison: 'would prefer any place to Newgate, and prefers the penitentiary to the *Euryalus*, because he is kept clean and gets a great deal more instruction'.[39] Despite the complaints of contemporary commentators, and despite the disapproval of this fifteen-year-old, the prisoners themselves clearly preferred the more lax surroundings of Tothill Fields and Newgate, in preference to Coldbath Fields, where there had been early experimentation with punitive reformatory techniques (the prison was nicknamed the 'steele', or bastille), or the *Euryalus*, which in the 1830s was ubiquitously described as a harsh, dog-eat-dog environment.[40]

Samuel Ogilby, a ten-year-old witness to the 1835 Select Committee on Gaols, had favoured Newgate to the *Euryalus*. In the former he had been able to see his friends, and his mother and step-father had visited twice a week bringing him food and tea; however, for family and friends the journey to the *Euryalus* at Chatham was too far and too costly. Whilst he was unsure about transportation, he was certain about his dislike of the hulk: 'I do not like this Place.'[41] On the other hand the Millbank prisoner, described above, had found the regime on the *Euryalus* relatively disciplined, with a degree of self-control, secured by the adoption of a sort of head-boy system:

> One of the boys, was appointed to keep order and regularity, and to report to the Captain any one who made use of bad language, sung songs, or attempted to game; he was a steady boy, and reported three or four whilst he was on

36 SC *Gaols*, PP, 1835, 1st Report, xi, appendix 3, p. 36.
37 Ibid.
38 Ibid.
39 Ibid.
40 For more information on the use of the silent system at Coldbath Fields see Radzinowicz and Hood, *Emergence of penal policy*, 353; McConville, *English prison administration*, 244–5, 352, 243–7; for more general discussion of the separate and silent systems see Henriques, 'The rise and decline of the separate system'.
41 SC *Gaols*, PP, 1835, 1st Report, xi, appendix 21, pp. 260–1.

board, some for gaming and some for swearing; they were caned by one of the guards.[42]

Unquestionably the transformation of the prison into something more ordered and disciplined was a slow process, but even so it is debatable how effective such regimes were. Whilst on the surface a structured approach to discipline and reformation might seem successful, prison subcultures had a way of undermining the efforts of the authorities. Moreover, much of the discipline and stress on uniformity was counter-productive, causing resentment and consequently provoking challenges to the prison regime. Children, it was commented, were often more difficult to handle than adults, perhaps because they were less willing and less able to consider the long-term consequences of their behaviour. There is no doubt that the new-style prison regimes were difficult, and highly unsuitable, for young children. The silent system in particular was difficult for children. Comradeship was an essential component of surviving prison life and the imposition of silence was a major deprivation. Moreover, education offered little relief. The emphasis was strongly religious and doctrinally based. The basics of reading and writing were taught, with some skill training in carpentry or bootmaking. However, the 'good book' was the main educational medium, accompanied by lives of the saints and stories of religious conversion. A list submitted by the schoolmaster of Newgate to the 1835 Select Committee on Gaols included *Forty-one letters on religious subjects; The influence of the pious women in promoting the revival of religion; The young Sabbath breaker;* and *Persuasions to early piety*.[43] The ineffectiveness of such a pious diet was also reflected on in the 1850s when Captain William. J. Williams, inspector of prisons for the home district, commented that 'I think it is not sufficiently of a secular nature. I think in many of these boys there is a distaste almost created in them by constant reference to the Bible on all educational questions, making it rather a spelling book, or education book, or class book, than a sacred book.'[44] Whilst it is possible that children improved their reading in the prison school, it was unlikely that the substance of the classes did much to engage their attention. According to William Augustus Miles, the boys were all too eager to spend time with books so long as they were not force fed with religious fare:

> There is a library in the boys' ward at Newgate: it contains a great number of evangelical books and lives of a great number of dissenting ministers; among the other books, however, there are a few containing history and travels, and it is with these latter books that the boys are delighted; they read them with eagerness, and the more illiterate boys will subscribe portions of food to engage the services of a boy to read them aloud.[45]

---

42 Ibid. appendix 3, p. 36.
43 Ibid. 4th Report, xii, appendix 12, p. 529.
44 SC *Criminal Juveniles*, PP, 1852, vii. 19, evidence of Capt. W. J. Williams.
45 Miles, *Poverty*, 93.

According to the Revd Clay, of the Preston house of correction, there were problems with allowing juveniles access to the more sensational aspects of culture. A fourteen-year-old boy questioned at the New Bailey, Salford:

> thought this 'Jack Sheppard' was a clever fellow for making his escape and robbing his master. If I could get out of gaol I think I should be as clever as him; but after all his exploits he got done at last. I have had the book out of a library at Dole Field. I paid 2d a book for three volumes. I also got 'Richard Turpin', in two volumes, and paid the same. I have seen 'Oliver Twist', and think the Artful Dodger is very like some of the boys here. I am here for picking a pocket of 25l.[46]

There is little commentary in the interviews with juvenile offenders about their response to prison facilities, such as education or diet. Most of the comments concentrate on their lives before custody and then on the conflict between order and disorder within the institution. It seems clear that the prison authorities were keen to give some impression that their reformatory strategies were working. The 1835 Select Committee on Gaols contains a number of statements from prisoners all testifying that the silent system was preferable to the previous atmosphere of rowdiness and bad language. A seventeen-year-old in Millbank penitentiary claimed to 'prefer total Silence, and even total Separation, to mingling with other Prisoners; showed this by choosing to be alone before Trial, because he wished, as much as possible, to avoid such Discourse as is carried on in a Prison'.[47] Yet when boys were questioned more informally, the over-riding impression was that the boys were on the side of disorder.[48] Of course the whole terminology of 'reformation' was far broader and far-reaching than merely stemming the commission of crime. Indeed, as W. J. Forsythe notes in his study of Exeter borough prison:

> The registers of the prison make it plain that the prison had as its aim much more than merely the punishment of what today would be called crime. It also acted towards the enforcement of a wide range of moral and social disciplines, the importance of which seemed to increase as evangelicalism, utilitarianism and classical political economy – from different starting points – pressed towards the more regulated Godly behaviour at the bottom of society and towards the reduction of pauperism, petty offences and other refusals to obey legal and administrative structures and moral norms.[49]

However, it has already been pointed out that the gap between theory and practice was substantial, with the prison authorities fighting a losing battle against the corruption of juveniles. The extremities of the silent and separate

---

[46] SC *Criminal Juveniles*, PP, 1852, vii, appendix 2, p. 421.
[47] SC *Gaols*, PP, 1835, 1st Report, xi, appendix 3, p. 41.
[48] I refer more generally to boys here since there is so little commentary either on girls in prison, or from girls about their experience in prison.
[49] Forsythe, *A system of discipline*, 39.

systems could not be applied to juveniles without the possibility of damage. Prison Inspector Whitworth Russell reported that 'there is an elasticity about childhood and youth which it is essential to maintain, but which I think can hardly be maintained under a system of separation' and so it seems children carried on communicating with adults and with each other.[50] Whilst commentators remarked on the prevalence of gambling and the constant discussion of criminal activity, prison insiders described an atmosphere where bullying and intimidation were substantial problems. This was particularly so on the *Euryalus*, possibly because once boys were removed to the ship, depending on their age, they would have had to wait a considerable time before actual transportation. Similar problems occurred at Parkhurst prison, where boys were also in waiting for transportation. Captain Hall, governor there in 1847, despaired of hardened juvenile offenders: 'the only voluntary activity they manifest is a continual effort by persuasion, by threats, by false promises, or by ridicule, to make other prisoners pursue their vicious example in opposing all means which may be tried for moral improvement'.[51]

Intimidation, both physical and mental, was an unavoidable component of prison life, the more so with rapid institutionalisation. The extent of violence in institutions is particularly difficult to uncover since, whilst it is recognised that prisons are not peaceable places, the presence of violence and bullying indicate a lack of control. However, institutional violence should not be underestimated, particularly amongst young men. Criminologist Joe Sim made the following observation about young offenders' institutions and detention centres: 'Here physical violence, psychological intimidation and constant bullying provide the chilling and stark context in which everyday decisions are made, lives controlled and bodies and minds sometimes broken and destroyed.'[52] There had been complaints about the management of the *Euryalus* for some time. Thomas Wontner in particular was a strong opponent of the hulk. In 1833 he stressed that keeping such a large number of boys on board, in such deleterious conditions (apparently between 500 and 800 boys shared wards of between thirty or forty), was hardly better than the situation in their former lodging-houses.[53] The most damning evidence about the *Euryalus* came from the prisoners themselves. An adult prisoner, Thomas Dexter, had occasionally worked as a nurse in the juvenile convict hospital which received boys from the *Euryalus*. Dexter described a subculture of violence and intimidation, a situation on the ship whereby gang-rule held sway. The Nobs had the ascendancy, creating an environment of fear, which

---

50 Second General Report of Prisons, 162, cited in Carpenter, *Reformatory schools*, 297.

51 Carpenter, *Reformatory schools*, 323.

52 J. Sim, 'Tougher than the rest? Men in prison', in T. Newburn and E. A. Stanko (eds), *Just boys doing business? Men, masculinities and crime*, London 1994, 100–17, esp. quotation at p. 103.

53 Wontner, *Old Bailey experience*, 360. See also *Morning Herald*, 14 Mar. 1830, and SC *Police*, PP, 1828, vi. 53, evidence of John Wontner, keeper of Newgate.

necessarily precluded boys from saying anything to those in charge. Moreover, strict codes of honour, as well as plain fear, held the 'Noseys' in check. Such was the fear of the Nobs that boys would purposely injure themselves in order to get into the hospital ward:

> I have known the Boys take an old Copper Button and apply it hot to the Skin, and then apply Soap and Rum to a Sore occasioned by a hot Button, and wrap it up for Two or Three Days, and then show that wound to the Doctor, and then come to the Hospital in a State piteous to behold. . . . I have known several Cases in which they have broken their Arms to get into the Hospital; they held their Arms upon a Form, and let the Edge of the Table drop upon them to break them in two.[54]

This violence was confirmed in horrifying detail by one of the boys interviewed on the *Euryalus*. William Johnson had been on the hulk for nearly two years and nine months. He had arrived from Newgate with thirteen other boys, a number of whom bullied him relentlessly. On arrival on the *Euryalus* William was placed in a cell with two of the boys who, already acquainted with children already on the ship, took pains to turn as many as possible against him, while continuing to torture him in their cell. William 'never made any complaint because if he had he would have been knocked about by the other Boys'. After persistent intimidation, William decided to attempt to be moved to the hospital ward by sticking pins into his hands. Unfortunately he also decided to take the advice of his torturers who recommended a blow to the eye, which they would gladly supply. Early one morning, at 4.30a.m., an hour before the ship usually rose, 'they pricked my eyes with needles – I was just awaking – took the needle held my eyes up . . . as I laid in the corner of my cell in my hammock – and jagged the needle three or four times in each eye'. William had expected some violence, but as he told his interviewer 'I did not care what had come of me then.' The attack was not reported for two days for fear of reprisal, and William stayed in the corner of his cell until a guard found him and took him to the captain, Mr Briant. The boys were punished, one by the cane and one by the black hole, although the investigation was shoddily carried out, taking only ten minutes at the most. For William Johnson the consequences were more long-lasting, his sight permanently damaged: 'can see shadow of a person – can see Daylight – one eye quite blind'.[55] Another child, Nicholas White, aged nine when he entered the *Euryalus*, also referred to the threat of intimidation. He described a network

---

[54] *SC Gaols*, PP, 1835, 1st Report, xi. 323, evidence of Thomas Dexter.

[55] PRO, HO 73/16, rough notebook iv, evidence of Harris in the name of Johnson. William Johnson's parents, John and Sarah Harris, had petitioned the Home Secretary about their son's case after his trial in January 1833. Whilst they drew attention to the 'misfortune of his losing one eye, with the probable decay of the other, and his sickly habit of body', no mention was made of how such debilitating injuries had been acquired: PRO, HO 17/17/pt.1, Bs/sz, petition of William Johnson.

of fear and power directed by young boys. Like William Johnson he pointed out that many of the boys on the ship had known each other before their arrival on the hulk, either in prison or on the streets,[56] the implication being that 'men' were quickly sorted out from 'boys', or 'nobs' from 'skunks' or 'noseys' in their stay on the *Euryalus*. It is difficult to envisage quite the levels of violence and emotional deprivation which these children experienced. Moreover, their removal from the hulk to the colonies was to provide little change in atmosphere. Indeed, records from Point Puer tell a continuing story of disobedience, confrontation and punishment.

In many ways juvenile offenders were useful guinea pigs for the evolving penal regimes: it was felt that for these prisoners at least, there was some possibility of redemption and reformation. Whilst penal commentators emphasised the efficacy of separation in the prisons at home, the ideology of removal and separation found its greatest expression in the reformatory experiments of transportation and colonial emigration. Whilst the essentially punitive nature of transportation remained, the increasing numbers of juvenile offenders sentenced to transportation matched a growing emphasis on removal as rather more than a temporary expedient. The following chapter explores juvenile offenders' attitudes to, and experience of, transportation and the closely paralleled colonial emigration. The interplay between reformation and recidivism, which transportation above all aimed to stem, ends this examination of the criminal child's journey through the justice system.

[56] PRO, HO 73/16, rough notebook v, evidence of Nicholas White.

7

Treatment: Transportation and Reformation

The use of transportation was integral to the punishment of young people, and particularly to the punishment of young men. Both practical and ideological considerations held sway. Thus it could be argued that young men had more chance of surviving the arduous sea passage and were more likely to acclimatise to the massive environmental challenge. Moreover, there was less likelihood that young men would be leaving a family; many of those transported to Australia were single persons. Lloyd Robson's quantitative work on the convict period demonstrated that more than 50 per cent of both male and female convicts were single or widowed.[1] Ideologically, for the reformers, transportation was sound. There had been a long history of transportation of children, often based on commercial calculations.[2] However it was really the eighteenth-century transportation to the American colonies which established the removal of convicts, and thus of infant felons, across the Atlantic. An act of 1718 permitted penal transportation of children aged between fifteen and eighteen to the North American plantations, provided they consented to go.[3] Cessation of transportation followed the War of Independence, to re-emerge in the late 1780s in the form of Australian transportation. For the reformers and politicians, transportation offered the best of both worlds. Offenders were removed from the cities and streets but at the same time were offered the possibility of redemption and reformation. The process of reformation, for juvenile criminals, meant a strong association between custody and removal. Moreover, the true number of children 'transported' was much higher when those children from the various voluntary institutions are considered.[4] The later history of such compulsory emigration has been

1 Robson, *Convict settlers*, 182–3, 187–8.
2 See G. Wagner, *Children of the empire*, London 1982, 1–18, for discussion of pre-transportation emigration of children.
3 Transportation Act, 4 Geo I, c.II (1718). See M. Ignatieff, *A just measure of pain: the penitentiary in the industrial revolution, 1750–1850*, London 1989, 19–20; R. Ekirch, *Bound for America: the transportation of British convicts to the colonies, 1718–75*, Oxford 1987.
4 Little has been written on the official transportation of children. However some coverage can be found in the following: P. Buddee, *The fate of the Artful Dodger: Parkhurst boys transported to Australia and New Zealand, 1842–52*, Perth, WA 1984; F. C. Hooper, *Prison boys of Port Arthur*, Melbourne 1967; A. G. Scholes, *Education for empire settlement: a study of juvenile migration*, London 1932. Child emigration schemes have been dealt with more thoroughly: Bean and Melville, *Lost children*; Bradlow, 'Children's Friend Society'; Hadley, 'Natives'; G. Wagner, *Barnardo*, London 1979; B. M. Coldrey, *The scheme: the Christian Brothers and childcare in Western Australia*, O'Connor, WA 1993 (this book was written and published by the Christian Brothers as a defence and vindication of their homes).

considered in detail with, for example, recent work on children sent from Barnardos. However, from the early nineteenth century the Philanthropic Society and the Children's Friend Society were sending their child inmates to Australia, Canada and the Cape. For juveniles, throughout the period of transportation, the distinction between transportation and emigration became increasingly blurred. This was particularly the case in the 1840s when boys from Parkhurst juvenile prison were 'apprenticed' to settlers in the new colony.[5] For juvenile offenders found guilty of the more serious larcenies, and for those with any sort of criminal record, it was fairly inevitable that transportation would occur at some point. There were a variety of responses to transportation. Some showed fear, some a resigned acceptance, others anticipation. Sixteen-year-old Henry Thompson, considering transportation, said: 'it is looked upon by each thief as an event which must occur some time or another, and the only point is to keep from it as long as they can'.[6]

Lloyd Robson's 5 per cent sample of prisoners transported to New South Wales and to Van Diemen's Land in the years between 1787 and 1852 drew a number of conclusions. Of the male convicts, 81 per cent were found guilty of a property crime (43 per cent of these for unspecified larceny), 50 per cent were single, 78 per cent were aged under thirty-five, and 19 per cent under twenty.[7] This story, of a young, single and mainly male population (only 15 per cent were female) is echoed by results from the Middlesex criminal registers sample. Thus 22 per cent of all indicted juveniles were sentenced to transportation, representing 14 per cent of all those thus sentenced. If death sentences are included (which were, except in a very few cases, reduced to transportation), 24 per cent of all indicted juveniles were transported. Larceny convictions accounted for 94 per cent of those juvenile offenders transported (a figure which does not include the very serious larcenies such as burglary and horse-stealing).[8] However, there is little real difference in the nature of the offending which resulted in transportation as opposed to imprisonment. Age and gender probably had some impact. Of the juvenile transports to be found in the Middlesex criminal registers sample 93 per cent were male. In real terms this means that only thirty-two of the sample female juveniles were sentenced to transportation as opposed to 410 males. Female juveniles sentenced to transportation tended to be slightly older: 94 per cent of females transported were aged between fourteen and sixteen, compared with 78 per cent of males.[9] The girls included sixteen-year-old Sophia

---

5   This was not a new idea, since assisted emigration schemes had been advocated, indeed acted upon by the Philanthropic Society and via the Brenton Asylum, for many years: Bradlow 'Children's Friend Society'; Hadley, 'Natives'.

6   PRO, HO 73/16, notebook 2, evidence of Henry Thompson.

7   Of these male offenders, 17% came from London: Robson, *Convict settlers*, 6–83, appendix II.

8   PRO, HO 26/5, 13, 23, 33, 43, 53.

9   Ibid. This reflected the fact that the female accused were generally slightly older: King, 'Female offenders', 65, fig. 2.

Groundhie who was transported for breaking and entering into the dwelling-house of Mary and Benjamin Ames, in Spicer Street, Mile End. Ann Gilby, Eliza Chapman and Sarah Attfield, were slightly older, aged seventeen, nineteen and seventeen respectively, and were transported for fourteen years on two convictions of stealing from shops.[10] Previous convictions were also significant, as were known criminal associations (known, presumably, through the vigilance of the police). Certain crimes tended to attract a sentence of transportation because such offenders were perceived as being more experienced criminals. This was particularly the case with pickpocketing. In 1815, in two separate cases, a fifteen-year-old, Levy Burnard, and a sixteen-year-old, Samuel Forster, were sentenced to life transportation for picking the pocket of an unknown person.[11]

Once again the evidence implies that young male offenders stood to be transported on a far narrower range of offences than their adult counterparts. Thus older prisoners were more likely to be transported for serious larcenies such as burglary, robbery and the theft of livestock. Moreover, it is necessary to incorporate the statistics of juvenile transportation into the context of the debate on reformation and the rationale of colonial remodelling. Hence juvenile boys were likely to be sentenced to transportation because of their youth and their potential rather than simply as a punitive mechanism. Amongst the boys interviewed on the *Euryalus*, many expressed indifference about transportation, some admitted to fear, and indeed some viewed transportation as a new start, preferring removal to the 'bay' to staying in England:

'Does not regret . . . going abroad . . . has a brother at the Bay – has been there about 2 years – heard he was at his trade & doing well . . . they were talking all night long about the bay – said he did not care about it – all he had to say against was the shortness of food – the work was nothing to him did not mind it – Anxious to be away – most everyone is glad to be out of the country' – William Johnson

'go abroad rather than go back to my bad companions' – Bowen

'go abroad cause do not want to bide in my country' – McEwen

'all expect to be lagged – make up their mind to it & wish to keep it up as long as they can – would as soon go out of the country' – L. Lloyd.[12]

The juvenile penal colony in Van Diemen's Land, Point Puer, had been established in 1834. During the late 1830s and 1840s over 1,200 young male convicts were sent there, travelling in specially appointed juvenile convict ships. On these ships, and at Point Puer, the strategies of separation were

---

10 *OBSP*, fourth session, 1802, no. 376, p. 235; second session, 1834, nos 223–4, pp. 149–50.
11 Ibid. first session, 1815, nos 57–8, p. 35.
12 PRO, HO 73/16, rough notebooks iii, iv, v.

continued in an attempt to avert the corruption of young boys by adult convicts. According to work carried out by Kim Humphery on juvenile transportation between 10,000 and 13,000 convicts aged eighteen and under were sent to Van Diemen's Land in the period 1803–53. About 90 per cent of them were boys. During the 1830s juveniles formed around 20 per cent of all convicts arriving in Van Diemen's Land – a figure that was, because of Point Puer, slightly higher than that for New South Wales, where juveniles accounted for more like 15 per cent.[13] Point Puer had taken over from the juvenile barracks in Sydney, Carters Barracks, which had closed in 1833. Throughout its lifetime (until 1849) Point Puer employed a variety of reformatory techniques, utilising separation and silence as well as discipline, occupation and Benthamite architecture.

As in Britain, the separation of juveniles from adults was double-edged. On the one hand it removed the children from exposure to corruption, on the other hand it categorised them as a problem in their own right. Thus in Australia too, young offenders could be viewed as being worse than their adult counterparts. Governor Arthur referred to such boys as 'a corrupt fraternity of little depraved Felons'.[14] Punishment was carried out with regularity within the colony. Charles O'Hara Booth, the superintendent of Point Puer, submitted a detailed report on the prison to the 1838 Select Committee on Transportation:

> The most trivial crime or irregularity is not permitted to pass without punishment in proportion to the degree or nature of the offence, which consists in confinement to the muster ground during cessation from labour, where no amusement is allowed, and the boys so confined are required to do the duties of scavengers. The next grade of punishment where a more refractory spirit is evinced, is to be placed in a cell immediately labour ceases, and receive their meals therein, where no talking or noise is permitted; they also sleep in them, but attend school, and are confined until they manifest a disposition to amendment.[15]

Apparently, corporal punishment was not resorted to 'until every means to reform have been tried without effect'.[16] However, an investigation into the boys' conduct registers – recorded due to a innovatory exercise by Governor Arthur – portrays a regime where both physical punishment and techniques of deprivation were used for a number of misdemeanours. Boys frequently spent time in solitary confinement, fed only on a diet of bread and water. A beating on the breech was also common, as was hard labour. Sentences could

---

[13] K. Humphery, 'Objects of compassion: young male convicts in Van Diemen's Land, 1834–50', *Australian Historical Studies* (Apr. 1992), 13–33, esp. pp. 13, 17.
[14] Cited ibid. 19.
[15] Ibid. 21.
[16] Ibid.

be extended, and boys who offended whilst they were indentured could be sent back to Point Puer.

The conduct registers initiated by Lieutenant-Governor Arthur ran from 1827 to 1843, and retrospectively to 1803, recording the convict's offences since their arrival in the colony and details of their conviction and behaviour prior to embarkation at Van Diemen's Land.[17] Certainly, solitary confinement was used extensively. For example, the record of seventeen-year-old Frederick Arnold, transported in 1836 for the theft of a handkerchief shows the following offences:[18]

July 22 1837:	Absconding	Existing sentence extended for 12 months, 25 lashes, & returned to Govt.
Oct 4 1837:	Absent without leave	4 days solitary confinement
Jan 8 1838:	Absent from barracks	6 days in cell, on bread and water
Sept 9 1839:	Absent from church muster	solitary confinement on bread and water
Nov 15 1839:	Being drunk	5 days in cell, on bread and water
Aug 26 1840:	Dancing in a public house	in cells, on bread and water
Feb 3 1821:	Neglect of duty	3 days in cells, on bread and water

Henry Underwood was placed in solitary confinement for a number of 'offences'. For example, for talking at the muster, for improper conduct at school, on suspicion of secreting potatoes, and for fishing on the rocks contrary to orders, he was each time put in solitary confinement for three or four days. After further 'insubordination' Henry's sentence was extended by one year.[19] In general solitary confinement was used in preference to physical punishment; mental and physical deprivation was thought more effective than the birch. Thomas Wontner was convinced that a boy would take a flogging rather than any other punishment: 'I have ever observed the boys have become bold, daring, and hardened, in proportion as they have undergone the most corporal punishment.'[20] On the whole physical punishment was resorted to when other punishments seemed to have failed. James Gavagan

17 AOT, Con 31. The primary purpose of these volumes was to record the behaviour of the convict whilst he underwent his sentence in the colony. The registers were kept for Van Diemen's Land between 1803 and 1843. Those referred to in this chapter are those which survive for a number of the boys interviewed by Miles, most of whom were transported to Van Diemen's Land between 1835 and 1837.
18 AOT, Con 31/2, no. 706, conduct register of Frederick Arnold.
19 AOT, Con 31/44, no. 31, conduct register of Henry Underwood.
20 Wontner, *Old Bailey experience*, 295.

was beaten for continued absenteeism.[21] Henry Underwood was transported in May 1836 and, as mentioned earlier, was placed in solitary confinement several times. But 1839 he was increasingly chastised physically rather than mentally. Thus in February he received '25 stripes on the breech' for insolence, in July he received twenty-five stripes for disorderly conduct, and by 1840 another incidence of insolence resulted in fourteen days hard labour in chains.[22] George Hickman, too, transported at the same time as Henry Underwood, was punished with solitary confinement or hard labour until 1838 when his behaviour worsened and he received a 'dozen lashes' for general misconduct and thirty-six lashes for violently assaulting another prisoner.[23] The registers indicate a long battle with authority by many of the boys. Thefts, neglect of duty, disobedience, drunkenness, gambling and absence leave a trail of confrontation and resistance throughout the boy's penal life. Whilst most boys were indentured soon after they arrived in Van Diemen's Land, they were very much convict workers, still subject to rules and regulations, and liable to be sent back to the penal colony. Essentially, until a convict received his pardon or ticket-of-leave, he remained policed in what was effectively a police state.

Increasingly, however, during the 1830s and 1840s, the gap between the juvenile and the penitentiary ideal was stressed. Hence juveniles should have their own system of justice, and the emphasis should be on reform rather than penality. Thus the language of transportation was gradually translated into the language of colonial emigration. Boys went to Parkhurst to be 'trained' for the colonies. No longer were they part of a criminal conglomerate merely transplanting to the other side of the world. Instead they were the new hope. Transportation was no longer a punishment, but a 'chance' for them to put the past behind them and start again:

> To transport them immediately, without having previously trained them to labour and endeavouring to instil into them habits of industry, is to burthen a colony with a worthless and a useless set of vagabonds. I therefore suggest that the destitute juvenile offenders, as well as the frequently re-committed juvenile thief, should be trained to work in this country; the one should be subsequently transported, the other subjected to compulsory emigration.[24]

The same ideology was extended to the many other semi-delinquent, orphaned or neglected children who populated the refuges, workhouses and houses of correction. As already described, by the mid nineteenth century a number of institutions were sending children abroad, not only to Australia, but also to Canada and South Africa. The Children's Friend Society, under the auspices of Captain Brenton, had been sending delinquent and neglected

---

[21] AOT, Con 31/16, no. 1148, conduct register of James Gavagan.
[22] AOT, Con 31/44, no. 31, conduct register of Henry Underwood.
[23] AOT, Con 31/21, no. 2059, conduct register of George Hickman.
[24] Miles, *Poverty*, 51.

children abroad since 1834; so did Parkhurst from 1838, and the London Ragged School Union from 1848. The Philanthropic Society also had its own juvenile emigration scheme during the same period. The ideology of colonial emigration fitted well with the need for British stock in the colonies. Children were thought better subjects for emigration, and they became the raw material upon which a colonial identity could be based. Increasingly, with the realisation of the strategic and political implications of emigration, there was some selectivity, and a growing emphasis on preparatory vocational training, such as had been practised at Captain Brenton's rural Hackney Wick Academy. As Elaine Hadley has pointed out, by the 1840s and 1850s it was no longer possible to send untrained children of dubious morality, since the colonies had begun to establish the roots of social stability.[25]

In 1852 Captain William J. Williams, the inspector of prisons, examined a number of boys in the Middlesex house of correction, at Westminster, judging them in terms of background and the degree to which they were 'hardened'. These boys were referred to Williams by the chaplain and governor; he in turn recommended them to the Philanthropic Society school for reformatory training, and thence to the colonies. One eleven-year-old boy had been four times in prison, three times in Tothill Fields, and once in Coldbath Fields:

I have been thieving three or four years. I went to school near Oxford-street. I first began to steal apples with other boys, and then to pick pockets, being taught by my elder brother how to do it . . . My mother has tried to keep me in, and has beat me; my step-father drinks. At times I have got clear off with as many handkerchiefs as I could carry, stowing them away in my trousers, and down my legs.

This boy was recommended to the Philanthropic Society. He was keen to go abroad and, according to Captain Williams, 'He has been wholly led away by his elder brother, and would, I think, if well looked after, and his peculiar disposition studied and treated accordingly, turn out well, or perhaps better than well.' Another boy, who told a sorry catalogue of death, drunkenness and neglect, was 'most willing to go to the school, and go abroad. I will conform most willingly to the rules.' Fortunately Williams concurred with this recommendation: 'I unhesitatingly recommend this boy for the school. His conduct in prison has been good. It is altogether a very sad case, his lapse from rectitude being clearly traceable to his father's misconduct.'[26]

It seems probable that the prison authorities were keen to 'sell' the idea of colonial emigration as opposed to transportation. By removing the patina of punishment, and grafting on ideas of colonialism and empire, transportation was transformed into a process that demanded that children show willingness and keenness to go abroad and to make a new start. In short, it demanded that these children rise above their situations:

25 Hadley, 'Natives', 423.
26 SC Criminal Juveniles, PP, 1852, vii, appendix 1, pp. 392–3.

'I wish to get out of this life, and would be most glad to do anything that would get me out of it. I promise to behave well, and would be glad to go abroad; my father would very much like me to go.'

'I wish, indeed, to quit this life; I would be happy to go to a school, and be very glad, indeed, to go abroad.'

'I want to leave off thieving; I would willingly go to the Philanthropic, and go abroad; I will be honest; I really want to get away from thieving.' [27]

These boys were all recommended to the Philanthropic, others were referred only grudgingly. Of one boy it was said: 'it is a doubtful case; but he pleads hard, and declares himself resolved to do better, and is quite willing to go abroad; he also seems much impressed with the dread of transportation, which he is well aware will be the consequence of his next conviction'.[28] The choice that was given to these children was clear: change your behaviour, turn your back on crime, go abroad now, with training, start afresh, be treated as a child; or carry on offending, carry on being punished, be transported, be treated as an adult. Certainly, some of the boys had little desire to go abroad: 'when I get out I shall go home; I do not want to go to a school, nor will I go abroad'. Williams could only express resignation: 'This boy's determination is so strong neither to enter a school or go abroad, that nothing is left but to allow him to follow his own course.'[29] Another lad was keen to go to the Philanthropic, but Williams could not recommend him:

> This boy came into prison dressed like a gentleman; he is very anxious to be sent to the Philanthropic; if he does not go he will be most certainly transported; he is extremely intelligent and acute; he has formed very dangerous connexions with a class of thieves very superior to the ordinary herd of juvenile offenders, as is shown by the description of his depredations. He will be remarkable either for good or evil, but on well weighing all the circumstances of the case, the experiment appears too hazardous for me to recommend a trial.[30]

Essentially, with the decline of transportation and the entrenchment of colonial emigration, there came a reaffirmation of classification, representing a further reconceptualisation of the poor. From the colonists' point of view, a destitute child was preferable to a delinquent child. These labels were convenient in that they could be thrown together or torn asunder as the situation merited. Within institutions, the differences between delinquent and destitute youth were often nominal. Certainly the reformatory school, or Parkhurst, may have been more punitive than the industrial school, or farm-school, but in terms of removal and uniformity the differences were minimal.

---

27 Ibid. 396–9.
28 Ibid. 397.
29 Ibid. 402.
30 Ibid. 401–2.

Yet once they were being promoted as New World stock, the differences became crucial. As Elaine Hadley has asked: 'were they criminals deserving of punitive transportation or paupers in need of the benefits of emigration? Were they slave labourers or British subjects deserving of protection? Were they hardened adults or impressionable children?'[31] Despite the stress on vocational training and aftercare – the welfare-orientated approach to juvenile justice – child emigration schemes encountered a constant barrage of criticism. Indeed, this criticism has pursued the subject of child migration throughout the following 150 years, and only now, in the late twentieth century, are the tangled legacies of its reality coming to light. Brenton's scheme for colonial emigration was one of the earliest nineteenth-century attempts at child migration, and to some extent served as a model for ensuing schemes.[32] However his methods, carried out under the auspices of the Children's Friend Society, were also a target of attack.[33] Brenton himself was particularly critical of his competitors. In his 1834 publication, *Observations on the training and education of Children in Great Britain*, he had little to say in favour of prison, reformatory school or of the juvenile hulk the *Euryalus*, and much to say of his own ideas:

> that thousands of poor children, instead of hundreds, may be trained to virtuous industry, is to prove that the Youth of this empire, and consequently adults, have been ruined by the very means employed for their reformation. . . . Increase of crime, and consequent necessity for Punishment, have been produced by the neglect and mismanagement of those who have had charge of the 'Children of the Poor'.[34]

Brenton perceptively made links between the workhouse and the prison, and recognised the need to avoid the creation of what was fearfully conceptualised as the 'criminal class of tomorrow'. However, despite what he claimed to be his 'visionary, flowery, utopian' ideas, the tables were soon turned on him and his organisation.[35]

Brenton's society was very much a commercial experiment, as well as a charitable one. There was an emphasis on supplying youthful labour, and

31 Hadley, 'Natives', 415.
32 For Edward Pelham Brenton (1774–1839) see *DNB* ii. 12–13; E. P. Brenton, *The Bible and the spade, or Captain Brenton's account of the rise and progress of the Children's Friend Society*, London 1837; Brenton, *Observations*, and, *A letter to the Rt Hon. R. W. Horton shewing the impolicy, inefficiency, and ruinous consequences of emigration and the advantage of home colonies by Edward. P. Brenton – esq – Capt. R.N*, London 1830. See also the account of the Children's Friend Society agricultural teacher, Charles Forss, *Practical remarks upon the education of the working classes; with an account of the plan pursued under the superintendence of the Children's Friend Society at the Brenton Asylum, Hackney Wick*, London 1835.
33 See, for example, the editorial on 'Children's kidnapping society' in *The Times*, 5 Apr. 1839, 4, col. b. For a full list of references in *The Times* to Brenton and the Society see Blackburn, *Children's Friend Society*, 303–5.
34 Brenton, *Observations*, p. vi.
35 Ibid. p. xiii.

indeed the majority of Brenton's children went either to the newly settled Western Australia, where labour was needed to consolidate the burgeoning population, or to the Cape. Accusations of bad practice followed the scheme. In Africa, reports spoke of children being treated like slave labour, or sold like animals. The sale of children to would-be employers was known amongst the children as 'the white cattle market'.[36] William Tozer wrote to his father from the Cape in April 1838, commenting that 'when us boys come in this country we are sold for £7.10.0 that is in dutch money 100 rix dollars'.[37] Meanwhile, in Britain, it was argued that the colonies would be corrupted by sending over children with criminal backgrounds. Whilst Brenton argued that the vast majority of the children were poor and destitute but not criminal, his claim was patently untrue. Significant numbers of children were sent by magistrates to the Children's Friend Society. Of the sixty-nine Middlesex children who were subjects of petitions in 1838-9, fifteen were awaiting emigration via the Children's Friend Society.[38] For the children themselves, these schemes had mixed benefits. Clearly, as Captain Williams's evidence suggests, for some children emigration, and even transportation, was a relief, a chance to start again. For others it was a fearful prospect. With little or no chance to assert themselves, 'abroad' was yet another place to endure. For instance, the children displayed a variety of responses to colonial emigration. Letters from children at the Cape exhibit a number of feelings and emotions from fear, to pleasure, to excitement, at what was a very alien environment. William Tozer had little favourable to say about his position on arrival in the Cape:

> The first master I had he half starved me and the whole time I was there that was four months he never gave me no clothes and I must work that . . . my body and I left him four times and came to Mr Christian and he would not hear what I say to an englishman. Bring me to him and then he say he shall see that my master should do good for me and then he send me to my master and then he gave me 30 lashes with a shambung and then they made fast in a room for one week and when I got loose I went to the magistrate to complain.[39]

Another boy, William Henry Bay, wrote to his mother in 1838 complaining about his bad situation:

> I am learning no trade, but am only a servant, at which I was very much disapointed, and have not the best of masters. I am neither found in caps or shoes, from which I feel great inconvenience; and this is not all I have to encounter, for, on the other hand, I am placed amongst a parcel of slaves, and not thought much better of by the master nor by the slaves themselves, as there is no difference made between us.[40]

---

36 Cited in Bradlow, 'Children's Friend Society', 162.
37 Blackburn, *Children's Friend Society*, 236.
38 PRO, HO 19/8, 1838–9.
39 Cited in Blackburn, *Children's Friend Society*, 236.
40 Ibid. 2.

The problems of cultural assimilation were starkly apparent. Children had to come to terms with the difference of their masters and neighbours, as well as of the native slaves. A girl called Margaret wrote to Mrs Bourhill at the Royal Victoria Asylum: 'Now I will tell you about the Caffres – they are as black as can be, they wear nothing but a skin, even the king of them wears the same, only when they come out to town.'[41] The variety of experiences that faced these children on their arrival in the Cape – the elements of Dutch, German and African culture, the hard work, the heat and starkly different environmental conditions – made a number of children reflect upon their past life in Britain. As a fifteen-year-old boy commented in a letter written to his mother in 1835:

> I sometimes do not know what to do with myself, If I think of my conduct to you when I was in England, but I hope John does not take an example from his brother, but keeps the Fourth Commandment better than I have done.[42]

According to reformers the strongest argument for the transportation of juvenile offenders, and the colonial emigration of both offenders and children at risk, was what they saw as the ubiquitous problem of recidivism. The relationship between those children who reoffended and their ability to reform was a constant issue in working out the strategies of punishment and reformation that have been described.

Reoffending and reformation

> Dreadful, therefore, is the situation of the young offender: he becomes the victim of circumstances over which he has no control. The laws of his country operate not to restrain, but to punish, him. The tendency of the police is to accelerate his career in crime. If, when apprehended, he has not attained the full measure of guilt, the nature of his confinement is almost sure to complete it; and discharged, as he frequently is, pennyless, without friends, character, or employment, he is driven, for a subsidence, to the renewal of depredations.[43]

In 1815 the committee formed to investigate metropolitan juvenile delinquency was well aware of the paradoxical relationship between offending, prison, punishment and reformation. Whilst it sought to remove the child from what it understood as the corrupting influence of his or her home environment, and the perils of peer pressure, the very institutions to which convicted children were sent only added to the process of recidivism. The problem of reoffending came increasingly into focus throughout the early nineteenth century. Whilst it undoubtedly underpinned the organisation of

41 Ibid. 226.
42 Ibid. 232.
43 Report . . . juvenile delinquency in the metropolis, 25.

classification systems, particularly the division of juveniles into 'perishing' and 'dangerous', it was also recognised in the legislation. Hence, the Vagrancy Acts had historically been informed by an essential belief in the 'career criminal'.[44] The Vagrancy Act of 1824 made it a criminal offence to be a 'reputed thief'.[45] Finally, the Habitual Criminals Act of 1869 gave full vent to the idea of a criminal class and the professional criminal.[46] However, this legislation could not possibly supply any real picture of the extent of reoffending. Rather, instead of assessing the relationship between recidivism and custody, it added more strength to the belief that there was a class of 'hardened' offenders, for whom little could be done. Throughout the decades before the mid century, institutions increasingly tried to get some idea of their inmates' offending behaviour prior to their present conviction. There was a recognition that indicted crime was not the true story of an inmates 'career', that many people had been processed summarily, and hence might have charges for vagrancy and disorderly behaviour for example. The register of boys in Parkhurst prison from 1838 made some attempt to assess their inmates' 'character'.[47] Of 596 Middlesex boys the character of 25 per cent was unknown, 12 per cent were good or well-behaved previously, 10 per cent were dull, tolerable or bad, and 53 per cent (313 boys) had been convicted previously. Concentrating on this latter group of boys, 68 per cent had been convicted at least once (this includes both those boys where it is stated that they have only been convicted once, and those boys who were said to have been convicted 'frequently' or 'often'); 21 per cent twice; 5 per cent three times; 2 per cent four times; and 3 per cent five times. Of the remaining 1 per cent, three boys had been convicted six times; one boy seven times; two boys eight times; and one boy had been convicted an astounding ten times. Hence, 33 per cent of these boys, at least, had been convicted more than once.

These boys included seventeen-year-old George Taylor, who had been received at Parkhurst in April 1848.[48] George had been convicted at the Middlesex sessions, at Clerkenwell, in November of the previous year for stealing a pair of boots. He had no trade, and could read and write only a little. George had previously been convicted of felony ten times, and was this time sentenced to seven years' transportation. He was sent to Van Diemen's Land in August 1852. Similarly Patrick Barry, aged sixteen, entered Parkhurst in November 1848.[49] Patrick had been convicted of pickpocketing

---

[44] Sharpe, *Crime in early modern England*, 100–3.
[45] Magarey, 'Invention', 20.
[46] Habitual Criminals Act, 32 & 33 Vict. c.99 (1869). See also Emsley, *Crime and society*, 133, 135.
[47] The following information, extracted from the Parkhurst prison register (PRO, HO 24/15, 1838–63), is based on the details of Middlesex boys only, for the period from December 1838 to November 1848.
[48] Ibid. received into Parkhurst on 17 Apr. 1848.
[49] Ibid. received on 21 Nov. 1848.

at the Middlesex sessions in June 1848 and sentenced to transportation for ten years. Patrick was a labourer with little literacy, who had previously been convicted five times of felony, and three times of a misdemeanour. He was sent to Western Australia in July 1851. The nature of the conviction (i.e. for felony or by summary proceedings) was supplied in the case of 114 boys. Of these 11 per cent had been convicted summarily, 78 per cent for felony, and 11 per cent had both felony and summary convictions. For example, fifteen-year-old Samuel Dobson who had entered Parkhurst in April 1848, had been convicted twice of felony, once for assault, and once for vagrancy.[50] Not surprisingly, the older the child, the more convictions he had. In terms of the type of crime for which children had been convicted (leading to their imprisonment in Parkhurst rather than previous convictions), of the whole sample of 596 boys, 93 per cent were convicted for larcenies. Their offences ranged from simple larceny to larceny from the person, and larceny by the servant. Other boys were convicted of serious larceny, such as burglary, indirect property crime, crimes against the person and miscellaneous felony. John O'Connor, aged thirteen, had been sentenced to seven years transportation at the Middlesex sessions in March 1845 for the theft of two books.[51] John had previously been convicted twice as a reputed thief. Sixteen-year-old chair-maker William Gibbs (alias Smith) entered Parkhurst in January 1848, convicted of larceny with a previous conviction, and a charge of burglary.[52] He was passed on to the Hampshire county police in November of the same year. Nevertheless, the overwhelming message from these figures supports the findings from the Middlesex criminal registers that the vast majority of children were convicted and imprisoned for comparatively minor crime.

Of those boys known to have been convicted before, seventy-three had previously been in custody in one form or another, 67 per cent at least once, 25 per cent twice, 4 per cent three times, 3 per cent four times, and 1 per cent five times. For example, fourteen-year-old John Hurley had been in prison five times before.[53] This time he had been found guilty of stealing a wooden bowl at the Middlesex sessions at Clerkenwell in December 1845. He was transported to Western Australia in October 1848. One boy had not only had a previous period of imprisonment in Parkhurst, but had been transported before. This was sixteen-year-old George Gales who had been convicted of larceny by the servant at the Central Criminal Court in August 1847.[54] George, a shoemaker, received another sentence of transportation and was sent to Van Diemen's Land in March 1850. Whilst these figures can show only a limited picture of reoffending they do imply a causal relationship between imprisonment and reoffending. The Parkhurst solution presented

---

50 Ibid. received on 17 Apr. 1848.
51 Ibid. received on 24 May 1845.
52 Ibid. received on 17 Apr. 1848.
53 Ibid. received on 11 Dec. 1845.
54 Ibid. received on 2 Mar. 1848.

the ultimate solution, the experience of reformatory custody, followed by transportation to the colonies.

It hardly needs stressing that colonial emigration, along with institutional-based regimes at home, was suffused with the concept of reformation. All but the very 'hardened' prisoners were felt to have the potential to reform; and to the extent illustrated in the reformatory schemes, both the state and the philanthropist were prepared to encourage that potential. Whilst many contemporary commentators were determined to portray criminals as a subclass who were irrecoverably hardened, a few enlightened individuals did make the link between lack of employment and crime, and the ideas of such people did occasionally surface into the mainstream of penal thinking.[55] The components of reformation have already been explored, resting largely as they did on religious and moral training, occupational training, limited education and separation from their previous, tainted environments. This separation, as should be clear, was often seen as literally geographical rather than merely physical. Whilst a number of the young offenders who were interviewed expressed willingness to reform, the reality was that reoffending rates were high. In 1852 a return of boys under seventeen committed to Middlesex houses of correction showed a depressing tendency towards reconviction. For example, in Westminster house of correction, as far as could be ascertained, 698 out of 1,987 boys had been previously committed, 152 of these four times or more. This was despite the 'improvements' of the previous seventeen years. In 1835 Chesterton had cited from a report of the Glasgow Bridewell to the Select Committee on Gaols. According to this report, which supported the move towards longer sentences, the prisoners sent for fourteen days had a 75 per cent chance of returning, those sent for thirty days a 60 per cent chance . . . and so on with the recommittal rate decreasing as the sentence length increased. The report omitted to point out that this was not necessarily due to the effectiveness of longer sentences, but rather to the fact that long-term imprisonment took away the physical means of offending.[56] The reasons for the high rates of recidivism were generally put down to the temptations and corruption provided by former companions, although undoubtedly unemployment and poverty played a major role, particularly given that it could be difficult to hide a prison record: 'it fixes too dark a stain on their characters'.[57]

For the boys interviewed c. 1836, there was an understandable ambivalence about reformation. Certainly a number of them expressed a willingness to reform, perhaps to learn a trade or to go abroad. Yet a number of the boys

[55] Such as the members of the Prison Discipline Society, or individuals such as Mary Carpenter, Matthew Davenport Hill or the Revd Sydney Turner.
[56] SC *Criminal Juveniles*, PP, 1852, vii, appendixes 2, 3, pp. 388–9; SC *Gaols*, PP, 1835, 1st Report, xi. 93.
[57] *Select Committee of House of Lords*, PP, 1847, evidence of Justice Coltman, cited in Carpenter, *Reformatory schools*, 303.

thought that the chance of them reforming was hopeless. Some of the boys who were moved from prison to Brenton's Academy or to the Philanthropic Society to embark on a programme of reformation did not find it to their liking. Michael Skully, a fifteen-year-old from Marylebone convicted of stealing a ten-shilling spoon, told Miles that he had spent some time at Captain Brenton's. He had spent about a month there, with the aim of going abroad: 'thought Captain Brenton would send him out – found it was no use to expect it and left him – there were other boys thought the same as he did'.[58] John Leary, who had been committed to Newgate several times, had little time for the Philanthropic Society: 'becoming restless under the restraint of its discipline, he effected an escape in a very daring manner by climbing up a chimney'.[59] He was eventually transported for life. As already noted, the Philanthropic Society had problems with inmates absconding.[60]

For some children, then, there was a constant conflict with authority that made reformation impossible. Certain children, such as John Leary, were labelled trouble-makers, and thus spent considerable time living up to their label. For other juvenile offenders the temptations of a life of crime proved too much. Rowland Bassett, a sixteen-year-old from Shoreditch, was released from Coldbath Fields, only to steal again, to pay some money he owed for a pair of trousers from the tally shop.[61] Many of the boys felt that as soon as they left prison they would offend again, if not through choice, then through the persuasions of their companions:

'as to reforming, I think many of the boys might get a place and wish for one, but it would only be for a day or two in order to rob their employers' – Samuel Holmes – thirteen

'no boy who has ever been a thief would turn honest – might get into a place but it would only be for a sound opportunity to rob his master' – Henry Thompson – sixteen

'Boys will not reform – the only way is to do away with the fences, penny plays, and gambling – is the cause – gambling especially' – William Johnson

'I would not trust a thief – they can never turn right – if they get a place it would be to run away after a month or so with any thing they could get hold of – as for myself I would rather go abroad – I have no friends and if I was to get into a place I should be enticed away again' – William Cook – fifteen.[62]

58 PRO, HO 73/16, notebook 1, evidence of Michael Skully.
59 Beck, *Peter Bedford*, 26–7. This incident is also mentioned in the SC *Police*, PP, 1817, 231, 543, evidence of H. S. Cotton and H. G. Bennett respectively.
60 Carlebach, *Caring for children*, 10–11.
61 PRO, HO 73/16, notebook 1, evidence of R. Bassett.
62 Ibid. notebooks 1, 2, 3, evidence of Samuel Holmes, Henry Thompson, and William Cook; rough notebook iii, evidence of W. Johnson.

Ultimately, there was a certain inevitability to the cycle of crime. Few juvenile thieves carried on interminably. It is likely that for many of them the relinquishment of crime came as a product not of deliberate choice, but of maturity, the increase of responsibility, and this was especially the case amongst those fortunate enough to find some sort of secure employment. For those juveniles who did get caught the outcome was also fairly inevitable. Despite the emphasis upon willingness to reform and upon self-help, many children were trapped in a web of poverty and delinquency that was only compounded by the newer approaches to juvenile justice. The emphasis on institutional punishment, or reformation, stressed removal from corruption, but periods of imprisonment marked the child as a criminal, and made chances of regular employment even more remote. One young man interviewed c. 1836, 24-year-old William Hay, whilst older than the juvenile offenders with whom he was imprisoned in the City Bridewell, summed up the situation for the boys:

Upon my remarking to him that the evil Course of Life he was now pursuing would lead him to the Gallows or to Botany Bay, he exclaimed with great Animation, 'Well! Sir, and what am I to do? Nobody will give me a Shilling to buy a Meal of Victuals, nobody will give me a Bit of Food, nobody cares about me, nobody will give me a Character, and without a Character who will give me Work? I cannot starve, so I make a Shilling where I can get it, never mind how!'[63]

---

[63] Ibid. loose papers, Select Committee on Gaols (secret), 10.

Conclusion

Public anxiety, political debate and popular fascination have continued to reflect a preoccupation with the incidence and nature of juvenile crime, and a concern for the various ways and means by which this 'problem' could be solved. The systems of juvenile justice which have developed in the twentieth century are rooted in the separate categorisation of the juvenile criminal which evolved in the early nineteenth century. However, the concerns and anxieties of that period were not without precedent. Indeed there was a strong continuity in the debates about adolescent and disorderly youth which can be traced through the early modern period.[1] Even before that period, under Anglo-Saxon law, child delinquency was a matter for consideration:

The Laws of King Aethelstan [AD 924]
Council of Greatanlea
Of Thieves
1. First: that no thief be spared who may be taken 'handhaebbende', [i.e. with the goods in his hand] above XII. years, and above eight pence . . .

Judicia Civitatis Lundoniae
Twelfth:
1. . . . He then said, that it seemed to him, and to those who counselled with him, that no younger person should be slain than XV. years, except he should make resistance or flee, and would not surrender himself; that then he should be slain, as well for more as for less, whichever it might be. But if he be willing to surrender himself, let him be put into prison, as it was ordained at 'Greatanlea', and by the same let him be redeemed.[2]

Despite this, there can be little doubt that it was not until the early decades of the nineteenth century that a specific definition of the criminal child, particularly in legal discourse, really started to emerge. Then began the deluge of pamphlet literature, from organisations such as the Prison Discipline Society, for example. Then began the numerous parliamentary select committees concerned with policing and punishment. And by the mid nineteenth century, there had been enacted various measures concerned both peripherally and specifically with the trial and punishment of juvenile offenders, notably the Industrial and Reformatory Schools Acts.[3] Whilst the concept of a specific 'invention' of juvenile crime, as posited by Susan Magarey, Magaret May and Leon Radzinowicz, is perhaps inappropriate, it is true that in this period

---

1 Griffiths, *Youth and authority*.
2 Sanders, *Juvenile offenders*, 3–4.
3 See bibliography for a list of the relevant parliamentary committees.

public concern and political anxiety combined to influence the treatment of, and attitudes to, juvenile offenders over that century and into the next.[4]

Moreover, it seems clear that this concern was born of the growing perception that juvenile crime was increasing. Yet criminal statistics are, of course, notoriously difficult to interpret, and, while indictments of children did increase, their importance lies not in any 'truth' which they might hold as to the increase of such crime, but rather in the way in which the perceived rise of crime combined with public concern and action to produce a recognisable watershed in the long history of juvenile delinquency. London played a central role in the conceptualisation of juvenile crime; a close association was made in the minds of contemporaries between the social problems of the metropolis and the rise of juvenile crime. The mythology of the 'criminal underworld', the subterranean world of the 'criminal classes' was historically associated with London. According to popular lore and literature there existed in London the dark alleys, the alsatias, the rookeries, which housed the criminal poor; a criminal poor which thrived on the vast display of wealth and consumerism provided by the capital. Moreover, London's youthful population, and the ubiquitousness of institutions for the criminal and the poor, meant that the delinquencies of children were perhaps more visible, more remarked upon, than in other settings. However, despite the centrality of London to this study, the history it describes has a national relevance. Certainly there were differences in the nature and incidence of juvenile crime in provincial towns. For example, discussion of juvenile offending in northern textile towns such as Manchester and Salford were tied much more strongly into political and class fears, and into contemporary concerns with child employment.[5] However, the concentration on urban Middlesex is indicative of the role that metropolitan crime undeniably played in shaping the fears and expression of both official and unofficial commentary.[6]

During the early nineteenth century, a combination of factors led to more indictments of juveniles, more imprisoned juveniles, and more transported juveniles. It has been argued here that the very combination of rising indictments, the growing trend towards custody (not forgetting those children who were placed within institutions through summary processing), together with the use of transportation and colonial emigration, resulted in a situation where many more children than previously were incorporated into the criminal justice system. Moreover, because of changing definitions of criminality, and changing legal demarcations, children who previously had been dealt with fairly informally were henceforth exposed to a much more formal, disci-

---

4   Magarey, 'Invention'; May, 'Innocence and experience'; Radzinowicz and Hood, *Emergence of penal policy*.
5   Pearson, *Hooligans*, 156–82.
6   However, an article by Peter King will use comparative provincial information from Gloucestershire, Berkshire, Shropshire, Bristol and Lancashire: 'The rise of juvenile delinquency in England, 1780–1840', *Past and Present* clx (1998), 116–66.

plined and punitive process. The changing treatment of criminal children was to a large extent generated by changing attitudes to youth and adolescence, to the working classes, and to the working out of notions of reformation which were closely tied into education, occupation and religion. Whilst it was not until the mid nineteenth century that the division between 'dangerous' and 'perishing' juveniles was formalised in the context of the reformatory and industrial schools, this ethos pervaded much of the discussion and handling of criminal children throughout the years between 1790 and 1850. This can be seen, for example, in the division of the Philanthropic Society inmates into the Reform (for what Mary Carpenter would by the mid century call 'dangerous' juveniles) and the Manufactory (for the 'perishing'). Thus in terms of the official development of policy on juvenile crime, the key words could be 'culmination' and 'codification'. Hence the 1820s, 1830s and 1840s saw a culmination of concerns and fears, and the codification of such issues into a complex legal apparatus for processing juvenile crime. This was not a simple linear progression. Rather it was the product of a variety of complex, and frequently confused debates, and an often torpid search for a suitable penal strategy. A lack of willingness to overlook the crimes of children, combined with the decreasing use of acquittal verdicts and the growth of secondary punishments, implies a conscious inclination to draw children into the criminal justice system, suggesting that to some extent the problem of juvenile crime was exacerbated, though not created, by the policy-makers of the time. This becomes even more apparent when the offences for which juveniles were being imprisoned and transported are considered; for the vast majority of juvenile offenders were indicted for petty and minor crime.

Whilst this study has sketched the development of penal policy and the emergence of the pamphlet literature that was concerned with juvenile crime in the early nineteenth century, its strongest endeavour has been to humanise the juvenile offender. No account of historic juvenile crime has paid any real attention to researching these offenders as children who commit and are accused of crime, rather than as one group within a panoply of criminal offenders. It is worth remembering that the subjects of historical research, whether they be working-class, middle-class or upper-class, whether children or adults, had an existence, an identity, a name.[7] Too often the reader is left with little impression of the lives with which the research has supposedly been concerned. In the case of juvenile crime in particular the pamphlet literature is so broad and so pervasive that it is perhaps understandable that historians have tended to perpetuate the characterisations and perceptions of social commentators and policy-makers rather than try to get under the skin of the offenders themselves. In truth, any reconstruction of the lives

---

[7] Recent work on the history of crime has begun to rectify this. See, for example, Davies, 'Youth gangs'; Linebaugh, *London hanged*; Gatrell, *Hanging tree*; G. Walker, 'Women, theft, and the world of stolen goods', in J. Kermode and G. Walker (eds), *Women, crime, and the courts in early modern England*, London 1994, 81–105.

of juvenile offenders is bound to be circumscribed. The nature of the surviving sources means that these lives are being constantly viewed through the
lens of their criminality. In a sense, the only reconstruction possible is that of
criminal lives. However, such experiences were not, as contemporaries often
expressed, generally peculiar to juvenile offenders, but were typical of the
lives of many working-class children.

For example, many working-class children experienced problems at home,
exacerbated by poor housing, ill health, unemployment, the drudgery of
menial and often erratic work, and limited educational opportunities.
Fourteen-year-old James Edwards, who was found guilty of burglary at the
Central Criminal Court in March 1835, lived and committed his crime
around Kingland Road, Hackney. Here he lived with his mother, a clog-
maker. His father had left, and since then James's mother had taken to drink.
Her situation was no doubt worsened by worry over James (who had previously spent time in prison) and about his brother who was on board the
Euryalus under sentence of transportation. James had two other siblings, a
married sister and another brother still at home. He had had some limited
education, attending a national school. However he could neither read nor
write. Clearly he felt thieving to be a remunerative occupation, considering
between 8s. and 10s. 'a middling day's work'. The family were on the verge of
destitution, making up a meagre income by a variety of methods. All the
family went out begging, James sang and sold matches. His mother also made
extra money by purchasing old leather from a bellows shop in Bethnal Green
and after cleaning it, selling it on to a Shoreditch shoemaker for 9d. or 1s.[8]
This story of debilitation, of poverty, of the makeshift strategies of the poor is
recognisable in a number of the sources. Countless tales in the records of
Euraylus and metropolitan prison interviews, in the *Old Bailey sessions papers*,
in *The Times*, in the accounts from social commentators, tell of similar sorry
circumstances. However criminal children could also emerge from far less
desperate situations, less meagre lives. For example, a boy identified only by
the initials G. W. was, like James, interviewed on the *Euryalus*. He too came
from Hackney, but there the similarity ends. Unlike James G. W. was from a
'highly respectable' background, and was 'well brought up'. Even so, he was
not immune to the same pleasures as his less 'worthy' comrades: 'The reason
of his committing the crime which reduced him to his present state was to
obtain money to indulge in those expensive habits which were induced by
the dissipated society he met at the theatres.'[9] This boy remained anonymous
since it was felt by Miles that to name him or to give any fuller details of his
background and parents would result in him being 'branded and marked'.[10]

Despite the contemporary representation of negligent, even cruel parents,
the situation of many parents was often one marked by frustration, sadness

[8] PRO, HO 73/16, notebook 1.
[9] Ibid. notebook 3.
[10] Ibid.

and desperation. As the father of James Scott, a twelve-year-old boy sentenced to transportation for the theft of a gown, stumblingly wrote to the Home Secretary in 1835: 'your Honer this is the humble petition of a broken hearted father for the loss of his boy James Scott who was sent away from him at the age of 12 yeares on the 22nd of . . . march for the term of seven yeares'.[11] Moreover, despite such grim tales of poverty and misery, the role of agency should not be overlooked. Whilst all too often historians, as well as contemporary commentators, paint a picture of an inexorable slide into crime, with little or no choice as to where their actions lead them, it should also be recognised that these children could make decisions of their own, and adopt particular strategies pertinent to their situations. Whilst circumstances often forced children into considering offending, they also offended for a variety of other reasons. Hence, peer pressure, street-life, adolescence and excitement were all factors which influenced a child's course in crime. The ubiquitous Henry Thompson pointed with some alacrity to the conflicting advantages and disadvantages of offending: 'money never does them any good – nor the Boys as fast as it comes it goes – comes like dirt and goes like dirt – father frequently told you – an honest shilling is worth 5 shilling stolen'.[12] Moreover, then as now, children of all classes pursued what can be roughly interpreted as delinquent behaviour and managed to move out of it relatively unscathed. Underlying the definition of criminal is the truism that a criminal only really becomes a criminal when he or she is caught and catalogued by the machinery of the law. Much of the behaviour that these children indulged in was understood by them as part of the normal, everyday, street scenery. The idea of professionalisation, of career criminality, is to a large extent an anomaly. Children did not generally make an active decision to become criminals; equally, most did not spend all their lives in the commission of crimes.

Certainly, however, the notion of criminal as victim should not be underestimated alongside the role of 'agency'. As this study has made clear, children involved in criminal offending in this period were at the mercy of a system that sought both to protect and punish them, but that ultimately created its own momentum, and hence created a legacy of the 'invention' of juvenile crime. From the mid nineteenth century, a more formal machinery of juvenile justice was put into place. Commentators like Mary Carpenter and Matthew Davenport Hill were increasingly recognised as juvenile crime professionals. Legislation was enacted that crystallised many of the developments and evolutionary processes of the preceding years. Consequently, the study of juvenile crime after 1850 has become one more closely focused on institutional histories, police court records and the records of social welfare agencies.

11 PRO, HO/84, Pv/36, petition of James Scott.
12 PRO, HO 73/16, rough notebook iii, evidence of Henry Thompson.

J. J. Tobias's study of nineteenth-century crime situated juvenile offenders in a context that supported much of the mythology and rhetoric of early nineteenth-century commentators: 'in the nineteenth century youngsters who were rejected and criticised by respectable society found acceptance and even praise in criminal society, whose standards they could meet by tales of real or imaginary crimes'.[13] In this study of juvenile crime before 1850 it has been shown that historians can no longer merely accept elite representations, but need to listen to the tales of real or imaginary crimes and very real punishments in the suprising range of records that still lie within reach.

---

[13] J. J. Tobias, *Crime and industrial society in the nineteenth century*, London 1967, 255.

APPENDIX 1

Interviews with Juvenile Offenders

It is axiomatic that, except in rare cases, authentic criminal autobiography does not exist.[1] The majority of everyday offenders did not leave written accounts of their lives and their offending. Does this necessarily preclude an understanding of offending from the offenders' point of view? Overwhelmingly, the answer has to be yes. Interviews conducted under the auspices of parliamentary investigation and inquiry, or in the course of criminal proceedings, are understandably skewed to the viewpoint of the individual who collates the material and to the fulfilment of a particular objective. However, such textual evidence should not be jettisoned completely. Whilst it is clear that it should be approached with caution, and with rigorous interrogation, it is possible to find source material which can help develop a greater understanding of the criminal 'careers' of offenders. For the purpose of this study material has been derived from various statements, interviews and accounts provided by juvenile offenders, mainly male, in the early to mid nineteenth century. That such accounts exist at all is a testament to the Victorian obsession with causation. Thus a number of interviews with juveniles were conducted as part of the investigations into the constabulary in the late 1830s. Around the same period a number of interviews were also conducted by William Augustus Miles, sometimes as part of the same constabulary commission, but also on his own initiative.

The sets of interviews, which are classed at the Public Record Office under HO 73/16 and HO 73/2 are closely related. Most of them derive from interviews that took place on the *Euryalus*, the juvenile hulk that was moored at Chatham between 1825 and 1843.[2] The other interviews come from metropolitan prisons, certainly Tothill Fields, and possibly Brixton.[3] Whilst the latter was not a Middlesex gaol, the boys interviewed offended as much north of the river as south. The *Euryalus* interviews were recorded largely by William Augustus Miles and fall into two groups. The first is a set of notebooks which were probably transcribed subsequently, and so are subject to the sorts of problems to be expected from selective accounts. They are largely in the first person, although occasionally the interviewer intervenes and the

---

[1] For a discussion of eighteenth- and nineteenth-century criminal biography see Bennett, *Oral history*; L. B. Faller, *Turned to account: the forms and functions of criminal biography in late seventeenth- and early eighteenth-century England*, Cambridge 1987; P. Rawlings, *Drunks, whores, and idle apprentices: criminal biographies of the eighteenth century*, London 1992.
[2] PRO, HO 73/16, notebooks 1, 2, 3; HO 73/16, rough notebooks iii, iv, v.
[3] PRO, HO73/2, pt 2, loose papers.

narrative transfers to second person. The second set of interviews were recorded by a variety of hands, although the most prominent is that of Miles. These interviews are extremely rough, and as far as can be ascertained are *verbatim*. They veer from the first person to the second. It is impossible to give exact references to these notebooks, since they are written and collated very roughly, on scrap paper, with no page numbering, precise dates or ages. However, many of these boys can be identified by a list submitted by J. H. Capper, the head of the hulks' establishment, to the 1835 Select Committee on Gaols.[4]

The prison interviews from Tothill Fields were recorded by Lieutenant Tracey, governor of Tothill Fields, and adhere to the general set of questions available under the same classification that were composed as part of the constabulary commission.[5] These questions deal mainly with the processes of offending. For example, offenders are asked about the circumstances in which they began offending; about the areas where, and the means by which, they committed crime; the amount of money they made; and about police corruption. The same questions are used in the second set of prison interviews, although in this case the identity of the recorder is unknown. The Westminster Bridewell interviews are supported by a letter from Lieutenant Tracey to Samuel Redgrave, editor of the criminal statistics, and representative of the constabulary commission, on 9 October 1837.. Tracey stressed the difficulty of finding prisoners suitable for interviewing, and the possibility of them being unreliable witnesses:

> The few prisoners that I have been enabled to select for this enquiry do not for the most part (as you will perceive) differ materially in their notions, on account of themselves, but I can, I think rely on their statements: these examinations were taken cautiously and without the possibility of their conferring with each other.[6]

Dating for all four sets of interviews is unclear, but they are no earlier than 1835 and no later than 1837. A final comment on ages: the boys interviewed on the *Euryalus* were all aged sixteen and under. Although age is not always given, many of the boys can be cross-referenced to the list submitted by J. H. Capper referred to above, where ages are supplied. The ages of the boys interviewed in the metropolitan prisons tend to be a little older, mainly between sixteen and twenty. However, since they were referring to offending behaviour over a substantial period of time, these interviews are particularly relevant to the present discussion. Finally, two long statements with reputed

---

4 SC *Gaols*, PP, 1835, 2nd Report, xi, appendix 21, pp. 263–6, evidence of J. H. Capper esq.
5 The questions can be found amongst the interviews in PRO, HO 73/2, pt 2, loose papers.
6 Ibid.

female thieves are also used. Again, these were recorded as part of the constabulary commission, in August 1837.[7]

Whilst much of the anecdotal evidence which has been used in this study comes from a limited period of years, and could thus be accused of being unrepresentative, the nature of the material is so scarce as to over-ride any such considerations. Moreover, it is highly likely that the responses of such children to their experiences varied little over the period. Whilst the levels and frequency of offending were possibly out of the ordinary, many of the experiences were common to all juvenile offenders. Certainly, supplementary forms of textual evidence suggest that this was the case. Hence the accounts of offending to be found in the *Old Bailey sessions papers* are invaluable, as are various newspaper accounts, criminal depositions (where they exist), and the evidence compiled on behalf of the various parliamentary select committees and from a number of the voluntary organisations committed to addressing the 'problem' of juvenile crime, for example the Philanthropic Society and the Children's Friend Society. It is debatable how much, if any, of this material could be said to be in the children's own words. Even though the narratives are from working-class children, caught up in the criminal justice system, the problem of atypicality still exists. Such children had generally run the gamut of the criminal justice system and were ensconced in prison or awaiting transportation. The words of the vast majority of children who passed in front of the magistrate and in and out of the penal institutions are irrecoverable.

---

[7] Ibid. loose papers, statements of reputed thieves Caroline Gadberry and Mary Mause, dated Aug. 1837.

APPENDIX 2

Patterns of Juvenile Crime and Punishment

Methodology

The statistics discussed in this study were drawn from the Middlesex criminal registers.[1] Before 1791, when the registers first appear, any systematic study of criminal age is impossible. Apart from isolated material recording age, consistent data for age is only available from 1791. With the appearance of the registers, some consistent work on age can be carried out, but only for indicted crime. Without extensive record linkage, it is impossible to assess the reliability of the age information in the criminal registers. However, scattered age data available for the eighteenth century has been analysed by Peter Linebaugh, who suggests that the difference in recorded ages is negligible.[2] The database covers a sample of six registers, taken at ten year intervals from 1797 to 1847 inclusive. All indictments were recorded, with the purpose of comparing the treatment of juvenile offenders to that of the whole Middlesex criminal population. Before the 1830s each register had a fairly large proportion of entries where no age is given. That occurred mainly in the case of indictments tried at the sessions at Clerkenwell and Westminster, for which the registers were not supplied with age related information.[3] Occasionally the age was missing for the Old Bailey/Central Criminal Court trials, for example in the case of misdemeanours which were generally tried at the petty sessions. Despite a probable level of inaccuracy, and the possibility that individuals may well have had good reasons for not giving their correct age, the registers still represent the earliest comprehensive source for age of indicted persons.

The Middlesex criminal registers date from 1791 to 1849, when they were combined with the registers for all England and Wales.[4] All the registers give details of sex (or gender), age, crime and sentence except for the five years from 1829 to 1833 inclusive for which age is not provided.[5] This allows a basic tabulation of the five types of information: sex; age; crime; sentence;

---

1 PRO, HO 26/1–56, Middlesex criminal registers, series 1.
2 P. Linebaugh, 'The ordinary of Newgate and his account', in J. S. Cockburn (ed.), *Crime in England, 1550–1800*, London 1977, 246–69, esp. p. 262.
3 These were jury trial courts hearing only indictments, with an equivalent level of jurisdiction to the county quarter-sessions courts, and the borough general sessions.
4 The registers for 1795, 1798, 1799 and 1802 do not fully survive.
5 Other information is provided, for example the name of the presiding judge or, occasionally, comments on literacy. The nature of the information does not remain constant over the period.

year. For the historian, the major distinctions to be made are between property crime and violent crime. For the study of juvenile crime, the latter category is less important since the vast majority of identifiable crimes committed
by juveniles were property crimes. However, there is some overlap between
the two as many crimes implied theft accompanied by violence, for example
burglary, robbery and highway robbery. Within property crime, there are
further divisions: between direct appropriation (grand and petty larceny) and
indirect appropriation (such as fraud, embezzlement, receiving, coining). So
far this produces four categories of offence – violent crime; burglary/robbery;
property crime; indirect property crime.

The coding of property crime is fraught with problems. Since the database
covers a period of sixty years, the first problem is that of the changing definitions of criminal behaviour. Thus changes in the criminal law meant that
many crimes which had previously been liable to the capital sentence were
made non-capital in the early nineteenth century.[6] For example picking
pockets, on the statute book as 'larceny from the person', was a capital
offence until repeal in 1808.[7] The critical reforms of the nineteenth century
make it impossible for the historian to make coding really precise, as do the
changes in the amount of detail supplied in the register.[8] In the registers for
the late eighteenth and very early nineteenth centuries, the offence was
recorded with some specificity, but increasingly during the nineteenth
century, descriptive detail was lost.[9]

Within the limitations of the data it was decided to create two categories
of direct property crime. The first category includes all larcenies, essentially
petty and grand larceny.[10] In addition this category includes those larcenies
which were capital at the beginning of the period, but for most of the period
unlikely to attract the death sentence, and certainly unlikely to result in

6   Between 1660 and 1800 successive legislation removed many of the more serious crimes
from the benefit of clergy. By the late eighteenth century the main distinction was between
capital crimes and non-capital crimes (i.e. grand and petty larceny). For a more detailed
discussion of benefit of clergy see *The reports of Sir John Spelman*, ed. J. Baker, ii, London
1978, 327–34; J. H. Langbein, 'Shaping the eighteenth-century trial: a view from the Ryder
sources', *University of Chicago Law Review* l (1983), 1–136.
7   Larceny (Pickpockets), 48 Geo. III c.129 (1808).
8   The situation was complicated further by Peel's reforms of the late 1820s which
removed benefit of clergy from many crimes. Yet in the legislation of 7 & 8 Geo. 4, c.28
(1827), which would have made theft of over a 1s. capital, another part of the same statute
allowed that persons convicted of felonies could only be sentenced to death if the felony
had been expressly made capital. The distinction between petty and grand larceny was also
removed (7 & 8 Geo. 4, c.29 (1827)), greatly reducing the number of capital felonies.
However this was merely making official a state of affairs that had existed informally for
some time.
9   The result of this ambiguity means that over time it is not always possible to identify less
serious capital crimes.
10 As John Beattie has pointed out, when, by the eighteenth century, sentencing policy for
both was identical, the distinction between petty and grand larceny was increasingly irrele-
vant: *Crime and the courts*, 182.

actual execution. By the late eighteenth and early nineteenth centuries such capital crimes as larceny from the person or larceny from the dwelling-house were more likely to result in imprisonment or transportation, usually via a partial verdict. Where such crimes did attract a death sentence they overwhelmingly resulted in a reprieve on condition of transportation. The second category includes the serious larcenies, those which were more likely to attract capital punishment, and to result in execution. These include serious capital larcenies such as burglary and housebreaking and livestock theft. Such a categorisation may seem rather simplistic, and certainly creates a very large larceny category. However, given the relationship between crime and punishment it was felt more worthwhile to give a sense of contemporary trial outcomes rather than to reflect the extremely complicated statutory divisions. Moreover, given that so many so-called capital crimes had been made non-capital by the 1810s and 1820s, it was felt that this two-fold division would provide a more realistic picture of the offending and punishment of juveniles.

Table 1 shows the categories for crime that were adopted, and the offences that fall within those categories. There are some overlaps and problems of marginal definition. For example within the categories of larceny and serious larceny there are blurred lines between robbery from the person, street robbery and robbery. Often picking someone's pocket might involve knocking into the victim, which suggests a physical assault. There are also problems with attempted crime. Attempted larceny from the person was a misdemeanour and has thus been placed in the misdemeanour category. However, attempted violent crime was placed with indicted violent crime. It was felt that what was most important was to focus upon the physical nature of the crimes rather than put them into misdemeanour, where the fact of 'intent' would be lost. Of the livestock thefts, horse-stealing was usually seen as being the most serious, although cattle-stealing and sheep-stealing were also often subject to the death sentence. Essentially, these categories are reliant on the pre-reform structures of the late eighteenth century. Hence trial outcome was the determining factor in the way in which the larcenies in particular were categorised. The three categories of misdemeanour, miscellaneous felony and miscellaneous should be explained. Misdemeanours were usually tried at the petty sessions in the nineteenth century. However some misdemeanours (for example some assault cases) were indictable, and dealt with at the quarter session level courts at Clerkenwell and Westminster. The two miscellaneous categories contain, in the first, those offences that are miscellaneous but known to have been felonies, and in the second non-felonious miscellaneous offences. For example, miscellaneous felonies included being at large from transportation, harbouring a convicted felon, conspiracy and piracy. Miscellaneous charges (those which were not felonies) included such diverse offences as being a person of evil fame, selling illicit spirits, curtilage (boundary) breaking, and impersonating a soldier.

It should be stressed that there are inherent limitations to the Middlesex criminal registers. This is partly a problem with any source that is used to analyse crime and criminality. Only recorded crime is shown, so only general statements can be made about patterns of crime. Coding involves an inevitable degree of subjectivity. More specifically, the registers only show indicted crimes.[11] Another limitation is that partial verdicts are not recorded. Partial verdict was the process by which the jury downgraded the crime of which the indicted person was accused. There were two ways of doing this. On the one hand the actual nature of the crime could be changed, hence its statutory description was changed and a lesser offence given. Another method was for the jury to reduce the value of the goods involved in theft. The lack of partial verdicts means that offence definition may have been further distorted since it is unclear whether the offence recorded in the Middlesex criminal registers was the offence shown in the original indictment, or the offence as defined by partial verdict.

Statistical analysis of sentencing, like crime, also has its drawbacks. However, unlike crime, the coding of sentences is far more straightforward. The main distinctions are between imprisonment, transportation, death and acquittal. Table 2 shows the breakdown of sentences, where applicable. It should be stressed that these were the sentences given in court. In some cases the sentences would subsequently have been reduced, or even the offender pardoned. Unfortunately the ultimate outcome of a case was not always given. The obvious example of this is in the case of death sentences where large numbers of offenders thus sentenced were subsequently transported or pardoned (although where an execution did take place details were inevitably supplied). The pardoning process, was, of course, extremely important, especially in the case of younger offenders where mercy was often recommended. A true picture of the outcome of any verdict could only be achieved by following the verdict from the Middlesex criminal registers through the entire records of prison, hulk and transportation.[12] Lastly, the 'miscellaneous' category includes a number of different sentences. These were cases where the individual was charged somewhere else or not charged at all (but not acquitted or not found).

---

11 Although the registers do also include those indictments which were 'not found' by the Grand Jury.
12 Such a task is beyond the scope of this study, given the breadth and depth of research which would be required. It would also face well-known problems of record linkage, which often prove much more complex and difficult in practice than they seem in prospect.

Table 1
Codes for criminal offences

Larceny	Mainly larceny (grand and petty); larceny from the person; robbery from the person; larceny from a dwelling-house, shop, warehouse, ship; navigable river; larceny over 40s
Serious larcenies (which are treated most seriously by contemporaries)	Mainly burglary; robbery; street robbery; house-breaking; livestock theft
Indirect property crime	Mainly fraud; coining; forgery; embezzlement; receiving
Crimes against the person	Mainly murder; manslaughter; maliciously shooting, wounding, cutting and stabbing; infanticide; sexual crimes
Misdemeanours	
Miscellaneous felony	Miscellaneous offences which were definitely felonies
Miscellaneous	All offences which do not fit into any of the above categories

Table 2
Codes for sentences

Imprisonment only	
Imprisonment and whipped	
Imprisonment and fined	
Death	Death execution and death pardoned where this information is supplied
Fined (singular)	
Acquitted/not found	Acquittal, discharged, not guilty, no bill
Whipped (singular)	
Transportation	7, 10, 14, 21 yrs, life
Miscellaneous	Bailed, removed to another county, discharged on sureties to appear, sent to navy, died, found insane

Table 3
Percentage distribution of criminal indictments by age, Middlesex, 1797–1847

N = 16,515 for all tables

Rows/bold: crime %								Columns/non-bold: age %	
	nil	juv.	17 – 25	26 – 35	36 – 45	46 – 55	56 – 65	66 – 75	75+	All ages
Larceny	**4.5**	**14.6**	**44.0**	**20.0**	**9.6**	**4.6**	**2.0**	**0.6**	**0.1**	**100.0**
	53.3	89.7	79.1	70.3	68.7	71.0	76.4	79.2	75.0	75.3
Serious	**0.8**	**8.2**	**56.6**	**23.5**	**7.1**	**2.6**	**1.0**	**0.3**	–	**100.0**
larcenies	0.8	4.0	8.0	6.5	4.0	3.1	3.0	3.1	--	5.9
Indirect	**11.7**	**6.0**	**33.4**	**24.5**	**15.0**	**6.5**	**2.2**	**0.7**	**0.1**	**100.0**
crime	16.7	4.5	7.3	10.5	13.1	12.2	10.0	10.4	8.3	9.1
Against	**13.3**	**2.3**	**27.1**	**32.2**	**15.5**	**6.7**	**2.1**	**0.5**	**0.2**	**100.0**
person	13.1	1.2	4.1	9.5	9.3	8.7	6.6	5.2	16.7	6.3
Misd.	**27.3**	**3.8**	**18.2**	**20.8**	**16.7**	**9.5**	**3.4**	**0.4**	–	**100.0**
	6.8	0.5	0.7	1.6	2.5	3.1	2.7	1.0	--	1.6
Misc.	**35.3**	**1.1**	**19.8**	**22.5**	**13.9**	**5.3**	**1.6**	**0.5**	–	**100.0**
felony	6.3	0.1	0.5	1.2	1.5	1.2	0.9	1.0	--	1.1
Misc.	**32.0**	**2.1**	**26.8**	**16.5**	**15.5**	**6.2**	**1.0**	–	–	**100.0**
	2.9	0.1	0.4	0.5	0.9	0.7	0.3	--	--	0.6
All	**6.4**	**12.3**	**41.9**	**21.4**	**10.5**	**4.9**	**2.0**	**0.6**	**0.1**	**100.0**
crimes	100.0	100.0	100.0	100.0	100.0	100.0	100.0	100.0	100.0	100.0

Table 4
Percentage distribution of crimes by sample years, Middlesex, 1797–1847

Rows/bold: crime %							Columns/non bold: year %
	1797	1807	1817	1827	1837	1847	All years
Larceny	**5.0**	**6.3**	**16.7**	**22.0**	**18.7**	**31.2**	**100.0**
	66.8	76.6	77.1	80.8	70.9	74.9	75.3
Serious	**12.8**	**8.7**	**24.5**	**20.8**	**14.9**	**18.3**	**100.0**
larcenies	13.5	8.3	8.9	6.0	4.4	3.5	5.9
Indirect	**4.5**	**6.0**	**15.9**	**18.9**	**21.2**	**33.6**	**100.0**
crime	7.3	8.7	8.9	8.4	9.7	9.8	9.1
Against	**4.3**	**4.5**	**6.4**	**8.5**	**34.0**	**42.3**	**100.0**
person	4.8	4.6	2.5	2.6	10.8	8.5	6.3
Misd.	**3.0**	**.8**	**14.8**	**9.1**	**28.0**	**44.3**	**100.0**
	0.9	0.2	1.5	0.7	2.3	2.3	1.6
Misc.	**25.7**	**5.3**	**12.8**	**20.9**	**20.9**	**14.4**	**100.0**
felony	5.2	1.0	0.9	1.2	1.2	0.5	1.1
Misc.	**14.4**	**7.2**	**10.3**	**12.4**	**23.7**	**32.0**	**100.0**
	1.5	0.7	0.4	0.4	0.7	0.6	0.6
All	**5.6**	**6.2**	**16.3**	**20.5**	**19.9**	**31.4**	**100.0**
crimes	100.0	100.0	100.0	100.0	100.0	100.0	100.0

Table 5
Percentage distribution of age by sample years, Middlesex, 1797–1847

Rows/bold: age %							Columns/non-bold: year %
	1797	1807	1817	1827	1837	1847	All years
Nil	**2.3**	**1.0**	**34.4**	**48.9**	**5.4**	**8.1**	**100.0**
	2.6	1.0	13.4	15.2	1.7	1.6	6.4
Juv.	**1.4**	**2.7**	**14.3**	**22.7**	**19.5**	**39.5**	**100.0**
	3.1	5.2	10.7	13.6	12.0	15.4	12.3
17 – 25	**4.5**	**4.9**	**15.8**	**19.6**	**21.2**	**33.9**	**100.0**
	33.7	33.0	40.5	40.1	44.8	45.4	41.9
26 – 35	**8.7**	**9.2**	**14.8**	**15.4**	**20.9**	**30.9**	**100.0**
	33.0	31.5	19.3	16.1	22.5	21.1	21.4
36 – 45	**8.0**	**10.2**	**15.0**	**16.9**	**20.4**	**29.5**	**100.0**
	14.9	17.1	9.6	8.7	10.8	9.9	10.5
46 – 55	**9.8**	**9.6**	**14.3**	**16.9**	**21.4**	**27.9**	**100.0**
	8.5	7.5	4.3	4.0	5.3	4.4	4.9
56 – 65	**8.2**	**11.2**	**13.0**	**16.9**	**21.8**	**29.0**	**100.0**
	2.9	3.6	1.6	1.6	2.2	1.9	2.0
66 – 75	**10.4**	**9.4**	**17.7**	**22.9**	**22.9**	**16.7**	**100.0**
	1.1	0.9	0.6	0.7	0.7	0.3	0.6
75+	**25.0**	**16.7**	**8.3**	**8.3**	**8.3**	**33.3**	**100.0**
	0.3	0.2	--	--	--	0.1	0.1
All ages	**5.7**	**6.3**	**16.4**	**20.5**	**19.8**	**31.3**	**100.0**
	100.0	100.0	100.0	100.0	100.0	100.0	100.0

Table 6
Percentage distribution of age by gender, Middlesex, 1797–1847

Rows/bold: age %			Columns/non-bold: sex %
	Male	Female	All gender
Nil	**80.8**	**19.2**	**100.0**
	6.7	5.4	6.4
Juv.	**89.3**	**10.7**	**100.0**
	14.2	5.8	12.3
17 – 25	**79.0**	**21.0**	**100.0**
	42.9	38.7	41.9
26 – 35	**71.8**	**28.2**	**100.0**
	19.8	26.5	21.4
36 – 45	**69.8**	**30.2**	**100.0**
	9.5	13.9	10.5
46 – 55	**70.5**	**29.5**	**100.0**
	4.5	6.8	4.9
56 – 65	**72.5**	**27.5**	**100.0**
	1.9	2.4	2.0
66 – 75	**70.8**	**29.2**	**100.0**
	0.5	0.7	0.6
75+	**83.3**	**16.7**	**100.0**
	--	--	0.1
All ages	**77.3**	**22.7**	**100.0**
	100.0	100.0	100.0

Table 7
Percentage distribution of crimes by gender,
Middlesex, 1797–1847

Rows/bold: crime %			Columns/non-bold: sex %
	Male	Female	All gender
Larceny	**75.7**	**24.3**	**100.0**
	73.8	80.6	75.3
Serious	**90.2**	**9.8**	**100.0**
larcenies	6.9	2.6	5.9
Indirect	**77.0**	**23.0**	**100.0**
crime	9.1	9.2	9.1
Against	**83.9**	**16.1**	**100.0**
person	6.8	4.5	6.3
Misd.	**69.3**	**30.7**	**100.0**
	1.4	2.2	1.6
Misc.	**86.6**	**13.4**	**100.0**
felony	1.3	0.7	1.1
Misc.	**85.6**	**14.4**	**100.0**
	0.7	0.4	0.6
All	**77.2**	**22.8**	**100.0**
crimes	100.0	100.0	100.0

Table 8
Percentage distribution of sentences by sample years, Middlesex, 1797–1847

Rows/bold: sentence %							Columns/non-bold: year %
	1797	1807	1817	1827	1837	1847	All years
Prison	**0.5**	**1.1**	**9.0**	**15.3**	**21.9**	**52.2**	**100.0**
only	3.3	6.3	20.5	27.7	41.0	61.7	37.1
Prison/	**8.0**	**3.8**	**26.9**	**26.5**	**10.5**	**24.1**	**100.0**
whip	3.8	1.6	4.5	3.5	1.5	2.1	2.7
Prison/	**39.9**	**52.1**	**0.4**	**0.3**	**3.1**	**4.2**	**100.0**
fine	12.2	14.4	--	--	0.3	0.2	1.7
Death	**13.6**	**11.3**	**33.9**	**34.2**	**6.1**	**1.0**	**100.0**
	9.1	6.9	7.8	6.3	1.2	0.1	3.8
Fine	**2.7**	**5.7**	**25.7**	**22.3**	**25.0**	**18.6**	**100.0**
	1.2	2.2	3.8	2.7	3.1	1.5	2.5
Acquit.	**7.9**	**9.5**	**21.5**	**21.4**	**16.9**	**22.8**	**100.0**
	42.8	46.0	40.1	31.9	25.9	22.1	30.5
Whip.	**11.7**	**13.2**	**23.3**	**43.9**	**7.9**	--	**100.0**
	2.4	2.4	1.6	2.4	0.5	--	1.1
Trans-	**5.2**	**6.0**	**17.8**	**26.8**	**26.2**	**18.0**	**100.0**
ports	17.8	18.7	21.1	25.3	25.6	11.1	19.4
Misc.	**39.0**	**1.1**	**2.8**	**1.7**	**21.5**	**33.9**	**100.0**
	7.4	0.2	0.2	0.1	1.2	1.2	1.1
Nil	--	**54.2**	**45.8**	--	--	--	**100.0**
	--	1.3	0.4	--	--	--	0.1
All	**5.7**	**6.3**	**16.4**	**20.5**	**19.8**	**31.3**	**100.0**
sentences	100.0	100.0	100.0	100.0	100.0	100.0	100.0

Table 9
Percentage distribution of sentences by crimes, Middlesex, 1797–1847

Rows/bold: sentence %							Columns/non-bold: crime %
	Larceny	Serious larcenies	Indirect crime	Against person	Misd.	Misc. felony	Misc.	All crimes
Prison only	**80.2** 39.6	**1.2** 7.3	**10.7** 43.4	**5.4** 32.0	**1.3** 30.7	**1.0** 31.6	**0.3** 16.5	**100.0** 37.1
Prison/ whip	**96.7** 3.5	– --	**1.8** 0.5	**0.4** 0.2	**0.9** 1.5	**0.2** 0.5	– --	**100.0** 2.7
Prison/ fine	**81.8** 1.9	**3.1** 0.9	**4.2** 0.8	**4.9** 1.3	**3.8** 4.2	**0.7** 1.1	**1.4** 4.1	**100.0** 1.7
Death	**33.4** 1.7	**51.7** 33.1	**7.7** 3.2	**4.0** 2.4	– --	**2.7** 9.1	**0.5** 3.1	**100.0** 3.8
Fine	**54.5** 1.8	**0.7** 0.3	**2.5** 0.7	**37.4** 14.5	**4.0** 6.1	**0.2** 0.5	**0.7** 3.1	**100.0** 2.5
Acquit.	**69.4** 28.1	**7.5** 38.7	**9.7** 32.5	**8.7** 42.3	**1.8** 34.8	**1.7** 44.9	**1.2** 59.8	**100.0** 30.5
Whip.	**94.7** 1.4	**1.6** 0.3	**3.7** 0.5	– --	– --	– --	– --	**100.0** 1.1
Trans- ports	**84.6** 21.8	**5.3** 17.3	**8.4** 17.9	**1.0** 3.2	**0.1** 0.8	**0.3** 4.8	**0.3** 10.3	**100.0** 19.4
Misc.	**15.5** 0.2	**11.9** 2.0	**4.8** 0.5	**23.8** 3.8	**34.5** 22.0	**8.3** 7.5	**1.2** 2.1	**100.0** 1.0
Nil	**63.6** 0.1	– --	**9.1** 0.1	**18.2** 0.2	– --	– --	**9.1** 1.0	**100.0** 0.1
All sentences	**75.3** 100.0	**5.9** 100.0	**9.1** 100.0	**6.3** 100.0	**1.6** 100.0	**1.1** 100.0	**0.6** 100.0	**100.0** 100.0

Table 10
Percentage distribution of sentences by age, Middlesex, 1797–1847

Rows/bold: sentence %									Columns/non-bold: age %
	Nil	Juv.	17 – 25	26 – 35	36 – 45	46 – 55	56 – 65	66 – 75	75+	All ages
Prison only	**5.4**	**11.9**	**42.5**	**20.9**	**10.6**	**5.1**	**2.6**	**0.9**	**0.1**	**100.0**
	31.5	36.0	37.6	36.3	37.3	38.8	48.0	55.2	50.0	37.1
Prison/ whip	**16.7**	**40.1**	**20.9**	**9.6**	**6.5**	**2.9**	**3.1**	**0.2**	**–**	**100.0**
	7.1	8.9	1.4	1.2	1.7	1.6	4.2	1.0	--	2.7
Prison/ fine	**2.1**	**2.5**	**29.0**	**29.7**	**18.5**	**12.2**	**4.2**	**1.4**	**0.4**	**100.0**
	0.6	0.4	1.2	2.4	3.1	4.3	3.6	4.2	8.3	1.7
Death	**0.6**	**6.6**	**53.4**	**23.3**	**10.2**	**4.5**	**1.1**	**0.3**	**–**	**100.0**
	0.4	2.0	4.8	4.1	3.7	3.5	2.1	2.1	--	3.8
Fined	**9.9**	**17.8**	**30.9**	**19.3**	**13.9**	**6.2**	**2.0**	**–**	**–**	**100.0**
	3.8	3.6	1.8	2.2	3.2	3.1	2.4	--	--	2.5
Acquit.	**10.7**	**9.0**	**39.0**	**23.4**	**10.8**	**4.8**	**1.7**	**0.6**	**0.1**	**100.0**
	50.9	22.3	28.4	33.4	31.3	30.0	25.7	31.2	33.3	30.5
Whip.	**4.2**	**49.7**	**22.8**	**9.0**	**6.4**	**4.2**	**3.7**	**–**	**–**	**100.0**
	0.8	4.6	0.6	0.5	0.7	1.0	2.1	--	--	1.1
Trans- ports	**1.1**	**13.8**	**51.0**	**19.9**	**8.9**	**4.0**	**1.0**	**0.2**	**–**	**100.0**
	3.4	21.8	23.6	18.0	16.4	15.7	10.0	6.2	8.3	19.4
Misc.	**7.9**	**1.7**	**22.0**	**33.9**	**24.3**	**7.9**	**2.3**	**–**	**–**	**100.0**
	1.3	0.2	0.6	1.7	2.5	1.7	1.2	--	--	1.1
Nil	**8.3**	**20.8**	**33.3**	**12.5**	**8.3**	**8.3**	**8.3**	**–**	**–**	**100.0**
	0.2	0.2	0.1	0.1	0.1	0.2	0.6	--	--	0.1
All sentences	**6.4**	**12.3**	**41.9**	**21.4**	**10.5**	**4.9**	**2.0**	**0.6**	**0.1**	**100.0**
	100.0	100.0	100.0	100.0	100.0	100.0	100.0	100.0	100.0	100.0

Table 11
Percentage distribution of sentences by gender,
Middlesex, 1797–1847

Rows/bold: sentence %			Columns/non-bold: sex %
	Male	Female	All gender
Prison only	**75.2** 36.1	**24.8** 40.5	**100.0** 37.1
Prison/ whip	**97.8** 3.4	**2.2** 0.3	**100.0** 2.7
Prison/ fine	**62.9** 1.4	**37.1** 2.8	**100.0** 1.7
Death	**88.7** 4.4	**11.3** 1.9	**100.0** 3.8
Fined	**79.7** 2.5	**20.3** 2.2	**100.0** 2.4
Acquit.	**72.5** 28.6	**27.5** 36.9	**100.0** 30.5
Whip.	**92.1** 1.4	**7.9** 0.4	**100.0** 1.1
Trans- ports	**83.9** 21.0	**16.1** 13.7	**100.0** 19.4
Misc.	**74.6** 1.0	**25.4** 1.2	**100.0** 1.1
Nil	**83.3** 0.2	**16.7** 0.1	**100.0** 0.2
All sentences	**77.3** 100.0	**22.7** 100.0	**100.0** 100.0

171

Table 12a
Count of Middlesex criminal registers, 1791–1848*

Year	Juveniles	Juveniles % of total	Girls only	Boys only	Girls % of juv.	Boys % of juv.
1791	104	7	18	86	17	83
1792	74	8	15	59	20	80
1793	60	6	11	49	18	82
1794	14	2	3	11	21	79
1796	44	5	9	35	20	80
1797	32	3	6	26	19	81
1800	83	10	15	68	18	82
1801	135	9	21	114	16	84
1803	76	7	15	61	20	80
1804	71	8	28	43	39	61
1805	68	7	32	36	47	53
1806	57	5	11	46	19	81
1807	53	5	15	38	28	72
1808	45	4	17	28	38	62
1809	100	8	34	66	34	66
1810	71	6	13	58	18	82
1811	71	6	18	53	25	75
1812	101	7	33	68	33	67
1813	100	6	25	75	25	75
1814	123	8	17	106	14	86
1815	147	7	19	128	13	87
1816	200	9	29	171	15	85
1817	286	11	21	265	7	93
1818	244	9	28	216	11	89
1819	261	10	24	237	9	91
1820	331	12	33	298	10	90
1821	322	13	40	282	12	88

Source: *Middlesex criminal registers*, 1791–1848; PRO, HO 26/1–56

Table 12b
Count of Middlesex criminal register, 1791–1848*

Year	Juveniles	Juveniles % of total	Girls only	Boys only	Girls % of juv.	Boys % of juv.
1822	316	12	27	289	9	91
1823	329	13	44	285	13	87
1824	377	14	52	325	14	86
1825	368	13	47	321	13	87
1826	440	13	45	395	10	90
1827	459	14	33	426	7	93
1828	427	12	41	386	10	90
1829	[age data missing]					
1830	[age data missing]					
1831	[age data missing]					
1832	[age data missing]					
1833	[age data missing]					
1834	602	15	102	500	17	83
1835	489	14	89	400	18	82
1836	503	15	98	405	19	81
1837	396	12	63	333	16	84
1838	475	14	68	407	14	86
1839	520	14	72	448	14	86
1840	506	14	69	437	14	86
1841	502	14	74	428	15	85
1842	526	13	83	443	16	84
1843	600	14	79	521	13	87
1844	540	13	76	464	14	86
1845	725	16	93	632	13	87
1846	760	16	92	668	12	88
1847	802	15	79	723	10	90
1848	597	12	83	514	14	86

Source: *Middlesex criminal registers*, 1791–1848, PRO, HO26/1–56

* These tables give the yearly counts and the yearly percentage distribution of juvenile offenders (0–16). They also give counts and % for both female and male juveniles. There may be some minor inaccuracies in these figures since they are based on a manual count of all the registers. The registers for 1791–1801 are not discrete (i.e. 1791–2 has been called 1791), and data is missing from some of these early years.

Bibliography

Unpublished primary sources

London, Borough of Hackney Archives, Rose Lipman Library
Refuge for the Destitute, apprenticeship indentures, 19 Sept. 1838
Refuge for the Destitute, minutes, 1819–47

London, British Library
MS Egerton 3710 Sir J. Silvester notebook, 1816

London, Corporation of London Record Office
209 c/13 Newgate prison visitors' book, Sept. 1823–Nov. 1825

London, Metropolitan Archive (formerly Greater London Record Office)
CRIM 4 Criminal indictments
MJ/SR Calendars of criminal indictments for London and Middlesex
MJ/SBB Order books for Westminster sessions
DL/C/404 (842–3) Consistory Court of London, register of wills and administration, will of Anne Sheen.

London, Public Record Office
CRIM 10 *Old Bailey sessions papers* (printed proceedings of the Central Criminal Court from 1834)
HO 8/7–78 *Euryalus* prison hulk, quarterly returns
HO 9/2 *Euryalus* prison hulk, quarterly lists
HO 10/1–64 Convict muster rolls for New South Wales and Tasmania
HO 11/10–12 Convict transportation records, 1835–41
HO 17 Petition archive, 1819–39
HO 18 Petition archive, 1839–54
HO 19 Petition archive register
HO 24/15 Parkhurst prison register, 1838–63
HO 26/1–56 Middlesex criminal registers, series 1, 1791–1849
HO 73/2 Constabulary Force, letters and papers, 1836–8
HO 73/16 Constabulary Force, letters and papers, 1835–7
HO 77/1–61 Printed lists of prisoners held at Newgate for trial
MEPO 4/12–30 Daily police reports, 1828–38
PCOM 1 *Old Bailey sessions papers* (printed proceedings of the London and Middlesex sessions, 1801–38)
PCOM 2/203 Newgate register of prisoners, 1834–6

London, Theatre Museum, Covent Garden
Miscellaneous files/fairs (1831)

Tasmania, Archives Office

Con 18 Description lists of male convicts, 1828–53
Con 22 Comprehensive registers of convicts, 1804–53
Con 23 Alphabetical registers of male convicts, 1804–39
Con 27 Appropriation lists of convicts, 9 May 1831, 4 Sept. 1834, 14 Oct. 1835, 27 Dec. 1836
Con 31 Conduct registers of male convicts, 1803–43
Con 32 Supplementary conduct registers
CSO 1 Colonial secretary's office correspondence records
MM 33 Miscellaneous microfilming of Tasmanian convict records
RGD 34 Register general's department

Official documents and publications (in date order)

Debates of the House of Commons, 3rd ser. cx, 1850; 4th ser. xiv, 1826
Report from the Select Committee on the State of the Police of the Metropolis, PP, 1816, v
Report from the Select Committee on the State of the Police of the Metropolis, PP, 1817, vii
Third Report from the Select Committee on the State of the Police of the Metropolis, PP, 1818, viii
Papers Relating to the Convict Establishment, PP, 1818, xvi
Report from the Select Committee on Criminal Laws &c., PP, 1819, viii
Report from the Select Committee on Criminal Commitments and Convictions in London and Middlesex, PP, 1828, vi
Report from the Select Committee on the Police of the Metropolis, PP, 1828, vi
Report from the Select Committee on Secondary Punishments, PP, 1831, vii
Report from the Select Committee on Secondary Punishments, PP, 1832, vii
Reports from the Select Committee of the House of Lords Appointed to Inquire into the Present State of Gaols and Houses of Correction in England and Wales, PP, 1835, xi–xii
Third Report from the Commissioners on Criminal Law (Juvenile Offenders), PP, 1837, xxxi
Report from the Select Committee on Metropolitan Police Officers, PP, 1837, xii
First Report of the Commissioners Appointed to Inquire as to the Best Means of Establishing an Efficient Constabulary Force in the Counties of England and Wales, PP, 1839, xix
Seventh Report of Her Majesty's Commissioners on Criminal Law, PP 1843, xix
First Report from the Select Committe of the House of Lords Appointed to Inquire into the Execution of the Criminal Law, especially respecting Juvenile Offenders and Transportation, PP, 1847, vii
Report from the Select Committee on Criminal and Destitute Juveniles, PP, 1852, vii
Report from the Select Committee on the Treatment of Criminal and Destitute Juveniles, PP, 1852–3, xxiii

Newspapers and periodicals

Annual Register
Cleave's Weekly Police Gazette
Morning Herald
Times

Contemporary books and articles

Adams, Coker, T., A letter addressed to Sir Eardley Eardley Wilmot, bart. in answer to his letter to the magistrates of England, on the increase of crime, &c, London 1828

Anon., The laws respecting women as they regard their natural rights or their connections and conduct . . . also, the obligations of parent and child, and the condition of minors . . . (etc) in four books, London 1877

Anon., A narrative of the facts relative to the murder of Richard Faulkner Taylor, Rochester 1831

Beames, T., The rookeries of London: past, present, and prospective, London 1850

Beck, W., Friends, ancient and modern, London 1908

Beggs, T., An inquiry into the extent and causes of juvenile depravity, London 1849

Bidwell, A., From Wall Street to Newgate, Hartford, Conn. 1895

Bidwell, G., Forging his chains: the autobiography of George Bidwell, Hartford, Conn. 1888

Brenton, E. P., A letter to the Rt.Hon.R.W.Horton shewing the impolicy, inefficiency, and ruinous consequences of emigration and the advantage of home colonies by Edward. P. Brenton – esq – Capt. R.N, London 1830

——— Observations on the training and education of children in Great Britain, London 1834

——— The Bible and the spade, or Captain Brenton's account of the rise and progress of the Children's Friend Society, London 1837

Buxton, C. F. (ed.), Memoirs of Thomas Fowell Buxton, baronet: with selections from his correspondence edited by his son, Charles Buxton, esq. BA, London 1848

——— (ed.), Memoirs of Thomas Fowell Buxton, London 1866

Buxton, T. F., An inquiry whether crime and misery are produced or prevented by our present system of prison discipline, London 1818

——— The substance of a speech of Thomas Fowell Buxton, esq. MP in the House of Commons, March 2nd, 1819: on the motion of Sir James Mackintosh . . . "that, a select committee be appointed, to consider of so much of the criminal laws as relates to capital punishment or felonies . . .", London 1819

Carpenter, M., Reformatory schools for the children of the perishing and dangerous classes and for juvenile offenders, London 1851, repr. London 1968

——— Juvenile delinquents, their condition and treatment, London 1853

Colquhoun, P., A treatise on the police of the metropolis: explaining the various crimes and misdemeanours which at present are felt as a pressure upon the community: and suggesting remedies for their prevention, London 1796

Dalton, M., The countrey justice, conteyning the practise of the Justices of the Peace out of their sessions . . ., 6th edn, London 1635

Dickens, C., *Oliver Twist*, London 1837–9

Fielding, H., *An enquiry into the causes of the late increase of robbers, &c with some proposals for remedying this growing evil*, London 1751

────── *An enquiry into the causes of the late increase of robbers . . . etc*, London 1752

Fielding, J., *An account of the origin and effects of a police set on foot by his grace the Duke of Newcastle in the year 1753, upon a plan presented to his grace by the late Henry Fielding, esq. To which is added a plan for preserving those deserted girls in this town, who become prostitutes from necessity*, London 1758

Forss, C., *Practical remarks upon the education of the working classes; with an account of the plan pursued under the superintendence of the Children's Friend Society at the Brenton Asylum, Hackney Wick*, London 1835

Greenwood, J., *The seven curses of London*, London 1869

────── *The wilds of London*, London 1874

Hanway, J., *Observations on the causes of the dissoluteness which reigns among the lower classes of the people . . . etc*, London 1772

────── *The defects of the police, the cause of immorality and the continual robberies committed, particularly in and about the metropolis*, London 1775

────── *The defects of the police, the cause of immorality . . . with various proposals for preventing hanging and transportation . . . etc*, London 1775

────── *The citizen's monitor*, London 1780

Hill, M. D., 'Practical suggestions to the founders of the reformatory schools', in J. C. Symons (ed.), *On the reformation of young offenders*, London 1855

Howard, J., *The state of the prisons in England and Wales: with preliminary observations . . . etc*, London 1777

Luson, H., *Inferior politics: or, considerations on the wretchedness and prolificacy of the POOR . . . on the defects in the present system of parochial and penal laws . . .*, London 1786

Mayhew, H., *London labour and the London poor, IV: Those that will not work, comprising prostitutes, thieves, swindlers and beggars by several contributors*, first edn, London 1861–2, repr. London 1967

────── and J. Binny, *The criminal prisons of London and scenes of prison life*, London 1862, repr. London 1968

Miles, W. A., *Letter to Lord John Russell concerning juvenile delinquency, together with suggestions concerning a reformatory establishment*, Shrewsbury 1837

────── *Poverty, mendicity, and crime*, ed. H. Brandon, London 1839

Neale, W. B., *Juvenile delinquency in Manchester: its causes and history, its consequences, and some suggestions concerning its cure*, Manchester 1840

Philanthropic Society., *First report of the Philanthropic Society: instituted in London, September, 1788, for the prevention of crimes*, London c. May 1789

────── *The Philanthropic Society, instituted September, 1788, for the prevention of crimes and the reform of the criminal poor . . .*, London 1789

────── *The memorial of certain persons calling themselves the Philanthropic Society*, London c. 1795

────── *Report of the committee appointed to examine the state of the Philanthropic Society*, London 1796

────── *An account of the nature and present state of the Philanthropic Society*, London 1804

Plint, T., *Crime in England, its relation, character and extent as developed from 1801–48*, London 1851

Prison Discipline Society, *Third report of the Society for the Improvement of Prison Discipline*, London 1821–2

—— *Sixth report of the Society for the Improvement of Prison Discipline*, London 1824

—— *Eighth report of the Committee of the Society for the Improvement of Prison Discipline and for the Reformation of Juvenile Offenders*, London 1832

Refuge for the Destitute, *The annual report of the Refuge for the Destitute, for the year 1832*, London 1833

Report of the committee for investigating the causes of the alarming increase of juvenile delinquency in the metropolis, London 1816

Report of the proceedings of a conference on the subject of preventive and reformatory schools, held at Birmingham, on the 9th and 10th December, 1851, London 1851

Robins, S., *A letter to the Right Honourable Lord John Russell on the necessity and mode of state assistance in the education of the people*, London 1851

Robson's London directory, for 1835, London 1835

Smith, W., *Mild punishments sound policy: or observations on the laws relative to debtors and felons . . .*, London 1778

Society for the diffusion of information about the punishment of death, London 1810

Tallack, W., *Peter Bedford, the Spitalfields philanthropist*, London 1865

Wade, J., *A treatise on the police and crimes of the metropolis; especially juvenile delinquency, female prostitution, mendicity, gaming . . . etc*, London 1829

Wakefield, E. G., *Facts relating to the punishment of death in the metropolis*, London 1831

Wild, J. (pseud.), *Begin. Sir, I am on the point of leaving England for Botany Bay, being convicted of picking pockets, etc* (A Suppositious Letter, 1810)

Wilmot, Eardley, J., *A letter to the magistrates of Warwickshire, on the increase of crime in general, but more particularly in the county of Warwick; with a few observations on the causes and remedies of this increasing evil*, London 1820

—— *A second letter to the magistrates of Warwickshire on the increase of crime in general, but more particularly of juvenile delinquency, with a few observations on the causes and remedies of this increasing evil*, London 1820

—— *A letter to the magistrates of England on the increase of crime; and an efficient remedy suggested for their consideration*, London 1827

—— *A letter to the magistrates of England on the increase of crime; and an efficient remedy suggested for their consideration*, London 1828

Wontner, T., *Old Bailey experience: criminal jurisprudence and the actual working of our penal code of laws: also an essay on prison discipline, to which is added a history of the crimes committed by offenders in the present day*, London 1831

—— 'The schoolmaster's experience in Newgate', *Frazer's Magazine* v (1832), 521–33

Worsley, H., *Juvenile depravity*, London 1849

Secondary sources

Anderson, M., 'The emergence of the modern life-cycle in Britain', *Social History* x (1985), 69–87

Andrew, D. T., *Philanthropy and police: London charity in the eighteenth century*, Princeton, NJ 1989

Ariès, P., *Centuries of childhood*, London 1962

Ascoli, D., *The queen's peace: the origins and development of the metropolitan police, 1829–1979*, London 1979

Baker, J. (ed.), *The reports of Sir John Spelman*, ii, London 1978

Bailey, V., *Delinquency and citizenship: reclaiming the young offender, 1914–48*, Oxford 1987

Bartrip, P. W. J., 'Public opinion and law enforcement: the ticket-of-leave scares in mid-Victorian Britain', in V. Bailey (ed.), *Policing and punishment in nineteenth-century Britain*, London 1981, 150–81

Bateson, C., *The convict ships, 1787–1868*, Glasgow, 1959

Bean, J. P., *The Sheffield gang wars*, Sheffield 1981

Bean, P. and J. Melville, *Lost children of the empire*, London 1989

Beattie, J. M., *Crime and the courts in England, 1660–1800*, Oxford 1986

—— 'London crime and the making of the "bloody code", 1689–1718', in Davison and others, *Stilling the grumbling hive*, 49–76

Beier, A. L., *Masterless men: the vagrancy problem in England, 1560–1640*, London 1985

Bennet, P. W., 'Taming "bad boys" of the "dangerous class": child rescue and restraint at the Victoria industrial school, 1887–1935', *Histoire Sociale – Social History* xxi (1988), 76–91

Bennett, J., *Oral history and delinquency: the rhetoric of criminality*, Chicago–London 1981

Berlanstein, L. R., 'Vagrants, beggars, and thieves: delinquent boys in mid-nineteenth-century Paris', *Journal of Social History* xii (1979), 531–2

Best, G., *Mid-Victorian Britain, 1851–75*, London 1971, repr. London 1985

Blackburn, G., *The Children's Friend Society: juvenile emigrants to western Australia, South Africa and Canada, 1834–42*, Northbridge, WA 1994

Bradlow, E., 'The Children's Friend Society at the Cape of Good Hope', *Victorian Studies* xxvii (1984), 155–77

Buddee, P., *The fate of the Artful Dodger: Parkhurst boys transported to Australia and New Zealand, 1842–52*, Perth, WA 1984

Burnett, J., *Destiny obscure: autobiographies of childhood, education, and family from the 1820s to the 1920s*, London 1982

Cale, M., 'Girls and the perception of sexual danger in the Victorian reformatory system', *History* lxviii (1993), 201–17

Campbell, C., *The intolerable hulks: British shipboard confinement, 1776–1857*, Bowie, MD 1993

Carlebach, J., *Caring for children in trouble*, London 1970

Chesney, K., *The Victorian underworld*, London 1970

Cohen, S., *Folk devils and moral panics: the creation of the mods and rockers*, London 1972

Cohen-Cline, P., 'Unregulated youth: masculinity and murder in the 1830s city', *Radical History Review* lii (1992), 33–52

Coldrey, B. M., *The scheme: the Christian Brothers and childcare in western Australia*, O'Connor, WA 1993

Colls, R., 'Oh happy English children! Coal, class and education in the north east', *Past and Present* lxxiii (1976), 75–99

Critchley, T. A., *A history of police in England and Wales*, 2nd edn, London 1978

Cunningham, H., 'The employment and unemployment of children in England, c. 1680–1851', *Past and Present* cxxvi (1990), 115–50

────── *The children of the poor: representations of childhood since the seventeenth century*, Oxford 1991

────── *Children and childhood in western society since 1500*, London 1995

Daunton, M. J., *Progress and poverty: an economic and social history of Britain, 1700–1850*, Oxford 1995

Davies, A., 'Youth gangs, masculinity and violence in late Victorian Manchester and Salford', *Journal of Social History* xxxii (1998), 349–69

Davin, A., *Growing up poor: home, school and street in London, 1870–1914*, London 1996

Davis, J., 'The London garotting panic of 1862: a moral panic and the creation of a criminal class in mid-Victorian England', in Gatrell, Lenman and Parker, *Crime and the law*, 190–213

Davison, L. and others (eds), *Stilling the grumbling hive: the response to social and economic problems in England, 1689–1750*, Stroud 1992

De Mause, L., *The history of childhood*, New York, 1974

Dictionary of western Australians, 1829–1914: II, *Bond – 1850–68*, ed. R. Erickson, Nedlands, WA 1979

Driver, F., 'Discipline without frontiers? Representations of the Mettray reformatory colony in Britain, 1840–80', *Journal of Historical Sociology* [Great Britain] iii (1990), 272–93

Egmond, F., *Underworld's: organised crime in the Netherlands, 1650–1800*, Cambridge 1993

Ekirch, R., *Bound for America: the transportation of British convicts to the colonies, 1718–75*, Oxford 1987

Emsley, C., *The English police: a political and social history*, Hemel Hempstead, 1991

────── *Crime and society in England, 1750–1900*, 2nd edn, London 1996

────── *Policing and its context, 1750–1870*, 2nd edn, London 1996

Erikson, E. H., *Identity: youth and crisis*, London 1968

Faller, L. B., *Turned to account: the forms and functions of criminal biography in seventeenth- and early eighteenth-century England*, Cambridge 1987

Feheney, J. M., 'Delinquency among Irish Catholic children in Victorian London', *Irish Historical Studies* xxiii (1983), 319–29

Forsythe, W. J., *A system of discipline: Exeter borough prison, 1819–63*, Exeter 1983

Foucault, M., *Discipline and punish: the birth of the prison*, London 1991

Gatrell, V. A. C., *The hanging tree: execution and the English people, 1770–1868*, Oxford 1994

────── and T. B. Hadden, 'Nineteenth-century criminal statistics and their interpretation', in E. A. Wrigley (ed.), *Nineteenth-century society: essays in the use of quantitative methods for the study of social data*, Cambridge 1972, 337–86

Gatrell, V. A. C., B. Lenman and G. Parker (eds), *Crime and the law: the social history of crime in western Europe since 1500*, London 1980

George, M. D., *London life in the eighteenth century*, London 1925, repr. London 1996

Gillis, J., *Youth and history: tradition and change in European age relations*, London 1974

——— 'The evolution of juvenile delinquency in England, 1890–1914', *Past and Present* lxvii (1975), 96–126

Goldstrom, J. M., 'The content of education and the socialization of the working-class child, 1830–60', in McCann, *Popular education*, 93–109

Graef, R., *Living dangerously: young offenders in their own words*, London 1993

Griffin, C., *Representations of youth: the study of youth and adolescence in Britain and America*, Cambridge 1993

Griffiths, P., *Youth and authority: formative experience in England, 1560–1640*, Oxford 1996

Hadley, E., 'Natives in a strange land: the philanthropic discourse of juvenile emigration in mid-nineteenth century England', *Victorian Studies* xxxiii (1990), 411–37

Hagell, A. and T. Newburn, *Persistent young offenders*, London 1994

Hanawalt, B. A., 'Historical descriptions and prescriptions for adolescence', *Journal of Family History* xvii (1992), 341–51

Haralambos, M. and R. M. Heald, *Sociology: themes and perspectives*, Slough 1980

Harris, R. and N. Timms, *Secure accommodation in child care: between hospital and prison or thereabouts?*, London 1993

Hay, D., 'Property, authority, and the criminal trial', in Hay and others, *Albion's fatal tree*, 17–63

——— 'War, dearth and theft in the eighteenth century: the record of the English courts', *Past and Present* xcv (1982), 117–60

——— and others, *Albion's fatal tree: crime and society in eighteenth-century England*, London 1975.

Hendrick, H., *Images of youth: age, class, and the male youth problem, 1880–1920*, Oxford 1990

Henriques, U., 'The rise and decline of the separate system of prison discipline', *Past and Present* liv (1972), 61–93

Hitchcock, T., P. King and P. Sharpe (eds), *Chronicling poverty: the voices and strategies of the English poor, 1640–1840*, London 1997

Hobbs, D., *Doing the business: entrepreneurship, the working class and detectives in the east end of London*, Oxford 1988

——— 'Professional and organised crime in Britain', in Maguire, Morgan and Reiner, *Criminology*, 441–68

——— *Bad business: professional crime in modern Britain*, Oxford 1995

Hooper, F. C., *Prison boys of Port Arthur*, Melbourne 1967

Horn, P., *Children's work and welfare, 1780s–1880s*, London 1994

Houlbrooke, R. A., *The English family, 1450–1700*, London 1984

Humphrey, K., 'Objects of compassion: young male convicts in Van Diemen's Land, 1834–50', *Australian Historical Studies* (April 1992), 13–33

Humphries, S., *Hooligans or rebels? An oral history of working class childhood and youth, 1889–1939*, Oxford 1981

Ignatieff, M., *A just measure of pain: the penitentiary in the industrial revolution, 1750–1850*, London 1989

Innes, J. and J. Styles, 'The crime wave: recent writing on crime and criminal justice in eighteenth-century England', *Journal of British Studies* xxv (1986), 380–435

Inwood, S., 'Policing London's morals: the metropolitan police and popular culture, 1829–50', *London Journal* xv (1990), 129–46

Jenkins, P. and G. W. Potter, 'Before the Krays: organised crime in London, 1920–1960', *Criminal Justice History: An International Annual* ix (1988), 209–30

Johnson, W. B., *The English prison hulks*, London 1957

Jordanova, L. J., 'Conceptualising childhood in the eighteenth century: the problem of child labour', *British Journal for Eighteenth-Century Studies* x (1987), 189–99

—— 'New worlds for children in the eighteenth century: problems of historical interpretation', *History of the Human Sciences* iii (1990), 69–83

Kean, A. W. G., 'The history of the criminal liability of children', *Law Quarterly Review* liii (1937), 364–70

Kett, J., *Rites of passage: adolescence in America, 1790 to the present*, New York 1977

King, P., 'Decision makers and decision making in the English criminal law, 1750–1800', *Historical Journal* xxvii (1984), 25–58

—— 'Female offenders, work and life-cycle change in late eighteenth century London', *Continuity and Change* xi (1996), 61–90

—— 'The rise of juvenile delinquency in England, 1780–1840', *Past and Present* clx (1998), 116–66

—— and J. Noel, 'The origins of "the problem of juvenile delinquency": the growth of juvenile prosecutions in London in the late eighteenth and early nineteenth centuries', *Criminal Justice History: An International Annual* xiv (1993), 17–41

Knell, B. E. F., 'Capital punishment: its administration in relation to juvenile offenders in the nineteenth century and its possible administration in the eighteenth', *British Journal of Criminology, Delinquency and Deviant Behaviour* v (1965), 198–207

Kray, R., *Born fighter*, London 1991

—— and R. Kray, *Our story*, London 1989

Langbein, J. H., 'Shaping the eighteenth-century trial: a view from the Ryder sources', *University of Chicago Law Review* l (1983), 1–136

Linebaugh, P., 'The ordinary of Newgate and his account', in J. S. Cockburn (ed.), *Crime in England, 1550–1800*, London 1977, 246–69

—— *The London hanged: crime and civil society in the eighteenth century*, London 1991

Lloyd Pritchard, M. F. (ed.), *The collected works of Edward Gibbon Wakefield*, London 1968

Low, D. A., *Thieves' kitchen: the regency underworld*, London 1982

McCann, P. 'Popular education, socialisation, and social control: Spitalfields, 1812–24', in McCann, *Popular education*, 1–40

—— (ed.), *Popular education and socialisation in the nineteenth century*, London 1977

McConville, S., *A history of English prison administration*, I: *1750–1877*, London 1981

Macfarlane, A., 'Review essay on Stone, *Family, sex and marriage*', *History and Theory* xviii (1979), 103–26

Magarey, S., 'The invention of juvenile delinquency in early nineteenth-century England', *Labour History* [Canberra] xxxiv (1978), 1'–27

Maguire, M., R. Morgan and R. Reiner (eds), *The Oxford handbook of criminology*, Oxford 1994

Mahood, L., *Policing gender, class and family*, London 1995

—— and M. Littlewood 'The "vicious" girl and the "street-corner" boy: sexuality and the gendered delinquent in the Scottish child-saving movement, 1850–1940', *Journal of the History of Sexuality* iv (1994), 549–78

May, M., 'Innocence and experience: the evolution of the concept of juvenile delinquency in the mid-nineteenth century', *Victorian Studies* xvii (1973), 7–29

Mays, J. B., *Growing up in the city: a study of juvenile delinquency in an urban neighbourhood*, Liverpool 1954

Morrison, B., *As if*, London 1997

Morton, J., *Bent coppers: a survey of police corruption*, London 1993

Nardinelli, C., *Child labor and the industrial revolution*, Bloomington, Ind. 1990

Newburn, T. and E. Stanko (eds), *Just boys doing business? Men, masculinities and crime*, London–New York 1994

Owen, D., *English philanthropy, 1660–1900*, Cambridge, Mass. 1965.

Paley, R., ' "An imperfect, inadequate and wretched system"? Policing London before Peel', *Criminal Justice History: An International Annual* x (1989), 95–130

—— 'Thief-takers in London in the age of the McDaniel gang, c. 1745–54', in D. Hay and F. Snyder (eds), *Policing and prosecution in Britain, 1750–1850*, Oxford 1989, 301–41

Palmer, S. H., *Police and protest in England and Ireland, 1780–1850*, Cambridge 1988

Paz, D. G., *The politics of working-class education in Britain, 1830–50*, Manchester 1980

Pearson, G., *Hooligan: a history of respectable fears*, London 1983

—— 'Hooligans in history', supplement to *History Today* (May 1984)

—— 'Youth, crime, and society', in Maguire, Morgan and Reiner, *Handbook of criminology*, 1169–91

Pearson, J., *The profession of violence: the rise and fall of the Kray twins*, London 1972

Philips, D., *Crime and authority in Victorian England: the Black Country, 1835–60*, London 1977

—— 'The royal bastard as policeman? William Augustus Miles and the Sydney police, 1841–48', in D. Philips and S. Davies (eds), *A nation of rogues? Crime, law and punishment in colonial Australia*, Melbourne 1994, 36–72

Pinchbeck, I. and M. Hewitt, *Children in English society*, II: *From the eighteenth century to the Children's Act 1948*, London 1973

Platt, A., *The child savers: the invention of delinquency*, Chicago 1969

Ploszajska, T., 'Moral landscapes and manipulated spaces: gender, class and space in Victorian reformatory schools', *Journal of Historical Geography* xx (1994), 413–29

Plumb, J. H., 'The new world of children in eighteenth-century England', in N. McKendrick, J. Brewer and J. H. Plumb (eds), *The birth of a consumer society: the commercialisation of eighteenth century England*, London 1982, 287–315

Porter, R., *London: a social history*, London 1994

Radzinowicz, L., *A history of English criminal law and its administration from 1750*, II: *The clash between private initiative and public interest in the enforcement of the law*, London 1956

—— *Ideology and crime: a study of crime in its social and historical context*, London 1966

—— and R. Hood, *A history of English criminal law and its administration from 1750*, V: *The emergence of penal policy*, Oxford 1990

Ramsland, J., ' "Cultivating a respectful and modest demeanour": children of the foundling, 1800–1926', *London Journal* xviii (1993), 95–112

Rawlings, P., *Drunks, whores, and idle apprentices: criminal biographies of the eighteenth century*, London 1992

Robson, L. L., *The convict settlers of Australia: an enquiry into the origins and character of the convicts transported to New South Wales and Van Diemens Land, 1787–1852*, Melbourne, 1965

Rose, L., *The erosion of childhood: child oppression in Britain, 1860–1918*, London 1991

Rudé, G. F. E., *The crowd in history: a study of popular disturbances in France and England, 1730–1848*, New York 1964

—— *Criminal and victim: crime and society in early nineteenth-century England*, Oxford 1985.

Rush, P., 'The government of a generation: the subject of juvenile delinquency', *Liverpool Law Review* xiv (1992), 3–43

Salgado, G., *The Elizabethan underworld*, London 1977

Samuel, R. (ed.), *East-end underworld: chapters in the life of Arthur Harding*, London 1981

Sanders, W. B., *Juvenile offenders for a thousand years: selected readings from Anglo-Saxon times to 1900*, Chapel Hill, NC 1970

Scholes, A. G., *Education for empire settlement: a study of juvenile migration*, London 1932

Schwarz, L. D., *London in the age of industrialisation: entrepreneurs, labour force and living conditions, 1700–1850*, Cambridge 1992

Sereny, G., 'A child murdered by children', *The Independent on Sunday*, 23 Apr. 1995, 8–12

—— *The case of Mary Bell: a portrait of a child who murdered*, 2nd edn, with new preface and appendix, London 1995

Sharpe, J. A., *Crime in early modern England, 1550–1750*, London 1984

—— *Judicial punishment in England*, London 1990

Shaw, C. R., *The Jack-Roller: a delinquent boy's own story*, Chicago 1930

Shoemaker, R. B., *Prosecution and punishment: petty crime and the law in London and rural Middlesex, c. 1660–1725*, Cambridge 1991

Shore, H., ' "An old offender tho' so young in years": the criminal careers of juvenile offenders in 1830s Middlesex', in T. Hitchcock, P. King and P. Sharpe (eds), *Chronicling poverty: the voices and strategies of the English poor 1640–1840*, London 1997

—— ' "Cross coves, buzzers and general sorts of prigs": juvenile crime and the criminal "underworld" in the early nineteenth century', *British Journal of Criminology*, special edition on *Histories of Crime and Modernity* xxxix (1999), 10–24

—— 'Home, play and street life: causes of, and explanations for, juvenile crime in the early nineteenth century', in A. Fletcher and S. Hussey (eds), *Childhood in question*, Manchester 1999

—— 'The trouble with boys: gender and the "invention" of the juvenile offender in the early nineteenth century', in M. Arnot and C. Usborne (eds), *Gender and crime in modern Europe*, London 1999

Sim, J., 'Tougher than the rest? Men in prison', in Newburn and Stanko, *Just boys*, 100–17

Sindall, R., *Street violence in the nineteenth century: media panic or real danger?*, Leicester 1990

Slack, P., *Poverty and policy in Tudor and Stuart England*, London 1988

Smith, D. J., *The sleep of reason: the James Bulger case*, London 1994

Springhall, J., *Youth, empire and society: British youth movements, 1883–1940*, London 1977

—— *Coming of age: adolescence in Britain, 1860–1960*, London 1986

Stack, J. A., 'Children, urbanisation, and the chances of imprisonment in mid-Victorian England', *Criminal Justice History: An International Annual* xiii (1992), 113–39

Steedman, C., *Policing the Victorian community: the formation of English provincial police forces, 1856–80*, London 1984

—— *Strange dislocations: childhood and the idea of human interiority, 1780–1930*, London 1995

Stone, L., 'Literacy and education in England, 1640–1900', *Past and Present* xlii (1969), 69–139

—— *The family, sex, and marriage in England, 1500–1800*, London 1979

Styles, J., 'From an offence between men to an offence against property? Industrial pilfering and the law in the eighteenth century', in M. Berg, P. Hudson and M. Sonenscher (eds), *Manufacture in town and country before the factory*, Cambridge 1983

Summers, A., ' "In a few years we shall none of us that now take care of them be here": philanthropy and the state in the thinking of Elizabeth Fry', *Historical Research* lxvii (1994), 134–42

Taylor, L., *In the underworld*, Oxford 1984

Thompson, E. P., 'The moral economy of the English crowd in the eighteenth century', *Past and Present* l (1971), 76–136

—— *Whigs and hunters: the origin of the Black Act*, London 1975

—— *Customs in common*, London 1991

Thompson, F. M. L., *The rise of respectable society: a social history of Victorian Britain, 1830–1900*, London 1988

Tobias, J. J., *Crime and industrial society in the nineteenth century*, London 1967

—— *Prince of fences: the life and crimes of Ikey Solomons*, London 1974

Vincent, D., *Bread, knowledge, and freedom: a study of nineteenth-century working class autobiography*, London 1982

———— *Literacy and popular culture: England, 1750–1914*, Cambridge 1989

Wagner, G., *Barnardo*, London 1979

———— *Children of the empire*, London 1982

Walker, G., 'Women, theft, and the world of stolen goods', in J. Kermode and G. Walker (eds), *Women, crime, and the courts in early modern England*, London 1994, 81–105.

Walkowitz, J., *City of dreadful delight: narratives of sexual danger in late Victorian London*, London 1992

Wall, R., 'The age at leaving home', *Journal of Family History* iii (1978), 181–202

Weisbrod, B., 'How to become a good foundling in early Victorian London', *Social History* x (1985), 193–209

West, D. J., *The young offender*, London 1967

Whyte, W. F., *Street corner society: the social structure of an Italian slum*, Chicago 1955

Willmott, P., *Adolescent boys of east London*, London 1966

Zedner, L., *Women, crime, and custody in Victorian England*, Oxford 1991

Unpublished theses

Davis, J., 'Law breaking and law enforcement: the creation of a criminal class in mid-Victorian London', unpubl. PhD diss. Boston 1984

Hartley, E., 'The institutional treatment of juvenile delinquency: aspects of the English reformatory and industrial school movement in the nineteenth century', unpubl. PhD diss. Leicester 1986

King, P., 'Crime, law and society in Essex, 1740–1820', unpubl. PhD diss. Cambridge 1984

May, M., 'A child's punishment for a child's crime: the reformatory and industrial schools movement in Britain, c. 1780–1860', unpubl. PhD diss. London 1981

Shore, H., 'The social history of juvenile crime in Middlesex, 1790–1850', unpubl. PhD diss. London 1996

Index

[*offenders names are listed under offenders, criminal*]

London, 2, 6n., 14, 15, 149; Bethnal
Green, 63, 151; Blackfriars Bridge, 89;
Bloomsbury, 43; the Borough, 76; Bow
Street, 26, 27, 81, 87, 91–2; Chelsea,
64, 98; the City, 15, 25, 83, 121;
Clerkenwell, 35, 42, 143; Commercial
Road, 77; Covent Garden, 47, 87; Field
Lane, 25, 46, 76, 78; Finsbury, 72; Fleet
Street, 89; Hackney, 11n., 40, 51, 65,
67, 96n., 111, 149; Hampstead, 90;
Holborn, 27, 41, 61; Homerton, 122;
Hyde Park, 87; Keates Street, 80;
Kensington, 83; Knightsbridge, 118;
Lambeth Street, 78, 83n., Leicester
Square, 91; Mansion House, 87;
Marlborough Street, 28, 39;
Marylebone, 90, 146; Mile End, 46,
134; Milton Street (also Grub Street),
78; Oxford Street, 85, 138;
Paddington, 53; Petticoat Lane, 76;
Russell Square, 22; Saffron Hill, 35, 76;
St Giles, 22, 25, 35, 36, 43, 76; Seven
Dials, 35, 60; Shoe Lane, 89;
Shoreditch, 146, 151; Soho, 40;
Spitalfields, 50, 71, 79, 124; Stepney,
46; Wentworth Street, 77, 79;
Westminster, 15, 35, 46, 78, 84, 138;
Whitechapel, 35, 77–80, 83n.;
Whitecross Street, 77; Wild Street, 88;
Woolwich, 47, 72, 110
London Ragged School Union, 138
Lush, Charles, 43
Luson, Hewling, 102

Magarey, Susan, 31, 148
Magdalen, see institutions, voluntary
magistracy, 5n., 11, 12, 24, 25, 26, 29,
31–3, 35, 56, 70, 75, 76, 81–2, 86, 92,
95, 96, 98, 141
Mahood, Linda, 11
Maidstone prison, see institutions, state
Manchester, 149
Marchant, William, 89–90
Marine Society, see institutions, voluntary
May, Margaret, 5, 42n., 148
Mayhew, Henry, 3, 4, 13n., 125
metropolis, unique influence of, 14–15,
19, 23, 149
metropolitan police, see police
Mettray, Colonie Agricole, 100
Middlesex, county of, 14, 15n., 21, 25, 37,
40, 63, 96, 102, 103, 117, 121, 133,
141, 143, 144, 145, 149, 155, 158
Middlesex criminal registers, 12, 56, 58,

59, 71, 72, 115, 118, 120, 122, 133,
144, 158–61
Miles, William Augustus, 1, 3, 4, 10, 26,
35, 40, 44, 48, 49, 60, 71, 72, 77, 78,
82, 84, 88, 94, 110, 112, 119, 122, 127,
136n., 151, 155–6
Millbank penitentiary, see institutions,
state
Miller, James, 21
Milnes, Mr (?), MP for Pontefract, 9
moral panic, 14, 21, 23, 64, 148
Morning Chronicle, 91–2

Napier, Sir George, 112
Napoleonic wars, 14, 23, 117n.
Neale, William Beaver, 3
New Bailey prison, Salford, see
institutions, state
Newgate prison, see institutions, state
Newman, J. A., 120
New Zealand, 113
Norman, Inspector (?), 50
nurseries of crime, 15, 24–6, 79, 102,
107–8, 115, 125

offences, criminal: assault, see juvenile
offenders, violent; burglary, 56, 59,
61–4, 73, 119, 121, 133, 134, 144, 151;
crimes against the person, 56, 144;
forgery, 121; highway robbery, 63, see
also offenders, criminal, highway
robbers; house breaking, see offences,
criminal, burglary; larceny, 56, 57–8,
122, 144, by a servant, 56, 72–3, 144,
see also domestic service, from a
dwelling-house, 51, 56, 62–3, 91, 118,
119, from a shop, 28, 61, 83, 119, from
a warehouse, 56, from the person, 59,
91, 144, see also, offences, criminal,
pick-pocketing and offenders, criminal,
pick-pockets, grand and petty, over
40s.; livestock theft, 56, 133, 134;
manslaughter, 64; murder, 28, 64–9, 78;
pick-pocketing, 28, 58–61, 73, 83, 85,
134, 143, see also offenders, criminal,
pick-pockets; receiving stolen goods,
fencing, 57, 75–8, 83, 86, see also
receivers of stolen goods; robbery, 61,
63–4, 77, 105, 134, see also criminal
offences, burglary. See also appendix 2
offenders, criminal: burglars, 55; highway
robbers, 121; pick-pockets, 27, 43, 55,
58–61, 73, 87, 88. See also receivers of
stolen goods